Make Way
for Reading

Make Way for Reading

Great Books for Kindergarten through Grade 8

Compiled and Edited by Karen Latimer
and Pamela J. Fenner

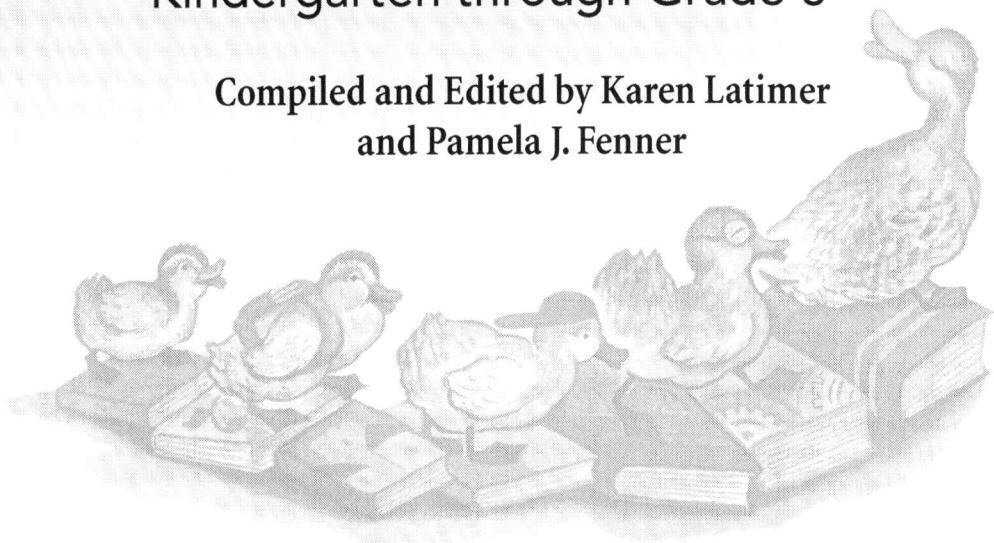

MICHAELMAS
PRESS

Make Way for Reading: Great Books for Kindergarten Through Grade 8
© 2012 by Pamela Johnson Fenner

Waldorf Student Reading List
© 1991, 1992 by Karen Rivers and Pamela Johnson Fenner
© 1993, 1995 by Pamela Johnson Fenner

Attention corporations, schools, libraries, and book clubs: if you would like to use this book as a fundraiser or premium, please contact the publisher.

Michaelmas Press
P. O. Box 702, Amesbury, MA 01913-0016
Telephone: +978.388.7066   Fax: +978.388.6031
E-Mail: pam@michaelmaspress.com
www.michaelmaspress.com

ISBN 978-0-9647832-5-8

Library of Congress Cataloging Data pending

Waldorf® is a registered mark of the Association of Waldorf Schools of North America.

Design: Toelke Associates, Chatham, NY
Illustrations by Durga Yael Bernhard

Printed in the United States of America

10 9 8 7 6 5 4 3 2 1

For my mother who read to me, took me to the library, and demonstrated by example her own pleasure in reading. To her I owe my love of literature and the teaching career which followed that passion.

K. L.

To all the parents, grandparents, siblings, aunts, uncles, friends, neighbors, librarians and bookstore staff who will share their love of storytelling and reading books to the children of the twenty-first century

P. J. F.

CONTENTS

Foreword

By Eugene Schwartz

In this second decade of the twenty-first century, it takes a particular kind of courage to publish a book that is a list of other books. I call it courage, because, even as I type these words on the screen of a computer, a debate rages from publishers' offices to the halls of academia to the schoolroom: is the physical book is still relevant? Many even pose the more vexing question: will the physical book even need to exist in the near future?

One answer to these questions has already been given by the publishing industry itself. The most powerful and universal cultural phenomenon that bridged the years between the end of the twentieth century and the beginning of the twenty-first was not a movie, or the trajectory of a rock star, or the ascent of an inspiring public figure. It was, in fact, a *children's book series* — the seven Harry Potter volumes — that captured the hearts and minds of hundreds of millions of children (and adults).

Harry Potter, an entity whose entire existence was encapsulated within the pages of a book, opened up the possibility of entirely new planes of possibility of children who themselves existed in a world of increasing rules and restrictions. It might be argued that the Harry Potter books were inevitably adapted into screenplays that fostered very successful movies. Yet those movies only served to heighten audiences' realization that the most spectacular and high-tech special effects could not compare to what they had *imagined*; and those imaginations were summoned up from the low-tech imprint of ink upon paper — the physical book.

Indeed, the computer being used to compose this Foreword is called a Mac*Book*, and the most successful "reading devices," e.g. the iPad, the Kindle, and the Nook, the are those that can simulate the texture and whiteness of paper, the turning of a page, the ability to insert a bookmark or to highlight text. So the most successful archrivals of books are devices that provide the best simulacrum of being . . . books.

Even as the adult sections of the big chain bookstores fill their shelves with drinking mugs and t-shirts, shopping totes and reading lights, the *children's* sections of those stores evince a remarkable continuity. Go there and you are far more likely to find real literary substance: the books that you read as a child (many of which are the books that your parents and perhaps even your grandparents read as children) are still on the shelves, and are still highly marketable items in the publishing world. The inherently conservative continuity of children's culture offers assurance that books have not yet had their day!

That being said, not only is the future of the book being questioned, but the viability of literacy itself. Notwithstanding ambitious school reading programs that attempt to compel children to read at any ever-younger age, illiteracy remains a stubborn statistical fact, while dyslexia and sheer lack of interest in reading are major issues in the American school system. It should not be surprising, then, that in the midst of the high-tech/low-tech, reading devices versus books debate, Waldorf education is coming to the fore.

Waldorf students do not merely *read* books; they create their own books, as well, for every subject that is studied, a Waldorf student writes and illustrates an artistic representation of what she learned. Such activities stimulate a love of learning, and a parallel love of, and respect for, books, and those who authored them. In the Waldorf setting, writing and reading are entwined, and the child feels at home in both worlds.

It is only fitting, then, that a reading list as rich and comprehensive as this would have been written by two Waldorf practitioners, Karen Latimer and Pamela Fenner. There are, of course, many ways of characterizing books and organizing such lists, but the most important from the Waldorf perspective is the grouping by age group, and this list excels in this respect. Waldorf schools teach in a way that is, above all, "age appropriate" and developmentally directed.

More than any other school activity, reading has the potential to pull children out of their dreamy sensibilities and thrust them into the wide-awake present-day world. It is more than just a matter of helping a child to coordinate seeing and hearing so that phonemes become familiar, or giving evermore sophisticated reading comprehension tests. Books can have a powerful effect on the changing *consciousness* of the child, and can serve as instruments of initiating him or her into successive stages of life. Books such as *Ann of Green Gables*, *The Secret Garden*, or *The Fellowship of the Ring*, that have awakened an entire "generation," and set before it a new vista of life, attest to the powerful effect of literature on the young.

The Russian psychologist Lev Vygotsky created the term "zone of proximal development" to characterize the way in which a child's inherent ability to learn something can be brought to fruition by an adult sensitive to the child's potential. This "scaffolding" effect, as later psychologists define it, can also describe the effect that a book can have upon a child — when that book is read at the right time, and under the right circumstances.

Our memories of the books that meant the most to us in our childhood are inextricably bound to the life experiences we had at the time — the friends we made or lost, the summer adventures we had, the joys and sorrows of the classroom. Rudolf Steiner once suggested that looking through a book that we read as a child, particularly if we had written something in it, could lead to a powerful recollection of our state of soul in our youth. But for that to happen we need the tangible, palpable, physical book that we held and earmarked and to which we once bid a reluctant farewell.

The dying King Lear, summoning up the lessons learned from a tempestuous life, says simply, "The ripeness is all." Even the best-written book with the most meaningful content can prematurely place unnecessary burdens on an impressionable child. With this guide in hand, however, parents and teachers are given gentle and sensible suggestions on finding the best book for the right age. May this book of books stand as the guardian of the road that leads to reading adventures.

Schwartz is the father of four, grandfather of seven, and the author of Millenial Child: Transforming Education in the Twenty-first Century. *A Waldorf teacher for 35 years, he is now an international educational consultant and lecturer. His articles and podcasts may be found at www.millenialchild.com*

Introduction

How Did We Begin?

The origins of this book can be traced to the experiences of two mothers searching for quality books for children. Both were former public school teachers, but were now part of the educational community at an independent Waldorf School, one of more than 1000 schools worldwide based on the educational philosophy of Rudolf Steiner.

One mother, Karen Rivers, was a teacher at the school and was inspired by requests from parents seeking help in selecting books to support the education of their children. The other, Pamela Fenner, was a parent searching for titles to add to a list she had maintained over the years for her three daughters. Seeing how their individual lists had much in common, Karen and Pam decided to combine their lists and make it available for the parents of the school.

Knowing that the list would be helpful to families and teachers of students in all kinds of learning environments from home schools to public, Pam published the list in a purple cover in a paperback format under her Michaelmas Press imprint. It was titled, Waldorf Student Reading List. In fact, many families may be familiar with what has become known as "the little purple book." Over the years, Pam—also Waldorf-trained—has updated and reprinted the list. An annotated reading list for the high school years can be found in *Books for the Journey,* also from Michaelmas Press.

When the time came for a complete revision, Pam asked me to undertake it. I had just retired from twenty years of teaching. She gave me the many book recommendations she had received over the years for inclusion in a future edition. I expanded the listings and added brief summaries, original publication dates, and awards. I omitted those titles no longer available even through online sources. The final section is a resource for adults who are looking for books with games, music, and crafts as well as for ideas to enrich family, seasonal, or cultural celebrations. The Appendix now includes multiple indexes and resources for further exploration.

What Are the Criteria?

Before I became a teacher, I took my two children to the local library, as my mother had taken me. We combed through the shelves looking for the books I had loved and stumbled accidently upon new favorites. However, today I would urge a more conscious process. I would learn more about child development and would also consult the trained children's librarian. The choice of reading material for children is too important to be left to random luck or chance. Only the very best literature should be presented; what sells is not always the best guide of quality; and the age of the child very much matters even when the selection is excellent.

Our aim is to offer children books that can inspire faith in the future, reveal the human spirit, widen the sense of self, nurture values, illumine history and natural science—and lead to a lifelong love of reading. We can measure the quality of a book by the degree to which an author does these. We can also expect to find our human capacity for humor and delight mirrored in the best examples of literature. Effective moral nourishment will come naturally through meeting well-crafted characters and plots as well as the archetypes of fairy tales and fables.

Another goal of this book is to provide an age-appropriate selection of literature; books are thus grouped in age and grade ranges. My understanding of the nature of growing children is significantly shaped by the view of human development articulated by Rudolf Steiner as he was founding the first Waldorf school. Guided by that understanding, I selected books to meet the developing child at each age range.

It is best to read a story first to see if it's appropriate for a particular child. This practice is especially important with collections of fairy tales and anthologies, which may include stories for a wide range of age or development. A list of suggested fairy tales in the Appendix offers some guidance.

In addition to reading unillustrated stories to stimulate a child's ability to make inner pictures, sometimes it is good to just tell a story rather than read one. This is also an excellent way to stimulate a child's pictorial imagination, a critical skill in reading. (Please see the article in the Appendix about learning to read.) You may learn a story "by heart" and retell it, or share your own living memories of your childhood or anecdotes of family history. Such personal storytelling has an important place in the treasure of "stories" we love.

How to Use this Book

The list of contents is the reader's guide. There are seven sections with an introduction for each followed by a reading list. I have put more information about choosing what to read in each introduction to help you make selections for a particular age group. You might use this book as a basis for evaluating titles that are not included here as well as newly published ones.

Some selections have a very wide range of appeal especially since they may be both read aloud or read independently. A child learns how to read at his or her own pace and reading skills vary widely. Naturally, there are books that overlap age ranges. The titles are listed under the earliest likely age range at which they will have wide appeal and/or reflect the grade at which a particular subject may also be studied in the Waldorf curriculum. For example, readers looking for books for a fourth grade student will also find choices among books listed in the earlier section as well as in Picture Books, Biography and Mythology, Legends and Folklore.

The joy of re-reading a beloved favorite from earlier times should not be overlooked, especially in times of illness, change, or stress. A book to be read aloud may appeal to a group that includes seventh graders as well as fourth graders—Kipling's *The Jungle Book* comes to mind. The indexes will prove helpful in this regard.

Books in the reading lists are in alphabetical order by title. The following chart shows the layout of each entry:

Book Title

Author, Illustrator   **Suggested Grades**

Annotation (Year of Original Publication)

★ = Book Award, if any

🔆 = A title that is recommended for a Waldorf Teaching Block
[See Appendix.]

As We Go To Press

It is challenging to keep up with the changes in the book publishing industry today, from the rise of online book sources, used bookstores, and book-related blogs, to almost "instant" publishing, in print or on electronic devices. Five or ten years ago we might not have included a particular "gem" of children's literature just because it was out of print and not easily found even in libraries. Though some recommended titles might cease to be available, these innovations in the industry offer a very hopeful picture for book "longevity."

For book lovers it is gratifying to see changes occurring at the local community level with bursts of activity on behalf of reading and literature. Library use has increased, as have literacy campaigns, book clubs for children as well as adults, and author visits in bookstores. Literary events and book festivals abound not just in major urban centers and suburban towns, but also in small villages. It is satisfying to contribute in any way to the goal of universal literacy. Pamela and I hope this reading list will inform and inspire all those who wish for every child a long and enriching lifetime of reading.

—Karen Latimer, Editor

Picture Books

KINDERGARTEN
TO GRADE 8

Sound and Rhythm

We crawl before we walk, babble before we speak meaningfully, and speak before we read. Mother Goose's rhythmic, repetitive rhymes delight the youngest children, who are interested in the sounds of language. Only gradually does the appeal of rhyme and rhythm give way to other characteristics of language such as imagery, imagination, or narrative content. Repetition engages little listeners more than novelty, as any parent who has read the same beloved storybook for the tenth time will testify. Like the joy of peek-a-boo, the pleasure in hearing a favorite verse, song, or simple story seems never-ending. Preschoolers and kindergartners experience the repetitive rhythm and rhyming elements of language most strongly, and like a ride on a carousel, the pleasure is circular and continuous in its ability to please.

Living Speech

The most important language experience for very young children is living speech. Reading aloud to children of this age is essentially an experience of speech rather than reading. A bedtime or naptime "story" of five or ten minutes of Mother Goose rhymes or traditional children's songs and lullabies can introduce the daily custom of listening to a story, which will gradually become the independent reader's daily reading habit. Adult readers in the home who model this habit give it importance and status for imitation. Reading one carefully chosen book, even once a week, is more effective than filling a child's room with books. Paramount to language development is the opportunity to experience living speech and interact with another human being. Reading books aloud is just one way to achieve that. A walk in the neighborhood or making cookies while talking about what is happening is just as effective for the youngest children.

Picture Books

Preschoolers opening a board book or picture book are learning the gross motor skills involved in sitting and looking at a book while also discovering the spatial orientation of books: front and back, top and bottom, left-hand page followed by right-hand page. This can be expanded to include additional sensory experiences in books like *Pat the Bunny*.

Because the young child's world of positive sensory experience builds a foundation on which fantasy and imagination develop over time, the quality of the pictures is the most important consideration in a "pre-reader" book. Many excellent artists contribute art of the highest aesthetic criteria to children's literature. The art of illustration is recognized in books honored with the Caldecott, Kate Greenaway or Golden Kite awards, and a review of these will help guide selection and develop an eye for the art of juvenile illustration. Luminous, light-filled color, richly detailed characterizations of subject matter, as well as the criteria of beauty, good taste, and truth that would apply to masterpieces of art should be considered when selecting illustrations for children's eyes

The appropriateness for the age of the child should certainly be considered. Just as we choose food to serve children's nutrition, so what they take into themselves with hungry eyes should be food for the inner soul of the child. Better to purchase a few beautiful books than waste even sixpence on a Mother Hubbard's cupboard full of empty, scary, or cartoon images. The introduction of electronic reading devices such as iPads to young children alters the experience of picture books in ways we have still to evaluate both for short-term and long-term effects.

When is the age of picture books over? Never, really. Illustrations continue to enrich the experience of books through out our lives. The illustrated coffee table book continues to enjoy a place on bookstore shelves when books themselves seem threatened by electronic technologies. In some cases a picture may be worth a thousand words, and because picture books introduce children to the world of books, they deserve special consideration.

Absolutely Positively Alexander: The Complete Stories

Judith Viorst; *illustrated by Ray Cruz and Robin Preiss Glasser*   2, 3

Three of the popular books that explore family values in the context of Alexander's various difficulties with bad days, money problems, and moving are collected here in one volume: *Alexander and the Terrible, Horrible, No Good, Very Bad Day; Alexander, Who Used to Be Rich Last Sunday; Alexander, Who's Not (Do You Hear Me? I Mean It!) Going to Move.* (1997)

Amos and Boris

William Steig, *illustrated by author*   1, 2, 3

A mouse and a whale become the closest of unlikely friends in a picture book with a story that is as delightful as the art by the Carnegie Medal-winning author/illustrator. (1977)

And Miss Carter Wore Pink: Scenes from an Edwardian Childhood

Helen Bradley, *illustrated by author*   1, 2, 3

Born in 1900, Helen Bradley was over sixty when she began to paint to show her small granddaughter what life was like when she herself was a child. Illustrated with full page, primitive-style paintings, the book depicts all of the detail of an idyllic life in the Edwardian period. See also, *Miss Carter Came with Us, 'In the beginning' said Great Aunt Jane,* and *The Queen Who Came to Tea.* (1971)

Around the World in One Shabbat: Jewish People Celebrate the Sabbath Together

Durga Yael Bernhard, *illustrated by author*   K+

Beginning in a market in Jerusalem, Bernhard takes the reader on a color-filled journey from one country to another around the globe showing the diversity and commonality as families prepare and observe the Jewish Sabbath. Named as a Sydney Taylor Honor Book. (2011)

Ashanti to Zulu: African Traditions

Margaret Musgrove; *illustrated by Leo and Diane Dillon*   2, 3

This lushly illustrated alphabet book describes life in twenty-six African tribes, from A to Z. (1976)

★ Caldecott Medal, Boston Globe-Horn Book

Autumn

Gerda Muller, *illustrated by author*   ☀ K, 1

Recently back in print from Floris Books, this is one in a quartet of seasonally themed small board books without text for very young children, showing regular activities of the day and of the year, or scenes from nature: *Winter*, *Spring*, and *Summer* follow. (2004)

Biggest Bear, The

Lynd Ward, *illustrated by author*   1, 2, 3

Little Johnny goes hunting for a bearskin to hang on his family's barn and returns with a small bundle of trouble. A meaningful story about "inappropriate or exotic pets" shows a hunting family in a positive light, but also considers the consequences that come when you set off to kill something for no reason. Ward, known as one of our greatest illustrators, is here author as well. (1952)

★ Carnegie Medal

Bread and Jam for Frances

Russell Hoban; *illustrated by Lillian Hoban*   2, 3

Francis the badger meets problems that concern many youngsters—a new sibling, making friends, the bedtime ordeal—and finds happy solutions in this amusingly illustrated beginning-to-read series that beginning readers can share with younger siblings. Look for: *A Baby Sister for Francis*, *Bedtime for Francis*, and others. (1960)

Chair for My Mother, A

Vera Williams, *illustrated by author*   1, 2

A child, her waitress mother, and her grandmother save dimes to buy a comfortable armchair after all of their furniture is lost in a fire. (1982)

Children of the Forest

Elsa Beskow, *illustrated by author*   ☀ K, 1

Beskow recounts in verse and charming illustrations the adventures of a family of small forest people throughout the four seasons. It is adapted from the Swedish *Tomtebobarnen* by William Jay Smith. All of Beskow's works can be recommended for very young listeners including *Christopher's Harvest Time*, *Peter's Old House*, *Woody*, and *Hazel and Little Pip*. (1910)

Clown of God, The: An Old Story

Tomie dePaola, *illustrated by author* 3, 4

A once-famous Italian juggler, now old and a beggar, gives one final perfor-mance before a statue of Our Lady and the Holy Child. This story is based upon an Italian folktale. (1978)

Complete Book of Flower Fairies, The

Cecily Mary Barker, *illustrated by author* 1–5

Barker's illustrations and poems made her one of the most successful and loved artists of the last century. Each plant is accurately drawn and also represented as a unique fairy. Her art is wonderful for the very young and the verses and botan-ical details serve as models for older students. This edition gathers together the works that originally appeared (and are still available) as individual volumes known collectively as *The Flower Fairy Series*. (2002)

Complete Brambley Hedge, The

Jill Barklem, *illustrated by author* 3, 4

This collection of popular illustrated stories about the mice of Brambley Hedge includes "Spring Story," "Summer Story," "Autumn Story," "Winter Story," "The Secret Staircase," "The High Hills," "Sea Story," and "Poppy's Babies," all of which are also available in single volumes. (1999)

Dandelion's Cousin, The

Gertrude Teutsch, *illustrated by author* K, 1, 2

Teutsch's book is a wonderful resource for sharing a love of and interest in nature. Through an imaginative story and beautiful illustrations, the reader is taken through the various stages of a tall relative of the dandelion that grew around the author's home. (2004)

Day in the Garden, A

Bettina Stietencron, *illustrated by author* K, 1

Enchanting illustrations invite us to discover all that is happening during "a day in the garden" in this picture book without text. (1992)

Each Peach Pear Plum

Janet and Allan Ahlberg; *illustrated by Janet Ahlberg*   K, 1

Rhymed text and illustrations invite the reader to play "I Spy" with a variety of Mother Goose and other folklore characters. (1978)

★ Kate Greenaway Medal

Eli

Bill Peet, *illustrated by author*   2, 3

A proud but decrepit lion learns a lesson about friendship from the vultures he despises. This is one of some thirty children's books written and illustrated by the Walt Disney artist whose work appeared in *Fantasia, Peter Pan,* and other animated films. (1978)

Eric Carle's Animals Animals

Compiled by Laura Whipple; *illustrated by Eric Carle*   4

Carle has illustrated the verses of various poets in which the unique qualities of particular pets and wild and domestic animals are characterized, providing a rich impression of the animal kingdom. (1989)

Flicka, Ricka, Dicka and their New Friend

Maj Lindman   1, 2

Flicka, Ricka, and Dicka are three little girls who live in Sweden. They have blue eyes, yellow curls, and look very much alike. Their simple adventures include: *Flicka, Ricka and Dicka and the New Dotted Dresses; Flicka, Ricka and Dicka Bake a Cake; Flicka, Ricka, and Dicka and the Little Dog* and others. (1942)

★ Caldecott Medal

Flowers' Festival, The

Elsa Beskow, *illustrated by author*   K, 1, 2

A little girl is invited to the Flowers' Midsummer Festival. At the top of the garden, Queen Rose sits on her throne surrounded by Lady Honeysuckle, Lord Bleeding Heart, and the rest of her court and welcomes all of the guests, the vegetables and flowers, the bumblebees and birds. Some of the guests have stories to share. Floris Books has reissued the works of the Swedish writer/illustrator who appeals to beginning readers and pre-readers. (1914)

Funny Little Woman, The

Arlene Mosel; *illustrated by Blair Lent*   K, 1

While chasing a dumpling, a little lady is captured by wicked creatures and escapes with the means of becoming the richest woman in Japan. (1972)
★ Caldecott Medal

Gift of the Sacred Dog, The

Paul Goble, *illustrated by author*   2, 3

The Great Spirit gives the sacred dog to a Plains Indians boy seeking relief for his hungry people. This traditional Native American tale is illustrated and retold in a simple easy-to-read text. (1980)

Grandfather Twilight

Barbara Helen Berger, *illustrated by author*   K, 1, 2

In the late afternoon as the evening shadows deepen, Grandfather Twilight takes an enchanted pearl, journeys through the forest to the ocean, and lifts the glowing pearl into the night sky, where it becomes the moon. The author's illustrations are luminous and convey the miracle of moonlight. Few illustrators for the very young convey such a sense of wonder and reverence. (1984)

John Greenleaf Whittier's The Barefoot Boy

Adapted and illustrated by Lisa Greenleaf   4+

Recall the freedom of running barefoot in the summer sun while perusing through the full-color realistic images drawn from Whittier's birthplace and reading his famous poem. The nineteenth-century poet was a contemporary of Longfellow and Emerson and was renowned as an ardent abolitionist and a mentor to women writers such as Celia Thaxter and Louisa May Alcott. (2011)

Keats's Neighborhood: An Ezra Jack Keats Treasury

Ezra Jack Keats, *illustrated by author*   K, 1

Keats is acknowledged as one of the first artists to feature realistic, friendly, multiethnic urban settings in his picture books. This collection brings together nine of his best-loved stories, including the Caldecott Medal-winning book *The Snowy Day* and the Caldecott Honor book *Goggles!*, plus *Whistle for Willie* and *Peter's Chair*. Illustrations may not be as large as in individual titles. (2002)

L M N O P and All the Letters A to Z

Howard Schrager; *illustrated by Bruce Bischof* K-2

Two teachers have created an imaginative book of phonetically-rich, easy-to-learn alphabet verses which may become a first reader. Each letter is illustrated with a series of colorful drawings that embody the letter's form, as is the custom in Waldorf schools. (2000)

Legend of the Indian Paintbrush

Tomie dePaola, *illustrated by author* **2, 3, 4**

A Native American boy paints the great deeds of his tribe. But making paints to match the colors of the evening sky eludes him. One night, a voice directs him to a special vantage point where he finds brushes filled with wonderful colors. He creates at last his masterwork, and the next day the brushes have rooted and become the brilliant flowers we now call Indian Paintbrush. (1988)

Lion and the Mouse, The

Jerry Pinkney, *illustrated by author* **K, 1, 2,**

Many storytellers have adapted Aesop's familiar fable, but Pinkney's wordless picture book is extraordinary. The award-winning artist uses pencils, colored pencils, and watercolors to render the African landscape. The only words are hints of animal sounds. The quality of the art makes this a book adults and children can relish together. (2009)

★ Caldecott Medal

Madeline

Ludwig Bemelman, *illustrated by author* **3, 4**

The charm of the author's award-winning illustrations and the humor of the must-read-aloud rhyming adventure of Miss Clavel's twelve little Parisian pupils continue to appeal. The fun continues in *Madeline and the Bad Hat, Madeline and the Gypsies, Madeline in London,* and *Madeline's Rescue.* (1939)

★ Carnegie Medal

Make Way for Ducklings

Robert McCloskey, *illustrated by author* K, 1

Mr. and Mrs. Mallard proudly return to their home in the Boston Public Garden with their eight offspring, hatched on a secluded island nearby. The McCloskey classic was based on an actual incident in which the duck family had to cross a street to get back home. Look for *Blueberries for Sal, One Morning in Maine*, and others. Appropriate for preschoolers. (1941)

★ Caldecott Medal

Medieval Feast, A

Aliki (Aliki Brandenberg), *illustrated by author* 2, 3

This is an early introduction to the tradition of the medieval feast by a popular writer/illustrator that includes colorful, amusing illustrations on every page and very little text. The foods, the customs, and the pageantry of a typical royal feast are presented in a story format. (1984)

Mia's Apple Tree

Nancy Jewell Poer; *illustrated by Eleni Mann* K–4

This enchanting children's book, written by a kindergarten teacher, celebrates nature's elemental helpers as they nurture a tiny seed in the earth. At the same time, a little girl is born to her waiting parents and grows up with her friend, the apple tree. Softly rendered color illustrations. (2004)

Miss Nelson is Missing

Harry Allard and James Marshall; *illustrated by James Marshall* 2, 3

The kids in Room 207 take advantage of their teacher's good nature until she disappears and they are faced with a vile substitute. The popular sequels are *Miss Nelson is Back* and *Miss Nelson has a Field Day*. (1977)

Museum ABC

The Metropolian Museum of Art K–3

There are countless alphabet books with pictures that correspond to a letter. These examples are taken from collections in New York's Metropolitan Museum of Art. Whether from a section of an Egyptian mural, a Japanese woodblock print, a Renaissance canvas, or a contemporary painting, readers will find them captivating. Others in the series are *Museum 123* and *Museum Shapes*. (2002)

Namaste!

Diana Cohn; *illustrated by Amy Cordova*   K, 1, 2

Nima, a young girl living near Mt. Everest in Nepal, greets passersby with "Namaste—the light in me meets the light in you" with her hands together and her head slightly bowed. She learns that she brightens the day for friends and strangers alike. Woven into the story are details about daily life in Nepal. Simple, bright illustrations from an awarding-winning artist accompany this gentle story. Includes a glossary of terms. (2009)

Negro Speaks of Rivers, The

Langston Hughes; *illustrated by E. B. Lewis*   6, 7, 8

The poem and stunning watercolor illustrations beautifully portray the experiences of African people throughout history, through the rivers they lived on in different parts of the world—the Congo, the Euphrates, the Nile, and the Mississippi. (2009)

★ Coretta Scott King Honor

Oliver Button is a Sissy

Tomie dePaola, *illustrated by author*   1, 2

Oliver would rather tap dance than play baseball and has to put up with the teasing of his classmates. DePaola is a prolific writer/illustrator and an award-winning one. This title is highlighted because teasing and bullying is the problem addressed, and we say bravo to the encouragement of individual interests that may not be popular. (1979)

Oxcart Man, The

Donald Hall, *illustrated by author*   ☀ 3

A year in the life of a nineteenth-century New England family of farmers is described in evocative pictures and simple, eloquent text. One could base the entire Waldorf Grade Three social studies block on this wonderful book. It can also serve as a class reader. (1979)

★ Caldecott Medal, New York Times Best Illustrated Book

Paddle-to-the-Sea

Holling Clancy Holling, *illustrated by author* ※ 4, 5, 6

Beautiful watercolor illustrations depict the geography of the Great Lakes region while the text tells an adventuresome tale about the perilous journey of a Native American carved toy canoe from Lake Superior to the Atlantic. Other picture storybooks by this author are also an excellent introduction to geography: *Minn of the Mississippi, Pagoo, Tree in the Trail, The Book of Indians, Seabird.* (1941)
★ Caldecott Honor, Lewis Carroll Shelf Award

Pelle's New Suit

Elsa Beskow, *illustrated by author* ※ 3

Pelle's sheep gives him wool for a new suit. Grandmother spins it into yarn, Grandfather dyes it, Mother weaves it, and the tailor cuts and sews it—while Pelle does errands for each. (1912)

Peter in Blueberry Land

Elsa Beskow, *illustrated by author* ※ K, 1

While looking for blueberries, Peter feels a light tap on his shoe, and a strange and magical adventure begins in which Peter meets the Blueberry King and Miss Cranberry. (1901)

Philipok

Leo Tolstoy; retold by Ann Keay Beneduce;
illustrated by Gennady Spirin K, 1

Little Philip's mother has told him he is too young to go to school, but one day he sets out to go on his own. Spirin's art, which combines traditional Russian technique with the traditions of the Renaissance, adds richness to a retelling that captures the simple style the author of *War and Peace* used in the stories he wrote for peasant children. See also *The Lion and the Puppy: And Other Stories for Children.* (2000)

Pocketful of Posies: A Treasury of Nursery Rhymes

Salley Mavor, *illustrated by author*   K, 1

Beautiful handcrafted, full-colored illustrations in fabric relief bring Mavor's collection of nursery rhymes to the level of enchantment that will delight children and parents alike. Mavor also incorporates natural materials such as acorn caps and driftwood along with plant-dyed wool in her fabric pictures. Not to miss. (2010)

★ Golden Kite Award, Boston Globe-Horn Book

Something from Nothing

Phoebe Gilman, *illustrated by author*   K–3

In this often-told tale from Jewish folklore, the author's exceptional art creates a shtetl (small Jewish town in Eastern Europe) within a book. Grandpa trims away the worn parts of Joseph's baby blanket to make him first, a jacket, then a vest, a tie, a handkerchief, and, finally, a button. Read aloud, the repetitive, rhythmic phrases invite children to join in. In an illustrated story within the story, a family of mice uses the scraps to build their own nest. (1993)

Story about Ping, The

Marjorie Flack; *illustrated by Kurt Wiese*   K, 1, 2

In this story set in China, a little duck finds adventure on the Yangtze River when he is too late to board his master's houseboat one evening. (1933)

Story of Babar, The

Jean and Laurent De Brunhoff, translated by Merle S. Haas; *illustrated by authors*   1, 2

The French series about an orphaned baby elephant that becomes a king, a husband, and a father to his own large family is an international success. Children will not detect the whiff of postcolonial political incorrectness that may strike the nose of some adults. (1931)

★ Carnegie Medal

Story of the Root Children

Sibylle Von Olfers; translated by Helen Dean Fish;
illustrated by author   ☀   K, 1

This nature story for very young children explains how the flower root children spend the winter asleep underground in the care of Mother Earth. When spring comes, they wake, sew new gowns and capes, and climb out into the warm spring sunshine. After they play in the meadows all summer, Mother Earth welcomes them back to their home underground. Delicate watercolor paintings illustrate the beauty of the seasons. See also *The Story of the Snow Children* and *The Story of the Wind Children*. (1906)

Sylvester and the Magic Pebble

William Steig, *illustrated by author*   1, 2

In a moment of fright, Sylvester the donkey asks his magic pebble to turn him into a rock but then cannot hold the pebble to wish himself back to normal again. How Sylvester is reunited with his family is a joyful story that put this book on many lists. (1969)
★ Caldecott Medal, Lewis Carroll Shelf Award

Tall Book of Mother Goose, The

Feodor Rojankovsky, *illustrated by author*   K–3

Reading verses aloud from Mother Goose nurtures language development and often is a child's first exposure to rhymes. With many versions to choose from, selections may be based on the quality and style of the illustrations, size of the book, age of the child, and variety of poems. One favorite is Rojankovsky's, which bursts with colorful, simple scenes, chubby-cheeked children and sprightly animals. The tall narrow size is easy for a child to hold alone and one poem and one or two pictures per page adds visual appeal and makes for easier reading. Those by Tommie dePaola, Tasha Tudor, and Blanche Fisher Wright are also favorites. Nursery rhymes are also found in anthologies such as *My Book House*. (1942)

Tear, The: A Children's Story of Transformation and Hope When a Loved One Dies

Nancy Jewel Poer, *illustrated by author*   K–8

For many years, Poer, a former kindergarten teacher, has worked with families experiencing threshold moments of birth and death. This is a sensitive story about the cycle of life told through a boy's close relationship with his grandmother. (2011)

Tomten, The

Astrid Lindgren; *illustrated by Harald Wiberg*   K, 1, 2

This story was adapted from a poem by the nineteenth-century poet, Viktor Rydberg, about a Swedish troll who saves farm animals from a hungry fox. Another volume, based on the same poem, is *The Tomten and the Fox.* (1961)

Tsubu the Little Snail

Carol Ann Williams; *illustrated by Tatsuro Kiuchi*   1, 2

When a poor rice farmer and his wife pray to a water god for a baby, "even a frog or a little snail," their prayers are answered—with a snail they call Tsubu, who can talk, sing, and even drive his father's horses. Tsubu marries a human, and when she demonstrates her love for him without regard for the opinion of others, he becomes human too. Kiuchi's dramatic paintings enliven this retelling of a Japanese fairy tale. (1995)

Under the Night Sky

Amy Lundebrek; *Illustrated by Anna Rich*   3-6

Follow a mother and son and their neighbors as they enjoy a special moment watching the spectacular aurora borealis or Northern Lights from their home in the city. The pages are graced with exquisite, almost luminescent illustrations. (2010)

Waldorf Alphabet Book

Famke Zonneveld, *illustrated by author*   1, 2, 3

Parents and young children can share in the joy of discovering the world of letters in this imaginative alphabet book. Each upper and lower case letter comes to life in the vivid pictures by the art teacher/author. Also known as *The Living Alphabet*, this most recent edition includes an informative essay, "Learning to Read and Write in Waldorf Schools," by William Ward. (2005)

When the Sun Rose

Barbara Helen Berger, *illustrated by author* 1, 2

A lonely little girl forms a very special friendship with an enchanting playmate who comes and goes with the sun. This warm story is illustrated with the same award-winning style as *Grandfather Twilight* and *The Donkey's Dream*. (1986)

Wise Enchanter, The: A Journey Through the Alphabet

Shelley Davidow; *illustrated by Krystyna Emilia Kurzyca* 1, 2

Over the course of twenty-six stories, four children are on a quest to save language from the forces of darkness. As they save each letter, one at a time, the reader is pulled into a magical journey. Soft black-and-white drawings reveal the form of each letter as it is rescued using the same picture-out-of-a-story approach used in Waldorf classrooms. (2005)

Yeh Shen: A Cinderella Story from China

Retold by Ai-Ling Louie; *illustrated by Ed Young* 2, 3

Beautiful watercolor paintings illustrate this folktale from China that predates the European Cinderella by one thousand years. (1982)

★ Boston Globe-Horn Book

Zomo the Rabbit: A Trickster Tale from West Africa

Retold and illustrated by Gerald McDermott;
translated by Nina Kuettel K, 1

Zomo the rabbit, a West African trickster, is given three apparently impossible tasks to complete before the Sky God will give him the wisdom that Zomo seeks. This is a colorfully illustrated version of a traditional tale from West Africa. (1992)

Grades
One to Three

AGES SIX TO NINE

Children's dependence on illustration falls away as they begin to develop more reading skills. Their own imaginations form the images of the characters, settings, and actions of the story. Because the development of these skills is gradual, there is an "in-between place" in which illustrated storybooks fall. As the text slowly becomes more and more of the page, illustrations appear farther apart, until we hardly want a picture to challenge the one built by our own imagination.

Building Literacy

In young children physical development predominates, including the brain and nervous system upon which intellectual abilities depend. Therefore, progress toward the ability to read abstract symbols or extract from them multiple levels of meaning is very gradual; rushing this process can be harmful.

Waldorf teachers often compare the growing intellectual abilities of the child to the root system of the plant. Force-feeding, overwatering, extending "sunlight" with electric lamps or checking root growth by pulling the stem out of the ground will not produce a stronger mature plant, even if such methods may force a short-lived blossom to appear. We can compare the process of forcing blossoms to educational practices that hurry reading by assigning homework packets on top of classroom drills; emphasizing reading programs over art, music, or physical exercise; and testing to establish progress.

What, then, should we do to preserve the vitality of childhood in the face of concern that there may not be enough time to teach everything needed to thrive in modern culture? While everyone agrees that literacy is an essential life skill in today's world, human development does not keep pace with culture, and brain development cannot be fast-forwarded. Reading will continue to be a necessity, even if printed books become an old curiosity shoppe novelty. How then do we encourage literacy skills that support creative thinking and imagination, abilities that remain vital today and in the future? Fostering a love of language and joy in the power of stories told and read will go further to promote the cause of literacy than tests and drills. In my experience that is also the consensus of teachers, librarians, and literacy workers.

Fairy Tales

In Waldorf kindergartens all over the world, we begin by telling fairy tales. You may be surprised that, in addition to Rudolf Steiner's indications to the teachers of the first Waldorf School, we have this advice from one of the most respected intellectual geniuses of our era as reported in *The Braid of Literature: Children's Worlds of Reading* by Shelby Ann Wolf and Shirley Brice Heath, 1992:

> An eager and anxious mother approached Albert Einstein for advice. Her young son was a budding scientist, and she needed help in laying out an appropriate course for his studies.
>
> "What should I read to him?" the mother queried.
> Einstein nodded his cloud of white hair and replied, "Fairy tales."
> Startled, the mother came back with, "Fine, but then what?"
> Einstein peered at the woman over his spectacles and said, "More fairy tales."
> Exasperated, the mother persisted, "And after that?"
> Einstein leaned closer to the woman, "Still more fairy tales."

Fairy tales—told by the teacher, retold enthusiastically the next day by the children, and perhaps acted out in little dramas or reviewed in puppet shows—are part of the curriculum for the first grade as well as an important part of the rich kindergarten curriculum in Waldorf schools. Books for this age group are weighted heavily with the richest source of imaginative archetypes of human experience and images of human transformation. Although analysis is inappropriate for children, adults may benefit from considering every character in a fairy tale as a part of the whole human being. While best shared without illustrations to encourage individual pictorial imagination, you simply cannot go wrong choosing a fairy tale or traditional folktale. And the magic may continue well into the later grades for some children.

Illustrated Storybooks

The text of an illustrated storybook is as important as the illustrations. The pictorial quality of language is now accessible, even though rhythm and rhyme continue to be enjoyed. Writers paint with words, and the text of picture storybooks now shares responsibility for quality, beauty, and truth. In addition, the world of nature and the human spirit, as represented in books, helps children to discover both the inner and outer worlds.

However, the way in which truth is revealed must be age-appropriate. The sense of wonder and curiosity about the natural world in grades one, two, and three is well met by stories that characterize but do not analyze nature, such as those of Thornton Burgess and many Native American tales. For younger children, the darker side of human nature is safely embodied in an archetypal figure such as the witch, the wolf, the giant, or the ogre. Villains are all bad and shades of grey do not play a part. Good triumphs. Evil is punished. The child can feel secure.

Second Grade

Second graders appreciate the stories of heroes who overcome hardships and challenges by the strength of their own character. Stories of saints and other holy people who follow their own inner voice of wisdom, make sacrifices, and perhaps break with their own past or tradition in order to effect change are particularly suitable. Fables illustrate how the greedy, selfish, or cruel creature learns a lesson; kindness and gentleness are rewarded. Aesop's fables abound in humorous moral lessons, as do the works of modern fable writers such as Lobel and Lionni. Children do not absorb morality from books unless it is present in their environment. However, literature can highlight the admired or disapproved characteristics, and fables speak to this age group without being heavy-handed.

Third Grade

For third graders the difficulties of human existence begin to take on meaning. The trials of the Hebrew people as recounted in legends and the Old Testament are representative of the historical evolution of all peoples seeking a way to live on the earth. Now is a time of natural interest in practical experiences such as gardening and cooking. Stories of how people learn to provide food, clothing, and shelter for themselves strengthen children to meet a time in which they naturally feel themselves separate individuals in a new way. Fiction about children who survive by their wits and skills (orphans abound!) fascinate and reassure.

Generally, if you find an author included here, any book by that author may be considered with some confidence. Chapter books and series are marketed to this age group as independent reading emerges. There are quality choices to be found, but tread carefully among the many being offered.

Across the Wide Dark Sea: The Mayflower Journey

Jean Van Leeuwen; *illustrated by Thomas B. Allen* 2, 3, 4

Based on entries from William Bradford's actual diary, this historical fiction tells the story of a young boy and his father who make the dangerous sailing journey from England to escape religious persecution in 1620. The story is told in a way that reflects a universal immigrant experience. Soft charcoal pencil and pastel illustrations complement this storybook for older or younger readers. It can be a family book to read aloud at Thanksgiving. (1995)

Adventures of Mole and Troll, The

Tony Johnston; *illustrated by Wallace Trip* 2, 3

Two very good friends, Mole and Troll, plan for Mother's Day, go to the beach, dig tunnels, and experiment with new shoes in this first of a charming beginning-to-read series with simple vocabulary. Tripp's droll illustrations make you smile, as always. More amusing adventures continue in *Night Noises, Mole and Troll Trim the Tree*, and *Happy Birthday Moll and Troll*. (1972)

Adventures of Pinocchio

Carlo Collodi; *illustrated by Roberto Innocenti* 3, 4, 5

Look for recent translations in 2009 by Geoffrey Brock or in 2005 by M.A. Murray of this Italian fairy tale about a wooden puppet that wishes to become a real boy. The villains are more sinister than in the cartoon movie, and it is, therefore, not so suitable for very young listeners. Confident readers can enjoy it alone. (1883)

Aesop's Fables

Retold and illustrated by Jacob Lawrence 2

Twenty-three of Aesop's Greek fables are translated into English with the full complement of Lawrence's illustrations to make this a special edition, but many other editions of Aesop may also be recommended. (1997)

Andy and the Lion

James Daugherty, *illustrated by author* 2, 3

In this modernized retelling of Aesop's *Androcles and the Lion*, Andy meets a lion on the way to school and wins his friendship for life by removing a thorn from his paw. (1938)

Animal Stories

Jakob Streit; translated by Jacob Piening   2, 3, 4

Twenty-five original animal stories by a master storyteller (and Waldorf teacher) are recommended to teachers as a resource for stories to tell in the classroom. (1974)

Animalia

Barbara Helen Berger, *illustrated by author*   2, 3

Berger showcases thirteen brief tales of wise and holy people who have lived gently with animals, including St. Francis, Buddha, and others from European and Asian legends. Intricate borders, full-color paintings, and calligraphy give this book the look and feel of an illuminated manuscript. (1982)

As My Heart Awakes

Arthur M. Pittis; *illustrated by Ausa M. Peacock*   3

The author has created a five-book "Waldorf Reader Series" that includes more than 125 stories and poems to complement a language arts curriculum. Three readers accompany the third grade with fables, saint stories, and poems— both ancient and modern—from Christian, Jewish, Islamic, Hindu, and Buddhist traditions. Pittis structures the series to move from simple to more complex language and syntax, which become progressively richer in sight words and phonetic vocabulary development. This volume and the next, *When I Hear My Heart Wonder*, follow the seasons. See also *Fee Fi Fo Fum* (Grade 2), *Snip, Snap, Snout* (Grade 3), and *Sun So Hot I Froze to Death* (Grade 4). (2005)

At the Back of the North Wind, The Princess and the Goblin, The Princess and the Curdie

George MacDonald   3–6

These three modern-age fairy tales were published in one volume in 1979, but are also available separately or in other anthologies. MacDonald, who died in 1905, is a masterful storyteller whose original fantasies engage older children as well as younger ones. *The Light Princess and other Tales* is another collection. (1832–1872)

Bear Called Paddington, A

Michael Bond; *illustrated by Peggy Fortnum*   3, 4

This is the first of ten titles that make up the original chapter-book series about a bear from Peru found in Paddington Station by an English couple. The content is suitable for younger children when read aloud, but confident beginning readers will not find the British prose too challenging. (1958)

Betsy-Tacy

Maud Hart Lovelace; *illustrated by Lois Lenski*   3, 4

Five-year-old girls from different traditions grow up together in the small Midwestern town of Deep Valley. The text in the first six appealing, easy-to-read chapter books grows appropriately more challenging as the girls grow older: *Betsy-Tacy and Tib, Betsy and Tacy Go Over the Big Hill, Betsy and Tacy Go Downtown, Heavens to Betsy*, and *Betsy in Spite of Herself*. Additional volumes follow the girls through high school, college, and marriage. (1940)

Book of Fairy Princes, The

Isabel Wyatt   1, 2

Seven of Wyatt's magical tales take us from ivory towers and colorful kingdoms to great forests and golden lands. Floris Books reissued it in 1994. Any of Wyatt's works for children that can be found are recommended. (1949)

Cat Heaven

Cynthia Rylant, *illustrated by author*   K–3

A comforting book for children who have lost a pet, this happy story paints in vibrant colors and rhyming text a feline paradise that would appeal to every cat. There is gentle humor, warmth, and much cheerful detail about the heaven that all cats know how to find. This Newberry and Caldecott Honor author knows how to reach the hearts of children and adults. See also *Dog Heaven*. (1997)

Catwings

Ursula K. Le Guin; *illustrated by S. D. Schindler*   3, 4

Four kittens, born with wings, venture an escape from the dangers of their urban home into the countryside. Short, well-written chapters and the watercolor illustrations make this a good fantasy series for younger readers. Other titles: *Catwings Return, Wonderful Alexander and the Catwings*, and *Jane on Her Own: A Catwings Tale*. (1988)

Charlotte's Web

E. B. White   3, 4, 5

A life-saving friendship between a common barn spider and a pig is the unlikely story behind one of the most popular children's books ever written. (1952)

★ Laura Ingalls Wilder Medal

Child's Garden of Verses, A

Robert Louis Stevenson   3, 4, 5

Stevenson's enduring collection of poems written for children was one of the first such volumes and is still one of the best. The 1986 edition illustrated by Tasha Tudor makes a fine read aloud for even very young listeners. (1885)

Child's Calendar, A

John Updike; *illustrated by Nancy Ekholm Burkert*   3, 4, 5

A New England year is described in a dozen verses by one of America's leading authors. A revised edition in 1999 with new illustrations by Trina Schart Hyman made this volume a Caldecott Honor-winner. (1969)

★ Caldecott Honor

Child's Own Book of Verse, A: Book One

Ada M. Skinner and Frances G. Wickes; *illustrated by Maud S. Fuller and Michael (Miska) Petersham*   K–3

While the cover may seem old-fashioned to modern parents, this book is full of delightful rhymes, jingles, and poetry certain to appeal to a young child's ears, heart, and imagination. The charming illustrations are by an award-winning husband/wife team. Books Two and Three are designed for the four primary years. The set is made available by the Baldwin Online Children's Literature Project that offers online resources at no charge and grants permission to individuals to print copies of books such as this for personal or educational use. (1917)

Child's Treasury of Poems, A

Edited by Mark Daniel; *various illustrators* K+

Anonymous verses as well as selections from well-known children's poets are displayed, with reproductions of fifty full-color paintings and numerous small engravings of child subjects from the Victorian and Edwardian "golden age of childhood." The poems may be found in other collections, but the organization into meaningful sections and the addition of period art gives them new life. Other collections by the same editor: *A Child's Treasury of Seaside Verse, A Child's Treasury of Christmas Poems,* and *A Child's Treasury of Animal Verse.* (1986)

Classic Fairy Tales, The

Iona and Peter Opie 1, 2, 3

An internationally recognized team of folklorists whose publications include *The Oxford Book of Children's Verse* and *The Oxford Dictionary of Nursery Rhymes* compiled this collection of twenty-four best-known stories in the English language. Each tale has a historical introduction and is preserved in the exact words in which it was first published in English or from the earliest surviving text. The black-and-white illustrations reproduced from early children's books are also of interest. (1974)

Colour Fairy Books, The

Edited by Andrew Lang 1, 2, 3+

The Dover paperback facsimile series of Lang's opus presents an inexhaustible international anthology of fairy tales and folktales for those who can never get enough. Start with *The Rainbow Fairy Book,* which is an anthology from the series, then work your way through all twelve colors, each with a specific collection, from *The Red Fairy Book* to *The Lilac Fairy Book.* (1889)

Complete Grimms' Fairy Tales, The

Jacob and Wilhelm Grimm; translated by Margaret Hunt; edited by James Stern; *illustrated by Josef Scharl* K, 1, 2+

The Grimms' stories were originally collected in German and published between 1810–1814 and later translated into English. Stern revised Hunt's translations and his version is among those preferred. A popular 1976 edition by Pantheon is often recommended in Waldorf Schools and includes an introduction by Padraic Colum and commentary by Joseph Campbell. As it is a resource, please see the recommended fairy tales listed by ages in the Appendix. (1884)

Grades 1 to 3

Copper-toed Boots

Marguerite deAngeli, *illustrated by author* 1, 2, 3

A little boy, who wants most of all to own a pair of copper-toed boots and a dog, works hard to earn his boots and finds a dog, too, in a story set in pioneer-era Michigan. (1938)

Diary of an Early American Boy: Noah Blake, 1805

Eric Sloane, *illustrated by author* 3, 8

Based on Noah Blake's actual diary of his daily activities, from making nails to maple sugaring, the author illustrated the text with superb pen-and-ink drawings to give a detailed picture of what the farm looked like, how things were done, and with what equipment and tools. This is a prized resource for teachers and parents working on the Waldorf Grade Three social studies unit on food, clothing, and shelter. (1962)

Dragon Kite, The

Nancy Luenn; *illustrated by Michael Hague* 3, 4

A crafty thief constructs a magnificent kite, which he hopes will enable him to reach the golden dolphins that adorn the roof of a nearby castle. The story is based on the life of a historical Robin Hood figure in Japan in the late 1600s. (1982)

Early Moon

Carl Sandburg; *illustrated by James Daugherty* 3, 4, 5

This is a selection of seventy of the author's poems for young people illustrated by a renowned author/illustrator and organized by topics. (1930)

East O' the Sun and West O' the Moon and Other Norwegian Fairy Tales

Peter Christen Asbjørnsen and Jørgen E. Moe K, 1, 2

The Dover Juvenile Classics affordable edition is the definitive collection of Norwegian folktales compiled by Asbjørnsen and Moe in the nineteenth century and translated by George Webbe Dasent. A second version was published in 1992. (1970)

Ellen Tebbits

Beverly Cleary   3, 4

What Ellen Tebbits likes best about third grade is having Austine Allen for her best friend. This story tells of the ups and downs of their relationship as Ellen navigates growing up. (1951)

Elsie Piddock Skips in her Sleep

Eleanor Farjeon; *illustrated by Charlotte Voake*   1, 2, 3

Elsie is a born skipper and Andy-Spandy, the fairies' Skipping Master, bestows her with a magic skipping rope. When an evil lord threatens the community's skipping grounds she returns, a lady of 109, to save the day with her magical skipping. In addition to the positive image of aging and fitness, the details and varieties of Elsie's rope-skipping feats inspired an annual jump rope festival at one Waldorf School. This is a perfect fantasy adventure for those too young for Harry Potter. Other tales by this author are also recommended. (1937)

Enchanted Castle, The

Edith Nesbit   3, 4, 5

Three friends use an enchanted ring to travel from their English homeland to a magical world. Initially it is thrilling to use magic to their advantage, but eventually they discover that it is overpowering their lives. Authors H. G. Wells and Noel Coward loved this story. (1906)

English Fairy Tales

Edited by Joseph Jacobs   K, 1, 2

Jacobs wanted English children to have access to English fairy tales as they were primarily reading French and German tales. He edited five collections between 1890 and 1912, including *More English Fairy Tales, Celtic Fairy Tales, More Celtic Fairy Tales*, and *European Folk and Fairy Tales*. (1898)

English Fairy Tales

Edited by Flora Annie Steel; *illustrated by Arthur Rackham*   K, 1, 2

This is a collection of fairy tales with a unique origin in the English language. Another collection, by Joseph Jacobs under the same title and published in 1898, may be easier to find, but Rackam's illustrations are always noteworthy. (1918)

Feather and Tails: Animal Fables from Around the World

Edited by David Kheridian; *illustrated by Nonny Hogrogian*   2

Husband and wife, each having won awards, have combined their talents to create a handsomely designed anthology of animal fables, proverbs, riddles, and folktales. These are mostly ancient teaching stories. The retellings exhibit a satisfying variety, while the playful illustrations enliven the whole collection. (1992)

Fee Fi Fo Fum

Arthur M. Pittis; *illustrated by Ausa M. Peacock*   2

The author's "Waldorf Reader Series" begins during the second half of second grade with this title. For series details, see *As My Heart Awakes*. This volume includes twenty-four classic tales such as "The Gingerbread Boy," "The Brementown Musicians" and "The Three Billy Goats Gruff." See also *When I Hear My Heart Wonder, Snip, Snap, Snout* and *Sun So Hot I Froze to Death*. (2005)

Frederick's Fables: A Treasury of 16 Favorite Leo Lionni Stories

Leo Lionni, *illustrated by author*   2

A treasury of thirteen works published individually between 1960 and 1994 is here reprinted with a new introduction by the author and three additional tales. Illustrated on every page, this anthology contains Lionni's most popular animal fables, including three Caldecott Honor books—*Alexander and the Wind-Up Mouse, Swimmy*, and *Frederick*. (1997)

Frog and Toad Together

Arnold Lobel, *illustrated by author*   2, 3

Beginning readers relate well to the relationship between two friends, Frog and Toad, as they share simple day-to-day activities and humorous small adventures. There are three more: *Frog and Toad are Friends, Frog and Toad All Year*, and *Days with Frog and Toad*. (1972)

★ Newbery Honor

Golden Bird, The

Edith Brill; *illustrated by Jan Pienkowski*   2, 3

In this little-known fairy tale, an old Polish woman living in the forest is rewarded with magic powers after she helps the injured Golden Bird. (1970)

Hear the Voice of the Griot!
A Guide to the African Geography, History, and Culture

Betty K. Staley; *illustrated by Sonya Kane and Daniela Ubsdell* ☀   1–8

Staley, a long-time Waldorf educator, has written a comprehensive 400+ page resource for teachers, families, librarians and those who wish to bring more of the African culture into their lives. What a treasury: fairy tales, fables, myths, poems, music, art, history, geography and so much more! When the material comes alive, one then can become a "griot"—the storyteller, the minstrel, the bard. 1997

Henry and Mudge

Cynthia Rylant; *illustrated by Sucie Stevenson*   2, 3

This is a popular humorous series (over twenty volumes and still going strong) of easy-to-read books with simple vocabulary and repetition. Henry and his lovable dog, Mudge, have gentle adventures typical of family life. (1987)

Henry Huggins

Beverly Cleary   3, 4

Henry Huggins is already quite a character when we meet him in third grade. His mutt, Ribsy, is featured in all of Henry's misadventures, which continue in *Henry and Ribsy* and *Henry and the Clubhouse*. This boy and dog combo may draw boys into the large circle of fans who love the Ramona series. (1950)

Hundred Dresses, The

Eleanor Estes ; *illustrated by Louis Slobodkin*   3, 4, 5

Wanda wears the same faded dress to school every day, and because she is also different (a Polish immigrant), she is teased and made fun of. No one believes her boast that she has a hundred dresses until she wins the art prize for her perfectly drawn collection of a hundred dresses. The text is simple enough for younger readers, but the lesson is powerfully conveyed. (1944)
★ Newbery Honor

Hymn of the Sun, The

St. Francis of Assisi, *edited and illustrated by Tony Wright*   2, 3

Wright has edited a translation from the Italian and illustrated this well-known traditional hymn by Saint Francis of Assisi to create an excellent version for children that can be used as a class reader after the story of Saint Francis has been shared. (1990)

I'll Always Love You

Hans Wilhelm   K-3

Wilhelm tenderly deals with the relationship of a boy and his dog, their growing up together, sharing many secrets and adventures, and being best friends. As the dog ages and dies, the boy learns to grieve, cope, and finally love again. This story is sad, moving, but also triumphant. (1988)

Journey Through Time in Verse and Rhyme

Heather Thomas   1–8

The author's poetry collection is arranged by age group from six to fourteen, especially for grades one through eight. The poems support the subject matter of many lessons besides English and is popular with Waldorf teachers. (1998)

King Beetle-Tamer and Other Lighthearted Wonder Tales

Isabel Wyatt   2, 3, 4

Floris Books reissued this collection of stories about fairies, unicorns, and magical adventures. Independent grade three and four readers will enjoy these humorous tales, but they can be read aloud with success to younger listeners, too. (1963)

King of the Golden River

John Ruskin   3, 4, 5

The East Wind and the King of the Golden River turn two cruel brothers into black stones, but kindly Gluck, youngest in the family, is rewarded for his unselfishness. This fairy tale by the English author and art critic was written for his daughter. (1851)

King Thrushbeard

Kelly Morrow, *illustrated by author*   2, 3

The author has created a quartet of beginning readers, retelling classic tales such as this one from the Grimm Brothers' collection. She is a class teacher and a reading specialist. The humorous and adventurous stories in early chapter book form introduce simple punctuation and phonetic decoding skills introduced in this first volume. Others are: *Lazy Jack, The Prince and the Dragon,* and *Sylvan and Jacosa.* (2010)

Knocking-Door-Tree Forest and Other Bangalow Tales, The

Susan Perrow; *illustrated by Eleni Mann*   K, 1, 2

This collection of magical stories by a respected storyteller is geographically set within the forests and gardens of Bangalow, a pretty village in the Northern Rivers area of Australia's New South Wales, but their appeal is universal. Another collection, *Healing Stories for Challenging Behavior* (2008) is a resource for adults and offers therapeutic stories for all kinds of problems as well as chapters on the art of storytelling, and how to select stories for their ability to heal. (2004)

Lady of Guadalupe, The

Tomie dePaola, *illustrated by author*   2, 3, 4

The prolific author/illustrator recounts the story of the appearance of the Lady of Guadalupe to a poor Indian farmer in Mexico in 1531. He learned of this story while an art student and subsequently wrote and illustrated other saint stories including that of Saint Christopher. (1980)

Last Little Cat, The

Meindert DeJong; *illustrated by Jeff McMullan*   3, 4

In this tender story by Newbery author DeJong, the last little cat finds the perfect home. Simple vocabulary and repetitive text make this a good beginning-to-read selection. (1963)

Lazy Jack

Kelly, *illustrated by author*   2, 3

This retelling of the humorous English folktale about a boy who never does anything right but becomes rich in spite of himself is part of the author's four-volume series of early chapter-book readers. See *King Thrushbeard* for series details. (2010)

Lion and the Puppy, and other Stories for Children, The

Leo Tolstoy; translated by James Riordan   1, 2, 3

A collection of twenty-five warm, earthy stories Tolstoy wrote for children, each based on Russian folklore with a definite moral or lesson to be learned. Like the best fables of Aesop, the morals naturally spring from the stories. (1988)

Liputto: Stories of Gnomes and Trolls

Jakob Streit; translated by Nina Kuettel;
illustrated by Susanne Mitchell   K, 1

Good and courageous gnomes run into setbacks from the mischievous trolls, adding suspense to these wonderful stories. This prolific author will delight children of all ages with the humanity and grace of the gnomes. (1992)

Little Bear

Else Holmelund Minarik; *illustrated by Maurice Sendak*   2, 3

The gentle adventures of Little Bear and his family and friends manage to entertain despite the carefully controlled vocabulary in this beginning-to-read series. The illustrations add to the amusing charm of these stories that delight younger listeners when read aloud. Others in the series are *A Kiss for Little Bear, Father Bear Comes Home, Little Bear's Visit,* and *Little Bear's Friend.* (1957)

Little Pear: The Story of a Little Chinese Boy

Eleanor Francis Lattimore   3, 4

The adventures of Little Pear, a mischievous five-year-old boy living in China in the early 1900s, are presented in chapter book format making this a good beginning-to-read selection. (1931)

Mare's Egg, The

Judy Varga, *illustrated by author*   3, 4

A crafty fox's wits lead him to serious trouble when he convinces Russian villagers to try to hatch a mud-covered pumpkin. (1972)

Moffats, The

Eleanor Estes; *illustrated by Louis Slobodkin*   3, 4, 5

Four children and a hard-working widowed mother live together on New Dollar Street in the village of Cranbury. Their seemingly quiet lives are studded with almost daily, unexpected adventures. (1941)

Mrs. Piggle-Wiggle

Betty Bard MacDonald   3, 4

She knows how to cure Answer-Backers and Won't-Go-to-Beds. Mrs. Piggle-Wiggle has a hilarious answer for every misbehavior—from eating too many sweets, to not putting away toys. Fun to read aloud at bedtime and the unmistakable lesson of each story is better "to sleep on" than a parental lecture. (1947)

My Book House

Edited by Olive Beaupré Miller   K+

For several generations, the primary and treasured source of enriching literature for children came from this twelve-volume set. "To give children the best in literature" was Miller's goal. It was the first collection whose verses, rhymes, folktales, and stories matched the developing needs of the child up through high school. Every volume lured one to read one more. Look for them in used and online bookstores and book fairs. (1920)

My Father's Dragon

Ruth Stiles Gannett, *illustrated by author*   3, 4

Elmer Elevator uses his clever imagination to rescue a baby dragon from Wild Island. This is the first of a winsomely illustrated early reader series of three titles, which includes *Elmer and the Dragon* and *The Dragons of Blueland*. (1948)
★ Newbery Honor

Old Mother West Wind

Thornton W. Burgess; *illustrated by Harrison Cady* ☀ 2, 3, 4

Burgess creates one of the earliest and still one of the best introductions to nature's creatures. Each short chapter is a complete story about an animal character. The features of the landscape and the forces of nature, such as the Merry Little Breezes, are characters too. *Mother West Wind's Children* is another volume of stories. Many of the stories are also available in individual volumes and can be enjoyed by independent readers. (1910)

Patter-Paws the Fox

Brian Masters; *illustrated by Brian Gold* ☀ 2, 3

This British beginning-to-read chapter book of animal fables, composed by Waldorf teacher Brian Masters, uses carefully chosen vocabulary, repetition, and rhyming. (1992)

Peacock Pie: A Book of Rhymes

Walter de la Mare; *illustrated by Barbara Cooney* ☀ 3, 4, 5

An extraordinary collection of poems for children features the capers of fairies, witches, giants, beasts, princes, kings, and children. Cooney illustrated it in 1961, and Louise Brierley was inspired again in 1989. Another fine collection is *Come Hither: A Collection of Rhymes and Poems for the Young of All Ages* (1928). (1913)

Phantom Tollbooth, The

Norton Juster; *illustrated by Jules Feiffer* 3, 4

Milo is bored until a peculiar turnpike tollbooth arrives, complete with Tock, a watchdog companion. The two enter a remarkable world of wacky adventures. Linguistic invention and sensible nonsense make this a fun book to read aloud. (1961)

Pigeon Post, The

Arthur Ransome   3, 4, 5

In the series, a group of independent children, ages two to twelve, play at being explorers in England's lake country in the 1930s. Often their adventures are aboard a boat called *The Swallow*, but in this sixth adventure they abandon the lake and go prospecting for gold. *Swallows and Amazons* was the first volume, and there are many others with quite a following, a website, and a fan club, The TARS (The Arthur Ransome Society). (1936)

★ Carnegie Medal

Pippi Longstocking

Astrid Lindgren; *illustrated by Louis S. Glanzman*   3, 4, 5

Although the series was written originally in Swedish, the irrepressible character of the pig-tailed unconventional comic heroine is one that translates in any language. Her zany adventures continue in *Pippi Goes on Board, Pippi on the Run,* and *Pippi in the South Seas.* (1950)

Poems for Children

Eleanor Farjeon   1–4

Farjeon was an adult writer of poems and plays, but is so renowned for her writings for children that an annual prize is given in her name for contributions to children's literature. This collection includes "Meeting Mary," "Sing for Your Supper," "Over the Garden Wall," "Joan's Door," "Come Christmas," and others. (1951)

Prince and the Dragon, The

Kelly Morrow, *illustrated by author*   2, 3

A classic story of a prince and a dragon that threatens the kingdom is retold in the third volume of the author's four-volume series of early chapter-book readers. See *King Thrushbeard* for series details. (2010)

Puck the Gnome

Jakob Streit; translated by Nina Kuettel;
illustrated by Georges A. Feldmann   K–4

This story is one of the most original children's stories to appear in quite a while. The story of Puck, who has one foot facing forward and one backward, illuminates the world of the hard-working gnomes. The moral insights, wisdom, humor, and true goodness found in Puck's adventures charm both children and adults. The illustrations are truly magical. (2004)

Rabbit Hill

Robert Lawson   2, 3

Unlike Farmer McGregor and Peter Rabbit, in this story the human family and the neighboring rabbits do arrive at a friendly solution to sharing the bounty of the family's garden. (1944)

★ Newbery Medal

Random House Book of Poetry for Children, The

Edited by Jack Prelutsky; *illustrated by Arnold Lobel*   K+

Every publisher has a big fat anthology of children's poems, so why this one? The editor is also a children's poet whose many works are highly recommended. Five hundred poems are divided into subject areas such as seasons, living things, children, and home. The poems of Emily Dickinson, Robert Louis Stevenson, Robert Frost, Langston Hughes, Gwendolyn Brooks, Lewis Carroll, Edward Lear, Ogden Nash, and Shel Silverstein ensure that the collection will carry any poetry lover through childhood and beyond. Indexed by title, author, first line, and subject with cheerful illustrations on every page. (1983)

Ring-A-Ring O' Roses and a Ding Dong Bell: A Book of Nursery Rhymes

Compiled and illustrated by Alan Marks   K, 1, 2

Marks has selected and artfully illustrated these classic nursery rhymes in a collection that has become a treasure and standby in Waldorf schools. His first book, *Storm*, won a Carnegie Medal. (1991)

Rukia Goes to School

Susan Cook; *illustrated by Ilana Stein* 1–5

Cook, a Waldorf teacher, has written a unique reader for children in grades one through five. She relates a day in the life of Rukia, a third-grade student at the Rudolf Steiner School in Mbagathi south of Narobi, Kenya. Readers learn about the culture of an African Waldorf school and see the differences and similarities to Waldorf schools in North America. (2009)

Russian Fairy Tales

Aleksandr Nikolaevich Afanas'ev ⚜ K, 1, 2

This collection was translated by Norbert Guterman and originally published in 1945. Black-and-white illustrations enliven two hundred tales in the 1976 edition, the most comprehensive edition in English. (1855-63)

Sarah, Plain and Tall

Patricia MacLachlan 3, 4, 5+

Sarah came from Maine to the Midwest in the nineteenth century to answer the widower Jacob's advertisement for a wife and mother for Anna and Caleb. The tale is told from the point of view of young Anna and continues in *Skylark* and *Caleb's Story*. The story is rich enough to appeal to older reluctant readers who will find the text not too difficult. It works as a family read aloud for mixed ages, too. (1985)

★ Newbery Medal, Scott O'Dell Award for Historical Fiction

Saynday's People: The Kiowa Indians and the Stories They Told

Alice Marriott ⚜ 3, 4, 5

The two volumes combined here, *Winter-Telling Stories* (1947) and *Indians on Horseback* (1948), written by an ethnologist, give a window into this tribe's daily life and culture, and includes recipes, crafts, stories and myths. These would be best read aloud in light of the oral tradition of Native Americans. (1963)

Seven Year Old Wonder Book, The

Isabel Wyatt 1, 2

Floris Books reissued this collection of stories about fairies, magic, and enchantment, within a framework story of a little girl whose mother reads her a bedtime story each night. Wyatt is an author much recommended in Waldorf circles. (1994)

Sharing the Seasons: A Book of Poems

Edited by Lee Bennet Hopkins; *illustrated by David Diaz*   3, 4, 5

Poet Lee Bennet Hopkins has brought together a memorable collection of poems that will remind readers that all kinds of wondrous things are happening outside their doors and windows. There are twelve poems for each of the four seasons, each highlighted with energetic and colorful paintings by a Caldecott Medal-winning illustrator. (2010)

Silver Curlew, The

Eleanor Farjeon; *illustrated by Earnest H. Shepard*   3, 4, 5

In this fairy tale, which incorporates the story of Tom Tit Tot, a lazy girl becomes the king's bride by implying that she has woven twelve skeins of cloth when actually she has eaten twelve dumplings. See also *Poems for Children*. (1953)

Sing a Song of Popcorn: Every Child's Book of Poems

Edited by Beatrice Schenk de Regniers and others;
illustrated by nine Caldecott Medal artists   3, 4, 5

Various Caldecott Medal artists have illustrated this anthology of poems, which is organized thematically so you can suit the mood or the occasion. (1988)

Snip, Snap, Snout

Arthur M. Pittis; *illustrated by Ausa M. Peacock*   3

This is the fourth book in the "Waldorf Reader Series." Stories are kept short, but are never dull or contrived. Each story focuses on different word groups, sounds, punctuation, and grammar. See *As My Heart Awakes* for series details. (2005)

Stories for Children

Isaac Bashevis Singer   K, 1

Singer writes with wit and imagination; his tales reflect a deep appreciation of God and the natural world. Over thirty stories are here, perfect for reading aloud. Many of these have appeared in other collections of Singer's stories, and some have been issued as individual volumes. (1962)

Stories Julian Tells, The

Ann Cameron; *illustrated by Ann Strugnell*   2, 3

This easy reader relates, in short chapters, episodes in seven-year-old Julian's life. These adventures include getting into trouble with his younger brother, Huey, planting a garden, trying to grow taller, losing a tooth, and finding a new friend. Sequels include *More Stories Julian Tells* and others. (1981)
  ⋆ ALA Notable Children's Book

Stories of the Saints

Siegwart Knijpenga   ⚜   2

Thirty-seven stories of Christian saints are told in a way that will captivate and inspire children. Saints, like the rest of us, are very different from one another, but the thread that unites all of these stories is that the spirit of love transforms tragedy into victory and rejoicing. These stories can be learned and retold by adults or read to primary grade children. Middle-school children can enjoy reading the stories themselves. (2000)

Stuart Little

E. B. White   3, 4, 5

The human Littles, of New York, adopt a young mouse, Stuart, into their family. Stuart embarks on a hero's quest across the American countryside, encounters many delightful characters, and finds himself in one adventure after another. This is a story of leaving home, growing up, and discovering oneself. Like White's *Charlotte's Web*, it can be enjoyed read aloud to younger listeners or read alone by independent readers. (1945)

Sun & Spoon

Kevin Henkes   3–7

The death of a grandma can leave an empty space but can also draw those left behind closer. This is a story about a boy and his grandfather both coping with this loss. There is sibling fighting, lying, and hiding, but many lessons are learned and all ends well. (2007)

Sylvan and Jocosa

Kelly Morrow, *illustrated by author*   2, 3

Best friends who have been separated wander and search for each other in this magical tale. This fourth early chapter book in a series builds on the reading skills of *The Prince and the Dragon* by the same author. See *King Thrushbeard* for series details. (2010)

Tale of Peter Rabbit, The

Beatrix Potter, *illustrated by author*   K-3

Look for the Warne edition of this much-duplicated series. The author's distinctive art and gentle stories about familiar animals deserve careful reproduction. Peter Rabbit's adventures in Farmer McGregor's garden are just the beginning. Read these aloud to the youngest, and they will read them again in the years that follow: *The Tale of Benjamin Bunny, The Tale of Squirrel Nutkin, The Tale of Mrs. Tiggy-Winkle, The Tale of Tom Kitten,* and *The Tale of Jemima Puddle Duck.* (1902)

Tale of the Mandarin Ducks, The

Katherine Paterson; *illustrated by Leo and Diane Dillon*   2, 3

Rich illustrations in the style of Japanese paintings portray a fairy tale love story set in Japan: Shozo, the chief steward, helps a wild drake escape from captivity on his Imperial lord's estate. The drake, who had been pining for his mate, is reunited with her, and together the ducks help the steward and his love to escape their cruel master. (1990)

★ New York Times Best Illustrated Book

Tales of Tiptoes Lightly, The

Reg Down   K–4

Tiptoes Lightly is a gentle and wise fairy living in an acorn high in the branches of a great oak tree. These three innocent and magical tales originated from the author's teaching in kindergarten and the lower grades and are suitable for reading aloud or as a first chapter book for beginning readers. Others in the series include *The Festival of Stones, Big-Stamp Two-Toes the Barefoot Giant, Magic Knot and Other Tangles, The Lost Lagoon,* and others. (2004)

Ten Saints

Eleanor Farjeon; *illustrated by Helen Sewell*   2

Farjeon tells the traditional stories of Saint Christopher, Saint Martin, Saint Dorothea, Saint Bridget, Saint Hubert, Saint Giles, Saint Simeon Stylites, Saint Nicholas, and Saint Francis in a version suitable for young listeners. See *Poems for Children* and others by this renowned writer. (1936)

Tenth Good Thing About Barney, The

Judith Viorst; *illustrated by Erik Blegvad*   2, 3

This little gem deals with the death of a beloved pet, Barney, and is one of the best on the subject of loss and grieving for very young children. (1971)

Toad for Tuesday, A

Russell Erickson; *illustrated by Lawrence Di Fiori*   2, 3, 4

On Thursday, Wharton the toad is captured by an owl who saves him to eat on Tuesday, the owl's birthday, but the intervening five days change his mind. (1974)
  ⋆ ALA Notable Book

Twelve Tales from Aesop

Retold and illustrated by Eric Carle   2

The award-winning artist has retold and illustrated twelve of the famous Greek storyteller's fables. (1980)

26 Fairmont Avenue

Tomie dePaola, *illustrated by author*   2, 3, 4

Kicking off a chapter-book series by the same name, the first volume in the popular writer/illustrator's easy-reader series recounts memorable moments from his early years, surrounded by loving family members and friends. The primary focus is the plagued construction and landscaping of the family's first and only house in Connecticut from 1938 to 1939. The author's chapter-book memoirs continue in *Here We All Are*, *On My Way*, and *What a Year*, taking readers to the beginning of the author's first-grade year in 1940. (1999)
  ⋆ Newbery Honor

Velveteen Rabbit, The

Margery Williams; *illustrated by William Nicholson*   **2, 3, 4**

By the time Velveteen Rabbit is dirty, worn out, and about to be burned, he has almost given up hope of ever finding the magic called "Real." Like the rabbit, this story never dies. (1922)

Waldorf Book of Poetry, The

Compiled by David Kennedy   **K+**

Anyone who loves poetry will welcome this new anthology to share with children or treasure for oneself. The collection of 425 poems is arranged in subjects such as Animals, History, Seasons, Saints, Fables, Numbers, Shakespeare, Imagination and more. In the Foreword, Eugene Schwartz describes the value of poetry in a child's education, how children learn verses by heart, and poetry's place in the Waldorf Curriculum. Designed to cover the elementary and high school years, it is a resource for any subject: history, mathematics, social studies, language, science and geography. (2011)

Water Babies, The: A Fairy Tale for a Land Baby

Charles Kingsley; *illustrated by Jessie Willcox Smith*   **2, 3, 4**

The ways of living creatures, plants, rocks, rivers, and tides are woven into a fairy tale about a little chimney sweep and his adventures under the waves, which the author, a naturalist and tutor to the Prince of Wales, wrote for his youngest child. It has charmed generations and taught "what a fine thing it is to love truth, mercy, justice, courage, and all things noble and of good report." (1863)

When I Hear My Heart Wonder

Arthur M. Pittis; *illustrated by Ausa M. Peacock*   **3**

This volume is part of the "Waldorf Reader Series." Please see *As My Heart Awakes* for series details. Grade three stories recapitulate the previous year's language arts curriculum. (2007)

Why Noah Chose the Dove

Isaac Bashevis Singer ; translated by Elizabeth Shub;
illustrated by Eric Carle   3, 4

As each animal boasts of the qualities that make it especially worthy to go on the ark, Noah takes a particular liking to the dove. A celebrated Yiddish storyteller and an awarding-winning artist collaborate on this unique tale. (1973)

Winnie the Pooh

A. A. Milne; *illustrated by E. H. Shepard*   2, 3, 4

Pooh, Eeyore, Piglet, Kanga, and Tigger are among the most well-known figures in children's literature and for good reason. Start by reading aloud, and at some point, the world of Pooh Bear can be enjoyed reading alone, at nine or ninety-nine. *The House at Pooh Corner* is a sequel. Beware of Disney versions; one is honey, the other white sugar. (1926)

Wonderful Wizard of Oz, The

L. Frank Baum; *illustrated by W. W. Denlow*   3, 4, 5

The story of Dorothy from Kansas and her adventures in Oz with the Lion, the Tin Man, and the Scarecrow is reissued in a facsimile of the illustrated first edition. Some of the other titles in the series of this utopian world are by other authors. Start with the original, perhaps read aloud, and then enjoy the rest: *Ozma of Oz, The Patchwork Girl of Oz,* and *The Emerald City of Oz.* (1900)

Grades 1 to 3

Grades
Four and Five

AGES NINE TO TWELVE

A mind nurtured by meaningful literature receives the benefit of an ever widening understanding of history and the physical world. The capacities of human imagination make this understanding possible even for a body confined to a wheelchair and a life lived inside the boundaries of a neighborhood barrio. In a wonderful symbiosis, rich and meaningful language experiences nurture imagination, just as it offers an entrance into the richest depths of those experiences. The value of literature may be assumed, but the matter of choices that will ignite and fuel the fire of appreciation remains.

For this age group, independent reading skills have usually been achieved, although there will still be struggles for some, including second language learners. But all children of this age find it a challenging time on some level. In literature for older elementary and junior high school students, the more complex character of human nature is explored as well as the individual's struggle with the light and dark side of the Self. This is in keeping with moral development and the gradual growth of personal conscience.

Fourth Grade

In fourth grade, the stories of the Norse myths and the "Twilight of the Gods" help to meet the boisterous energy of children leaving the innocence of young childhood. Many children experience an acute sense of aloneness or a first taste of the existential dilemma intrinsic to our human individuality. A changing of worlds is depicted in the Norse myths as well as an experience of loss that cannot be ignored or denied. Another study that helps this transition is the animal kingdom, a first "formal" science in Waldorf schools. Animal fiction stories are a favorite with this age group when they are based on the actual nature of the animal. The classic "boy and dog" or "girl and horse" stories arise and hold interest more intensely at this time than any other. What we share with the animal kingdom, a body of sensation and feeling, is coming awake and to consciousness in children of this age, and will burst into the physical development of adolescence.

Fifth Grade

Greek myths and the history of the earliest civilizations of India, Persia, Egypt, and Greece are ideally studied at about the fifth grade. The rise of democracy parallels an appreciation of the importance of the spirit and contributions of the individual. Fifth graders are ready to embrace the idea of a pantheon of diversity that recognizes the virtues and limitations of each one. The powers of gods hold fascination, as will other legends and stories that explore the possibilities of magical powers and supernatural phenomena.

There is a desire to escape the world and, at the same time, a compelling wish to be part of it. Mysteries and miracles of nature can fascinate as deeply as the world of fantasy and magic, and in the study of plant reproduction we find a delicate echo of human sexuality that prepares the way for human physiology and anatomy studies in the upper grades.

Aida

Retold by Leontyne Price; *illustrated by Leo and Diane Dillon*   5

The celebrated African-American opera star retells the story of the Verdi opera for which she is best remembered. *Aida*, a romance set in ancient Egypt, is enhanced with illustrations by an award-winning team of artists. (1990)

★ Coretta Scott King Illustrator Award

Alice's Adventures in Wonderland

Lewis Carroll; *illustrated by John Tenniel*   5–8

From a master of fantasy, the story of Alice's surreal adventure down the rabbit hole into another world has passed the test of generations, and children as well as adults enjoy it read aloud. *Through the Looking Glass and What Alice Found There* is the sequel. When read aloud, even younger children can enjoy it, although the levels of satire and symbolism appeal to a more mature reader. (1865)

All-of-a-Kind Family

Sydney Taylor   4, 5

The life of a Jewish family with seven children growing up on New York's Lower East Side in the early twentieth century is the subject of this series. It includes *All-of-a-Kind Family Downtown, All-of-a-Kind Family Uptown, Ella of All-of-a-Kind Family,* and others. (1951)

Animal Family, The

Randall Jarrell; *illustrated by Maurice Sendak*   4, 5

A lonely hunter living in the wilderness beside the sea gains a family made up of a mermaid, a bear, a lynx, and a boy. Honors were heaped upon this book for the poet's language and for what it has to say about the meaning of family. (1965)

★ Newbery Honor, New York Times Best Juvenile Book

Animal Stories

Walter de la Mare   4

Animal Stories, Chosen, Arranged, and in Some Part Written by Walter de la Mare is the full title of this timeless collection. He won the 1947 Carnegie Medal in Literature for *Collected Stories for Children*. (1940)

Are You There, God? It's Me, Margaret

Judy Blume 5, 6

Faced with the difficulties of growing up and choosing a religion, adjusting to her family's move to the suburbs, and having to make new friends, Margaret, who is turning twelve, talks over her problems with her own private God. This book put Blume on the map as a funny, fresh voice in juvenile literature. (1970)

★ New York Times Outstanding Book of the Year

Artist to Artist:
23 Major Illustrators Talk to Children About Their Art

Eric Carle; *illustrated by author and other artists* 4+

Eric Carle, award-winning book designer, writer, and illustrator, has authored more than seventy picture books. In this anthology, twenty-three fellow picture book artists speak to children about what influenced and inspired them to become illustrators. This oversized book features fold-out pages with full-color reproductions of each illustrator's early work, as well as photographs of them as children and self-portraits.(2007)

★ School Library Journal Best Books of the Year

Bambi: A Life in the Woods

Felix Salten ☀ 4

This story was originally published in Austria in 1923 and offers a conservationist message against deer hunting which the Disney film also conveyed. It is a coming-of-age tale about facing and overcoming danger, grief, hardship, and fear. Adapted for many age levels, none compare to the original. John Galsworthy described Salten's story of a young deer growing to maturity as a "small classic." (1929)

Bat-Poet, The

Randall Jarrell; *illustrated by Maurice Sendak* 4, 5

A bat wanting to be a poet shares what he learns about the creative process as he writes poems about the other creatures. (1964)

★ New York Times Best Illustrated Book

Bats! Strange and Wonderful

Laurence Pringle; *illustrated by Meryl Henderson* 4

This is a first-rate introduction to the anatomy, lifestyle, and environmental benefits of these flying mammals, bats. Delightful watercolor paintings illustrate the unusual abilities, physical features, and habits of some of the individual species. (2000)

✳ School Library Journal Best Books of the Year

Beardance

Will Hobbs 5, 6, 7

While accompanying an elderly rancher on a trip into the San Juan Mountains, Cloyd, a Ute Indian boy, tries to help two orphaned grizzly cubs survive. (1993)

Beauty of the Beast, The: Poems from the Animal Kingdom

Edited by Jack Prelutsky; *illustrated by Meilo So* 4

Wet-on-wet watercolors brilliantly illustrate this outstanding collection of poems organized by species to include the whole kingdom, from insects and fish to reptiles, birds, and mammals. Highly recommended. (1997)

Because of Winn-Dixie

Kate DiCamillo 4, 5

India Opal, a motherless preacher's daughter, lonely in her new Florida home, welcomes a scraggly, smiling, stray mutt into her life. Together, they win over the town. (2000)

✳ Newbery Honor, School Library Journal Best Books of the Year

Bed-Knob and Broomstick

Mary Norton; *illustrated by Erik Blegvad* 4, 5

Three siblings, staying with their aunt, meet a kindly neighborly witch who gives them a gift that enables them to travel through time and space, leading to many magical adventures. This is a combined edition of two 1947 titles: *The Magic Bed-Knob* and *Bonfires and Broomsticks*. (1957)

Grades 4 to 5

Bee Book, The

Jakob Streit; translated by Nina Kuettel;
illustrated by Jesus Gaban   ☀ 4, 5, 6

Streit's father was a beekeeper, and it was in early childhood that the author developed a passion for the honeybee. This early science book factually and scientifically allows one to enter into the magic and mysterious world of the bees. (2010)

Beejum Book, The

Alice O. Howell; *illustrated by Brett Helquist and Glynis Oliver*   4+

Ten-year-old Teak travels through Europe in the 1930s with her family because of her father's work. She wishes for a real home, school, and friends. We enter with her into the adventurous inner magical world of Beejumstan and its many characters. Based on the real life of the author, it is a story that has entranced children and adults alike with its deep and simple truths. Charming illustrations. (2002)

Ben and Me

Robert Lawson, *illustrated by author*   4, 5, 6

This is history on the light side as told by a mouse who claims to have been Benjamin Franklin's companion. Two other titles by this Newbery author also feature an animal narrator: *Mr. Revere and I* and *Captain Kidd's Cat*. These are good for older reluctant history readers too. (1939)

Benjamin West and His Cat Grimalkin

Marguerite Henry; *illustrated by Wesley Dennis*   4, 5, 6

Henry collaborated with Dennis Wesley to write a fictionalized biography of the early American Quaker painter who was recognized on both sides of the Atlantic. (1947)

Big Red

James Arthur Kjelgaard   5, 6

The subtitle tells it all: *The Story of a Champion Irish Setter and a Trapper's Son Who Grew Up Together, Roaming the Wilderness*. Danny and his dog are featured in two more volumes, which appeal to boys and girls alike: *Irish Red* and *Outlaw Red*. Kjelgaard wrote other dog stories and history books for children. (1945)

Big Tree

Mary Buff, *illustrated by Conrad Buff* 5

Children will discover the vastness of time, the potential of life and the beauty of creation through the story of a giant five-thousand-year-old sequoia, called Wa-No-Na by the Native Americans. (1946)

Birchbark House, The

Louise Erdrich 4, 5

Erdrich, a member of the Turtle Band of Ojibwa and author of many novels for adults, writes her first children's story with a realistic portrayal of Native American daily life during the westward expansion of the United States. Told through the eyes of a seven-year-old Ojibwa girl, this story is partially based on Erdrich's own family's history and continues in *The Game of Silence*, which also won a Scott O'Dell Award. (1999)

★ Scott O'Dell Award for Historical Fiction

Black and Blue Magic

Zilpha Keatley Snyder 5, 6, 7

When clumsy Harry Houdini Marco helps a strange little man on the bus and receives a beautiful pair of magical wings, he's soon covered with bumps and bruises. Can he figure out how to use his special gift and learn to fly? (1966)

Black Beauty: The Biography of a Horse

Anna Sewell 4, 5, 6

Sewell wrote this novel in hopes of raising awareness of cruelty to animals, especially English carriage horses. The story has certainly moved the hearts of generations of readers and remains one of the most popular horse stories ever written. (1877)

Black Stallion, The

Walter Farley 5, 6

This is the first novel in the popular series about the beautiful black stallion shipwrecked on an island with the boy, Alex. Their adventures once off the island fill another eighteen volumes. (1941)

Blue Willow

Doris Gates   5, 6

Reflecting the experience of the California migrant workers during the Depression, this is the story of a little girl who dreams of attending a regular school and living in a real home in a valley like the one on a treasured Blue Willow plate. (1940)

Book of Nonsense, A

Edward Lear   4, 5

More than one hundred limericks and full-color drawings are reproduced in facsimile editions of Edward Lear's now-classic collection of ridiculous, exuberant, nonsense rhymes. (1876)

Borrowers, The

Mary Norton   4, 5

The award-winning adventures of the family of little people who live under the kitchen floor of a nineteenth-century house was so successful it spawned a series, which includes *The Borrowers Afield*, *The Borrowers Afloat*, *The Borrowers Aloft*, and others. (1952)

★ Carnegie Medal

Bronzeville Boys and Girls

Gwendolyn Brooks; *illustrated by Ronni Salbert*   4, 5, 6

Brooks, a Pulitzer prize poet of African-American descent, focuses these poems on children and their activities in the Bronzeville neighborhood of Chicago. First published in 1956 with black and white drawings, a 2006 edition bursts with vibrant colors by artist Faith Ringgold and features an urban setting, children of color and the universal play of childhood. (1956)

Caddie Woodlawn

Carol Ryrie Brink   4, 5, 6

Written by her granddaughter, this is the fictionalized biography of eleven-year-old Caddie and her tomboy adventures in a small town during pioneer days. *Magical Melons* is a sequel. (1936)

★ Newbery Medal, Lewis Carroll Shelf Award

Cave, The

Elizabeth Coatsworth 4

A young Navajo boy helps a Basque sheepherder take the ranch's sheep to summer pasture and is able to save the sheep when a sudden storm appears. (Coatsworth's books are somewhat rare but worth looking for.) (1958)

Children of Green Knowe, The

Lucy Boston; *illustrated by Peter Boston* 5, 6

The ancestral home in England, Green Knowe, is still mysteriously occupied by seventeenth-century children, a discovery made by their modern descendent, Toby, who is sent there to live with his grandmother. Quality writing continues in: *Treasure of Greene Knowe, The River at Green Knowe*, and *A Stranger at Greene Knowe*, which won a Carnegie award. (1954)

Chitty Chitty Bang Bang: The Magical Car

Ian Fleming 5, 6

Fleming's only children's book is about a flying, floating, driving-by-itself magical automobile that takes the Pott family on a riotous series of adventures as they try to capture a notorious gang of robbers. James Bond's creator continues to be fascinated with invented gadgets. (1964)

Chronicles of Narnia

C. S. Lewis 4, 5, 6+

Outstanding writing and meaningful themes make this fantasy series one not to miss. In *The Lion, The Witch and the Wardrobe*, four children and the noble lion, Aslan, oppose the White Witch who has the land of Narnia under her spell. Additional adventures follow in: *Prince Caspian, The Voyage of the Dawn Treader, The Silver Chair, The Horse and His Boy*, and *The Magician's Nephew*. A Carnegie Medal was award to the final title, *The Last Battle*. (1950)

Chronicles of Prydain, The (Quintet)

Lloyd Alexander 5, 6, 7

In the legendary Welsh land of Prydain, Taran, the pig keeper's young assistant, yearns for fame and glory. Titles in this fantasy quintet are *The Book of Three, The Black Cauldron, The Castle of Llyr, Taran Wanderer*, and *The High King*. (1965)

★ Newbery Medal for *The High King*, Newbery Honor for *Black Cauldron*

Cotton in My Sack

Lois Lenski, *illustrated by author*   4, 5

Lenski wrote wonderful regional stories about children with an excellent geographical sense of place. This one is about the hard life of sharecroppers picking cotton in Arkansas in the 1940s. (1949)

Courage of Sarah Noble, The

Alice Dalgliesh   4, 5

Remembering her mother's words, an eight-year-old girl finds courage to go alone with her father to build a new home in the wilderness and to stay with the Indians when her father must go back to bring the rest of the family. (1954)

★ Newbery Honor

Cricket in Times Square, A

George Seldon; *illustrated by Garth Williams*   4, 5

A Times Square newsstand is the home and starting point for the New York City adventures of Chester the cricket, Harry the cat, and Tucker the mouse. Their story continues in *Harry Kitten and Tucker Mouse* (the prequel), *Tucker's Countryside, Chester Cricket's New Home,* and *Harry Cat's Pet Puppy.* (1960)

Daughter of the Mountains

Louise S. Rankin; *illustrated by Kurt Weise*   5, 6, 7

Momo has always wanted a Lhasa terrier—like the sacred temple dogs of the Tibetan Buddhist priests. When a trader brings Pempa to her parents' teahouse, Momo's dream comes true. Then a band of robbers steals the valuable dog, and to recover him, Momo must make a dangerous journey she may not survive. (1948)

★ Newbery Honor

Dear Mr. Henshaw

Beverly Cleary   5, 6, 7

Four years after Leigh first began a correspondence with his favorite author during the second grade, he finds he is writing about coping with his parents' divorce, being the new boy in school, and generally finding his own place in the world. (1983)

★ Newbery Medal

Diamond War, The

Zilpha Keatley Snyder   4, 5, 6

Fast-paced and funny, with lots of dialogue, this is the first in a series introducing the Castle Court Kids from the three-time Newbery Honor author. The stories about a neighborhood group of ethnically diverse kids look at contemporary issues. Others are: *Secret Weapons*, *Ghost Invasion*, and *The Box and the Bone*. (1995)

Dog Who Wouldn't Be, The

Farley Mowat   5+

Set in the Canadian prairie in the early twentieth century when dogs and boys could roam free, this mostly true story about the author, his dog, and their adventures reflects a childhood full of imagination that led to his becoming a great writer. Each chapter is another hilarious adventure. (1957)

Doll's House, The

Rumer Godden   4, 5

For Tottie Plantagenet, a little wooden doll, life in the new dollhouse is not quite perfect with the arrival of the dreadful doll, March Pane. Can the dolls make a home together? A 1962 edition was illustrated by Tasha Tudor. (1948)

★ ALA Notable Children's Book

Down the Mississippi

Clyde Robert Bulla   5, 6

A Minnesota farm boy gets a much-desired opportunity to go down the Mississippi on a raft as the kitchen helper. Instead of curing him of his wish to work on the river, as his parents had hoped, it only strengthens his desire to become a river man. (1954)

Dragon Boy, The (Star Trilogy)

Donald Samson; *illustrated by Adam Agee*   4, 5, 6

The first in a trilogy, *The Dragon Boy* grew out of a teacher's desire to create a tale of courage and perseverance for his students. It is a captivating story of a young orphan boy, Straw, and his surprising relationship and adventures with Star, an emerald-green Luck Dragon. The author draws on the Asian picture of the dragon as a benevolent creature. The second book is *The Dragon of Two Hearts* and the concluding title is *The Dragon, The Blade and the Thread*. (2008)

Dragonsblood: An Environmental Fairy Tale

Eugene Schwartz; *illustrated by Kris Carlson*   4+

This is an epic environmental fable that spans continents and centuries, from Medieval Europe to modern America. Full of suspense and drama, it inspires with its themes of persistence and courage, which are powerfully illustrated with chalk drawings. (2010)

Egypt Game, The

Zilpha Keatley Snyder   5

A group of children, entranced with the study of Egypt, play their own Egypt game, are visited by a secret oracle, become involved in a murder, and befriend the professor before they move on to their next interest—Gypsies. (1967)

★ Newbery Honor, Lewis Carroll Shelf Award

Elin's Amerika

Marguerite deAngeli, *illustrated by author*   4, 5

The author's historically accurate story of a little Swedish immigrant and her adventures in America when her family settled in New Sweden (Delaware) in the mid-1600s is charmingly illustrated. (1941)

Ella Enchanted

Gail Carson Levine   5, 6, 7

In this Cinderella tale, Ella, a girl cursed by the gift of obedience, is, nonetheless, a take-charge, intuitive heroine who, despite her love for her particular prince, learns how to say no. (1997)

Escape to Witch Mountain

Alexander Key   5, 6

When a mysterious and evil man claims to be their uncle and acquires court custody, Tia and Tony run away to prevent him from enslaving their unusual powers. The sequel is *Return from Witch Mountain.* (1968)

Eyewitness Books (Series)

Various authors 5–8

Individual titles in this well-illustrated and extensive nonfiction series include *Bird*, *Skeleton*, *Rocks & Minerals*, *Pond & River*, *Tree*, *Mammal*, *Butterfly & Moth*, and many others. Recent volumes also include history subjects. (1988-Present)

Fantastic Stories

Terry Jones; *illustrated by Michael Foreman* 5–8

Multi-talented Terry Jones, perhaps best known as a scriptwriter and member of the Monty Python team, takes his offbeat, hilarious imagination into twenty-one stories for children, using traditional fairy tale archetypes and turning them into something utterly different. At times, the wit and wisdom are sophisticated, making some tales appropriate for older readers. (1993)

Finn Family Moomintroll

Tove Jansson; translated by Elizabeth Portch; *illustrated by author* 4, 5, 6

This is the third book in a Finnish animal fantasy series begun in 1945, but the first to be translated into English. The series begins with the *Moomins and the Great Flood* and is followed by *Comet in Moominland* in which many of the characters are introduced. Easier to follow when read aloud with a child. Some allusions and the sardonic humor may confound readers who otherwise would find the content appealing. (1958)

First Year, The

Enid Meadowcroft; *illustrated by Grace Paull* 4, 5, 6

Meadowcroft recounts the story about the Pilgrim's journey to America on the Mayflower and their experiences that first year establishing a colony, leading up to the first Thanksgiving. (1946)

Five Children and It

Edith Nesbit 4, 5

A quintet of English siblings discovers a sand fairy who grants wishes in this early example of the fantasy genre set in the 1850s. The slightly dated British prose may need warming up to; try reading it aloud for a start. If this one catches on, seek the other two: *The Phoenix and the Carpet* and *The Story of the Amulet*. (1902)

Flash: Dog of Old Egypt

Lynn Hall   5

The pharaoh's son tries hard to prove the pup whose life he saved is the best of the royal dogs, not knowing that to succeed means losing the dog forever. (1973)

Flat Tail

Alice Gall and Fleming Crew;
illustrated by W. Langdon Kihn   4

Flat Tail is a beaver, and his life story is told and illustrated in wood block prints. Companion volumes are *Wagtail* (the story of a frog with illustrations by Kurt Weise) and *Ringtail* (the story of a raccoon illustrated by James Reid.) Out of print now, this excellent nature study series is available in used book outlets and libraries. (1935)

Follow My Leader

James B. Garfield   5, 6

After being blinded in a freak accident at age eleven, Jimmy must relearn all of the things he used to know. With the help of a therapist and a school for the blind, he learns Braille, the use of a cane, and has a chance to have a guide dog. Learning to work with the dog is not easy, but Jimmy forges a friendship with the dog that forms the core of this story. (1957)

Four Dolls

Rumer Godden; *illustrated by Pauline Baynes*   4, 5

Four of the author's best-loved doll stories: "Candy Floss," "Impunity Jane: The Story of a Pocket Doll," "The Fairy Doll," and "Holly and Ivy" are collected in this volume. Originally published individually. (1983)

Fox, The

Margaret Lane; *illustrated by Kenneth Lily*   4

This nonfiction series is beautifully illustrated and describes how the animal is born, grows, lives, and finds food. Others in the series are *The Frog*, *The Squirrel*, and *The Bear*. (1982)

Freckle Juice

Judy Blume   4, 5

Andrew, a second grader, wants freckles so badly that he buys Sharon's freckle recipe for fifty cents. Hilarious adventures ensue. (1971)

From the Mixed-Up Files of Mrs. Basil E. Frankweiler

E. L. Konigsburg, *illustrated by author*   5, 6

Two children run away from their home and family in the suburbs and live inside the Metropolitan Museum of Art. Their plan has flaws, but works long enough for them to discover a mystery to be solved. The author is a two-time Newbery winner. (1967)

★ Newbery Medal

Gammage Cup, The

Carol Kendall; *illustrated by Erik Blegvad*   5, 6

In this fantasy, a handful of little people, the Minnipins, rise up against the leading family of their isolated valley. They are forced up the mountain into exile where they discover that their ancient enemy is preparing to attack. In the sequel, *A Whisper of Glocken*, the seemingly antiheroic Minnipins are prompted by a flood to attempt to restore an ancient treasure and make their valley safe again. (1959)

Gay Neck: The Story of a Pigeon

Dhan Gopal Mukerji   5, 6, 7

An Indian boy sends his prized carrier pigeon to be trained for service in World War I. Gay Neck serves his new masters heroically as he flies from the rooftops of India and soars through the Himalayan homes of eagles and among the circling planes of warring nations in the first air battles. (1927)

★ Newbery Medal

Gentle Ben

Walt Morey   5, 6

Growing up in a rugged Alaskan fishing town with his parents but with no friends, a kind-hearted boy falls in love with a bear that is mistreated by a local. A touching, suspenseful, and humorous story ensues. (1965)

Gib Rides Home

Zilpha Keatley Snyder   5, 6

Despite the harsh treatment he has endured at the Lovell House orphanage, ten-year-old Gib Whittaker manages to maintain his hopeful outlook when he is farmed out to help with the horses of a wealthy banker in 1908. *Gib and the Gray Ghost* is the sequel. (1998)

Gift of the River, The

Enid Meadowcroft; *illustrated by Katharine Dewey*   5

The details of everyday life for various individuals, from children to artisans to leaders, are woven into this first history of Egypt, which covers many centuries up to the sixth century B.C. (1937)

Ginger Pye

Eleanor Estes   4, 5

The Pye family of Connecticut adopts a dog, which they name Ginger. But they notice that ever since Ginger came to live with them, a mysterious stranger wearing a mustard-yellow hat has been hanging around their house. When Ginger disappears one day, they wonder if the mysterious stranger in the hat is involved. (1951)

★ Newbery Medal

Gone-Away Lake

Elizabeth Enright   4, 5

Portia and her cousin Julian discover summer adventure in a colony of forgotten houses on the shores of a swampy lake in this tale by a Newbery-winning author. *Return to Gone-Away* is the sequel. (1957)

★ Newbery Honor, Louis Carroll Shelf Award

Great Brain, The

John Fitzgerald; *illustrated by Mercer Mayer*   4

This is a humorous series about a boy who grows up in awe of his older brother who is called the Great Brain. Younger siblings can relate well. Other titles include: *The Great Brain at the Academy, The Great Brain Does It Again, The Great Brain Reforms,* and *The Return of the Great Brain.* (1967)

Great Gilly Hopkins, The

Katherine Paterson   5, 6

Gilly is an angry, alienated heroine who has been in one too many foster homes. The latest one is full of misfits, and Gilly wants no part of it, at first. This is a great story that also addresses prejudices of all kinds whether of race, class, or handicaps. (1978)

⭐ Newbery Honor; National Book Award

Hah-Nee of the Cliff Dwellers

Mary Buff; *illustrated by Conrad Buff*   4, 5

The Buffs bring us a beautifully illustrated story of the Southwest cliff dwellers and of the historical thirteenth-century drought that destroyed their rich native culture. (1956)

Half Magic

Edward Eager; *illustrated by N. M. Bodecker*   4, 5

Four children discover an ancient coin with magic powers. Each short chapter is a new adventure, whether to King Arthur's court or the Sahara desert, but the wish granted is often not quite the one expected. With magic, be careful what you wish for! Getting it exactly right proves challenging again in two more titles: *Magic or Not?* and *Magic by the Lake*. (1954)

Hans Brinker or the Silver Skates

Mary Mapes Dodge   4, 5, 6

When a new friend gives Hans and his sister, Gretel, enough money for one pair of ice skates, Hans insists that Gretel enter the grand skating competition, while he approaches a great doctor who consents to try to restore their father's memory. The author, who died in 1905, has created an enduring story about life in nineteenth-century Holland. (1865)

Harriett the Spy

Louise Fitzhugh   4, 5, 6

Would-be writer Harriet likes to keep a notebook of her daily observations, but when her friends find out what she has written about them, even clever Harriet needs help to put things right again. There are more adventures featuring Harriet and her gang. Look for *The Long Secret* and *Sport*. (1964)

Heidi

Johanna Spyri 4, 5, 6

An orphan is sent to live with her hermit grandfather in a simple cottage in the Swiss Alps and then to become a companion to an invalid girl in the great city of Frankfurt. Here is one not to miss. (1880)

Henner's Lydia

Marguerite deAngeli, *illustrated by author* 4, 5

Lydia tries hard to finish her hooked rug so she can take her first trip to the market with Pop, but so many other things divert her attention: a visit to the cider mill, a visit to a new baby, and a chase after a runaway pig. The story is set in rural Pennsylvania's Amish Conestoga Valley country in the 1930s. (1936)

Hiawatha and Megissogwan

Henry Wadsworth Longfellow; *illustrated by Jeffrey Thompson* 4, 5, 6+

In this short episode from Longfellow's 1855 popular epic poem, *The Song of Hiawatha,* Hiawatha battles the evil magician Megissogwon. Thompson's striking illustrations add to the drama of the story. Many editions of the complete poem exist, not the least of which is a rare 1908 version illustrated by Frederic Remington, Maxfield Parrish, and N. C. Wyeth. (2001)

Hieroglyphs for Fun: Your Own Secret Code Language

Joseph and Lenore Scott, *illustrated by author* 5, 6

This is an excellent introduction to the "lost language of the gods," which presents the authentic basic alphabet and sufficient additional hieroglyphs to develop written messages. It is accompanied by a brief discussion of related aspects of ancient Egyptian culture. (1974)

Hitty: Her First Hundred Years

Rachel Field; *illustrated by Dorothy Lathrop* 4, 5, 6

The adventures of a much-traveled wooden doll carved in 1829 is the subject of a historical novel that was reissued in 1999 with a larger format, new illustrations by Susan Jeffers, and a somewhat revised story edited by Rosemary Wells (which also eliminates racially biased slang such as "Injuns"). The original version is still around as well. (1929)

★ Newbery Medal

Homer Price

Robert McCloskey, *illustrated by author* 4, 5

Homer Price, boy resident of Centerburg, the small-town heart of a bygone America, has many humorous adventures including one with a donut machine on a rampage, musical mousetraps, Superman, and super weeds out of control. Grandpa Hercules and Uncle Ulysses, and other comic characters return with Homer in *Centerburg Tales*, the sequel. (1943)

I Am Phoenix: Poems for Two Voices

Paul Fleischman 4, 5, 6+

This unusual collection of poems celebrating the musicality of birds is to be read aloud by two voices or groups. See also a similar collection: *Joyful Noise: Poems for Two Voices*, which won the Newbery Award. (1985)

Immigrants: A Library of Congress Book

Martin W. Sandler 5- 8

Focusing on the period 1870–1920, this entry in the Library of Congress Book series is a collection of over one hundred photographs and illustrations loosely tied together by a general text for middle-grade readers. Quotes and photos combine to give an idea of what life was like for immigrants. The conclusion emphasizes cultural diversity as our greatest strength. (1995)

Incredible Journey, The

Sheila Burnford; *illustrated by Carl Burger* 4, 5, 6

Three loyal pets, two dogs and a Siamese cat, travel 250 miles across Canada to follow their master to a new home. Read it aloud or read it alone—it's a tear-jerker either way. (1961)

★ Lewis Carroll Shelf Award

Island of the Blue Dolphins

Scott O'Dell 5, 6, 7

Based on the true experience of "The Lost Woman of San Nicolas," this novel is about a Native American girl whose hunting and gathering skills allow her to survive eighteen years marooned on an island off California's coast. There is a sequel as well, *Zia*. (1960)

★ Newbery Medal

James Herriot's Treasury for Children: Warm and Joyful Animal Tales

James Herriot; *illustrated by Ruth Brown and Peter Barrett*   4–7

This collection of the Yorkshire country veterinarian's stories is selected especially for children, although not initially written for juvenile readers. It includes "Moses the Kitten," "The Market Square Dog," "Smudge, the Little Lost Lamb," and "The Christmas Kitten." Young adult readers may wish to continue with other collections of Herriot's stories like *All Things Bright and Beautiful*, which inspired the PBS series. (1992)

Jelly Belly

Robert Kimmel Smith   4, 5

The fattest kid in the fifth grade wants to lose weight, but not badly enough to starve. Smith's protagonists, usually middle-school-age boys, as in *Chocolate Fever*, *Baseball Billy*, or *Squeaky Wheel*, come across as real youngsters. (1981)

Joyful Noise: Poems for Two Voices

Paul Fleischman; *illustrated by Eric Beddows*   4, 5, 6+

Written for two voices or groups of voices, this is a special collection of poems that honor the insect world. These tributes to the six-legged kingdom recreate the "booming, boisterous, joyful noise" of insects and help us to see things from a "bug's eye view." (1988)

★ Newbery Medal

Jungle Book, The

Rudyard Kipling   4, 5, 6+

Kipling was England's first Nobel-winning author. His most popular tale is of the boy, Mowgli, raised and educated by jungle animals in central India. *The Jungle Book* and *The Second Jungle Book* are available in one or two volumes and any number of editions of selected stories. Simplified texts with cartoon illustrations based on the Disney film are also available, but the original is a classic of literature to be read aloud to young listeners or savored alone by confident young adult readers. (1893)

Justin Morgan Had a Horse

Marguerite Henry   5, 6

The many-times-honored author of horse stories here tells of a young colt that later becomes the father of the world-famous Morgan horse breed. (1946)

✳ Newbery Honor

Katie John

Mary Calhoun   4, 5

Ten-year-old Katie John Tucker is the central character of this series, which is imbued with a good feeling of locale, a strong sense of seasonal change, and, above all, a vigorous portrayal of an appealing heroine. Other titles are *Depend on Katie John*, *Honestly Katie John*, and *Katie John and Heathcliff* (1980) in which the former boy-hater falls in love for the first time. (1960)

Kavik the Wolf Dog

Walt Morey   5, 6

A wolf-dog instinctively travels two thousand miles from Washington to Alaska to return to the boy who once saved his life. See also Morey's *Gentle Ben*. (1968)

Keep the Wagons Moving

West Lathrop; *illustrated by Douglas Duer*   5, 6

This novel of the Oregon Trail recounts the adventures of two brothers on their way to the Oregon Territory. The elder is hired to accompany a cruel neighbor on a wagon train, while the younger secretly steals off from home on his own and is kidnapped by a French trapper who is also going westward. (1949)

King of the Wind: The Story of the Godolphin Arabian

Marguerite Henry; *illustrated by Wesley Dennis*   5, 6

The second novel by the much-honored author of horse stories traces the slightly romanticized biography of the actual Arabian stallion that became a founding sire of the Thoroughbred breed and of the mute Moroccan boy who tended him as long as he lived. (1948)

✳ Newbery Medal

Grades 4 to 5

Koko's Kitten

Francine Patterson; *photographed by Ronald H. Cohn*   ☀   **4**

This is an amazing true story of Koko, a gorilla who learned to use sign language. The kitten was a gift, a pet Koko loved, cared for, and grieved for when it died. Illustrated with photographs. (1987)

★ School Library Journal Best Books of the Year

Lad: A Dog

Albert Payson Terhune   **5, 6**

The author's first novel recounts the heroic and adventurous life of a thoroughbred collie devoted to his master and mistress. *Lad of Sunnybank* followed, and then several more dog stories that remain favorites because they are about animals that possess positive human qualities like courage, faithfulness, concern, loyalty, and cleverness. (1919)

Lantern Bearers, The

Rosemary Sutcliff   **5, 6, 7**

Sutcliff earned an award with this historical fiction about the fall of the Roman Empire in the British Isles to the Saxon barbarians and the beginning of the Dark Ages. She tells it from the point of view of a Roman soldier who chooses to stay in Britain. This is the gripping tale of "the lantern bearers," those who try to keep civilization alive through the darkest times in history. See also *Dragon Slayer, the Story of Beowulf.* (1959)

★ Carnegie Medal

Lassie Come Home

Eric Knight   **4, 5, 6**

Three times the loyal collie dog escapes and returns to Joe, the twelve-year-old boy she loves. Then, taken far into the northern regions of Scotland, she flees again and sets out on an epic trek homeward. Lyrically written and rich with the flavor of the English and Scottish countryside, this story continues to be enjoyed by children as well as adults, for whom it was originally published as a short story in the *Saturday Evening Post.* (1938)

Little Bee Sunbeam

Jakob Streit; translated by Nina Kuettel;
illustrated by Verena Knobel 4, 5

This natural science story relates the adventures of Little Bee Sunbeam, who searches for particularly good nectar to make honey when it suddenly becomes very cold. Honeybees cannot fly when the temperature drops so abruptly, and the little bee must spend the night alone in the forest where an exciting adventure unfolds. Parents may read this to children as young as third grade, but independent middle school readers can enjoy it on their own. (2010)

Little Britches: Father and I Were Ranchers

Ralph Moody 4, 5, 6

"Ralph Moody's series should be read aloud in every family circle in America," wrote fellow writer Sterling North. The autobiographical chronicle of the life of young Ralph begins with his New England family's move to a Colorado ranch in the early 1900s. Other titles (in chronological order) are: *Man of the Family, Mary Emma and Company, The Fields of Home, Shaking the Nickelbush, Horse of a Different Color,* and *The Dry Divide,* available from Beautiful Feet Press. (1950)

Little House on the Prairie, The

Laura Ingalls Wilder; *illustrated by Garth Williams* 4, 5

Her story is told in fascinating, realistic detail based on the author's prairie childhood and marriage. Younger readers might start best with *Farmer Boy,* although it is third in the series. The chronology begins with *Little House in the Big Woods,* followed by *Little House on the Prairie, Farmer Boy, On the Banks of Plum Creek, By the Shores of Silver Lake, The Long Winter, Little Town on the Prairie,* and *Those Happy Golden Years.* Four of the sequels won Newbery Honor and ALA Notable Awards. (1932)

Little Lord Fauntleroy

Frances Hodgson Burnett 5, 6

A young lad finds his life changed when he leaves the streets of New York City to become an English lord. This is a classic in children's literature. (1886)

Little Princess, A

Frances Hodgson Burnett 5, 6

Once rich, Sara Crewe becomes a penniless orphan, banished to a room in the attic of Miss Minchin's Select Seminary for Young Ladies. As a servant she is abused, cold, and hungry, but her lively imagination helps her transform her world and that of her fellows. Many editions of this best-loved story are available including abbreviated or simplified text versions. (1905)

Magic Maize

Mary Buff; *illustrated by Conrad Buff* 4, 5

A Mayan Indian boy of Guatemala, whose father is wary of new ways, plants some kernels of a new kind of corn and finds a jade earplug of the ancient Mayans, leading him to some unusual adventures. As with other titles by these author/illustrators, much cultural background and regional geography is incorporated into the tale. (1953)

★ Newbery Honor

Maniac Magee

Jerry Spinelli 5, 6

It's not just that this homeless twelve-year-old kid can hit a ball better and run faster than anyone else in Two Mills, Pennsylvania, but that he does unthinkable things, like crossing the boundary between the white West End and the black East End, confronting prejudice and racism head on. Spinelli addresses issues like bullying, prejudice, and stereotyping in his many novels for middle-graders. (1990)

★ Newbery Medal

Mary Poppins

P. L. Travers; *illustrated by Mary Shepard* 4, 5

A magical nanny has unusual talents and ways of traveling in this popular British series that includes *Mary Poppins Comes Back*, *Mary Poppins in the Park*, and *Mary Poppins Opens the Door*. Racism in the original has been removed in the revised 1962 edition. (1934)

Master Puppeteer, The

Katherine Paterson; *illustrated by Haru Wells*   5, 6, 7

Jiro, son of a poor puppet maker, runs away and apprentices himself to Yoshida, the master of Japan's Hanaza puppet theater. Jiro finds himself caught up in an intrigue involving a Robin Hood-like character who steals from the rich to help the poor during a lawless time in Japan's history. (1976)

 ✴ National Book Award

Matchlock Gun, The

Walter D. Edmonds; *illustrated by Paul Lantz*   ☀ 4, 5, 6+

In 1756, during the French and Indian War in upper New York State, ten-year-old Edward is determined to protect his home and family with the ancient, and much too heavy, Spanish gun that his father gave him before leaving to fight the enemy. This is based on a true story that may interest reluctant older readers studying history. (1941)

 ✴ Newbery Medal

Melendy Family, The

Elizabeth Enright   4, 5

This ever-popular series, now reprinted in one volume, follows the adventures of the lively Melendy family. The children—ages six through thirteen-—live with their father, a writer, and Cuffy, their beloved housekeeper, who takes on the many roles of nurse, cook, substitute mother, grandmother, and aunt. Individual volumes include *The Saturdays, Then There Were Five, Spider Web for Two*, and *The Four-Story Mistake*. (1944)

Miracles on Maple Hill

Virginia Sorenson   4, 5

Marley's father, having returned from being a prisoner-of-war in World War II, is suffering. Needing some back-to-nature healing, they leave the city and return to the farmhouse on Maple Hill where Marley's mother spent her childhood. This is a heartwarming story about healing, caring, and helping. (1957)

 ✴ Newbery Medal

Misty of Chincoteague

Marguerite Henry; *illustrated by Wesley Dennis*   4, 5, 6

This tender tale is about two children and a Chincoteague Island pony. Horse stories have always been popular with children, and none more so than this Newbery author's satisfying tales, which include two sequels, *Stormy: Misty's Foal* and *Sea Star: Orphan of the Chincoteague*, and many other great horse stories, including *The Album of Horses* and the Newbery winner *King of the Wind.* (1947)

★ Newbery Honor

Moon in the Cloud, The (Trilogy)

Rosemary Harris   5

Persuaded by Noah's son Ham to go to Egypt in his place and collect two temple cats, Reuben has many adventures before his mission is accomplished. First in a trilogy about ancient Egypt; the other two are *The Shadow on the Sun* and *The Bright and Morning Star.* (1968)

★ Carnegie Medal

Mouse and the Motorcycle, The

Beverly Cleary; *illustrated by Louis Darling*   4, 5

Ralph the mouse rides a toy motorcycle through this light-hearted series by an author with a large following. The others are *Runaway Ralph* and *Ralph S. Mouse.* (1965)

Mr. Popper's Penguins

Richard and Florence Atwater; *illustrated by Robert Lawson*   4, 5

A good-humored housepainter is gifted with two penguins and very soon has his own small flock. The slapstick humor makes it a great book to read aloud. (1938)

★ Newbery Honor, Lewis Carroll Shelf Award

Mrs. Frisby and the Rats of NIMH

Robert O'Brien   4, 5, 6

Having no one to help her, a widowed mouse with a sick son overcomes her fears and visits the neighbor rats whose former imprisonment in a laboratory gave them wisdom and longevity. (1971)

★ Newbery Medal, Boston Globe-Horn Book Honor

Mummies Made in Egypt

Aliki, *illustrated by author*   5

Like this author's *Medieval Feast*, this is an introductory level book about Egypt, whimsically illustrated with not too much text and appropriate for younger readers. Both titles may interest middle elementary students studying history. (1985)

My Mom's a Vet

Henry Horenstein, *photographed by author*   4

A young girl's firsthand impressions and full-color photographs provide a close-up look at the life and career of a country veterinarian as she travels from farm to farm, caring for ill pigs, goats, horses, and cows. When read aloud, younger listeners can enjoy hearing the story, but it is written at a middle-school independent reader level. (1994)

National Velvet

Enid Bagnold   5, 6

A fourteen-year-old English girl wins a horse in a raffle, trains it, and rides it in the Grand National, the world's greatest steeplechase. This has been a favorite horse book for decades. (1935)

Neverending Story, The

Michael Ende; translated by Ralph Manheim   5, 6

Shy, awkward Bastian is amazed to discover that he has become a character in the mysterious book he is reading and that he has an important mission to fulfill. By the author of *Momo*, translated from German. (1979)

On My Honor

Marion Dane Bauer   5, 6, 7

Weighed down by guilt, twelve-year-old Joel searches for the courage to tell the truth about the drowning of his best friend, Tony, while the boys were playing near the treacherous, and forbidden, Vermillion River. (1986)

★ Newbery Honor

Grades 4 to 5

One Day in the Alpine Tundra

Jean Craighead George; *illustrated by Walter Gaffney-Kessell* ☀ 5

A renowned nature writer relates a boy's adventure when he is alone on the alpine tundra on a stormy day. Subsequent titles in the series explore other biomes with an engaging story line and illustrations: *One Day in the Desert, One Day in the Prairie, One Day in the Tropical Rain Forest,* and *One Day in the Woods.* (1984)

Onion John

Joseph Krumgold 5, 6, 7

His friendship with an immigrant handyman, Onion John, causes a conflict between a twelve-year-old boy and his father in this penetrating story by the two-time Newbery author. (1959)

★ Newbery Medal

Peterkin Papers, The

Lucretia Peabody Hale 4, 5

The humorous adventures of a foolish family whose problems are righted by the ever-sensible advice of the Lady from Philadelphia. The sequel, *The Last of the Peterkins* (1886) is included in the one-volume edition, *The Complete Peterkin Papers.* (1880)

Pioneer Sampler, A: The Daily Life of a Pioneer Family

Barbara Greenwood, *illustrated by author* 4, 5, 6+

First published as *The Daily Life of a Canadian Family in 1840,* this fiction/non-fiction hybrid, chronicles a year in the lives of the fictional Robinson family. Illustrated historical notes enlarge on their social history and activities, from churning butter to predicting the weather. Readers are invited to try their hand at the tasks to experience a bit of pioneer life. The story and activities could be enjoyed by even younger listeners if read aloud, but at 240 pages with an extensive index, it is not a chapter book. (1994)

Pond Lake River Sea

Maryjo Koch, *illustrated by author*   4

A sequel to the immensely popular *Bird Egg Feather Nest*, this is an informative exploration into life found beneath the surface of ponds, lakes, rivers, and seas. Beautifully expressive watercolor illustrations and handwritten text provide a unique perspective on the complex network of aquatic life. Another in her series of science books for young readers is *Seed Leaf Flower Fruit*. (1999)

★ Scientific American Book of the Year

Puritan Adventure

Lois Lenski, *illustrated by author*   4, 5

A widow comes to New England to live with her sister's family whose way of life as Puritans of the Massachusetts Bay Colony are in sharp contrast to hers. This book features the author's distinctive artwork. (1944)

Pushcart War, The

Jean Merrill   5, 6

Children joyfully join the war between the huge trucks that block the New York City streets and the pushcart peddlers with a secret weapon: pea shooters armed with pins stuck through dried peas that flatten the truck tires. But can the push-carts win against a corrupt mayor who taxes the pins and prohibits the sale of dried peas? (1964)

Raft, The

Jim Lamarche, *illustrated by author*   4, 5

Spending the summer with his artist grandmother, a city boy discovers the joys of rafting and of sketching the wildlife he encounters. Luminous art filled with the wonders of nature reflect the text. (2000)

★ School Library Journal Best Books of the Year

Railway Children, The

Edith Nesbit   4, 5

When their father disappears suddenly and mysteriously, Phyllis, Peter, and Roberta must leave their wealthy London surroundings to live with their mother under poorer circumstances in the country. The resilient children become res-cuers—of babies, injured boys, trains, and eventually their own family. (1906)

Ramona and Her Father

Beverly Cleary   **4, 5**

Ramona Quimby, her family, and certain familiar friends first appeared in 1955 and new titles continued to appear as late as 1999. This novel deals with the effects on the family when father loses his job. Others include *Ramona the Pest*; *Ramona Quimby, Age 8*; *Ramona and her Mother*; *Beezus and Ramona*; *Henry and Beezus*; and *Ramona's World*. This is an extremely popular series. Humor and a feeling for the dynamics of family living characterize Cleary's work. She has been honored with many book awards and for her lasting contributions to children's literature. (1975)

★ Newbery Honor, Boston Globe-Horn Book

Rascal: A Memoir of a Better Era

Sterling North; *illustrated by John Schoenherr*   **4**

After the death of his mother and his father's preoccupation with his own grief, the author turns to a pet raccoon for solace. Rascal manages to get into just about everything in his human family's home, including their hearts. As the raccoon grows up, so does the author, who must let go and allow his friend to return to the wild. (1963)

Rebecca of Sunnybrook Farm

Kate Douglas Wiggin; *illustrated by Helen Mason Grose*   **4, 5, 6**

This is a beloved tale of the downtrodden but ever-optimistic Rebecca Rowena Randall who is left penniless when her father dies. Her two aunts—the stern Aunt Miranda and the kindly Aunt Jane, take in Rebecca. The beautifully produced facsimile edition (1994) features six full-color plates and thirty-two pen-and-ink drawings by the original illustrator. (1903)

Robber Ghost, The

Karin Anckarsvard; translated by Annabelle MacMillan;
illustrated by Paul Galdone   **5, 6**

In this novel, one of a juvenile mystery series translated from the Swedish, Michael and Cecilia, schoolmates in the small Swedish town of Nordvik, become involved in the mystery of the theft of money from the post office, which is located in the wing of an old castle. Look for others, such as *The Mysterious Schoolmaster* and *Madcap Mystery*. (1955)

Roller Skates

Ruth Sawyer   4, 5

In old New York of the 1890s, tomboy Lucinda is sent to live with her teacher for a year while her parents are abroad. Thank goodness Miss Peters understands the heart of a ten-year-old who wishes to roller skate to school. (1936)
★ Newbery Medal

Rootabaga Stories

Carl Sandburg; *illustrated by Michael Hague*   4, 5

Two-time Pulitzer prize author Sandburg wrote this collection of original fairy tales for his own two daughters at the beginning of his career. The 1988 edition wonderfully illustrated by Hague is presented in two volumes, *Part One* and *Part Two*. The poet's rich language and whimsical invention beg to be read aloud. (1922)

Santiago

Ann Nolan Clark   5, 6, 7

Santiago is a twelve-year-old Indian being brought up in an aristocratic Spanish household. Despite protests, an old Indian burden bearer comes and takes the boy back to his own Indian people. Santiago learns more about his ancestral people than he has known from his sheltered life in Guatemala City. (1955)

Schlemiel Went to Warsaw and Other Stories

Isaac Bashevis Singer; translated by author and Elizabeth Shub; *illustrated by Maurice Sendak*   4, 5, 6

Singer received the Nobel prize in 1978 for his Yiddish fiction evoking the vanished world of Polish Jewry before the Holocaust. This is his best-known book for children, a collection of stories that reflect Jewish folklore, culture, and humor. See also *Zlateh the Goat and Other Stories*. (1968)

Secret Garden, The

Frances Hodges Burnett   5, 6

Ten-year-old Mary, quite contrary, comes to live in a lonely house on the Yorkshire moors and discovers an invalid cousin and the mysteries of a locked garden in this beloved tale. Many editions can be found. Noteworthy illustrators include Graham Rust, Tasha Tudor, and Inga Moore. (1888)

Grades 4 to 5

Secret of the Andes

Ann Nolan Clark
5, 6

An Indian boy who tends llamas in a hidden valley in Peru learns the traditions and secrets of his Inca ancestors. See also *Santiago* by this author. (1952)

★ Newbery Medal

Secret Valley, The

Clyde Robert Bulla; *illustrated by Grace Paull*
4, 5

A family that moves to California to look for gold fails to find it, but instead discovers a beautiful valley in which to build a farm. The prolific and popular author grew up on a farm and during his lifetime wrote more than fifty books for children. (1949)

Seed Leaf Flower Fruit

Maryjo Koch, *illustrated by author*
5

Koch researched, wrote, and illustrated this engaging guide to the botanical world. She presents a unique blend of material on agriculture, food, ecology, homeopathy, and medicine, delightfully illustrated with watercolor paintings. This is one of a trio of award-winning youth science books; *Bird Egg Feather Nest* and *Pond Lake River Sea* are the other two. (1998)

Shadow of a Bull

Maia Wojciechowska; *illustrated by Alvin Smith*
5, 6

Manolo Olivar has to make a decision: to follow in his famous father's shadow and become a bullfighter or to follow his heart and become a doctor. (1964)

★ Newbery Medal

Shaw's Fortune

Edwin Tunis, *illustrated by author*
5–8

Tunis chronicles the growth of a Virginia tobacco plantation over several generations, beginning in 1650. Beautifully illustrated, it includes descriptions of daily life as well as a view into the lives of the plantation's slaves. (1966)

Shiloh

Phyllis Reynolds Naylor 4, 5, 6

Marty finds a lost beagle and tries to hide it from his family and the dog's mean-spirited owner. (1991)

★ Newbery Medal

Short Stories 1927-1956

Walter de la Mare 4, 5

Giles de la Mare, the author's grandson, has edited these stories, which are now preserved in one volume for those who especially treasure Walter's genius. See also the 1970 collection, *The Complete Poems of Walter de la Mare*. (2001)

Skippack School

Marguerite de Angeli 4, 5

The subtitle is *Being the Story of Eli Shrawder and of One Christopher Dock, Schoolmaster About the Year 1750*. In Pennsylvania, mischievous young Eli, recently arrived with his Mennonite family from Germany, tries to adjust to his new life and especially to the teaching methods of his schoolteacher. (1939)

Song of the Swallows

Leo Politi, *illustrated by author* 4

Every spring the swallows return to San Juan Capistrano, and every year young Juan rings the mission's bells to welcome them back. (1950)

★ Carnegie Medal

Soup

Robert Newton Peck 4, 5, 6

Rural Vermont during the 1920s is the setting for this nostalgic and humorous account of episodes in the lives of young Peck and his trouble-seeking pal, Soup. Many titles followed the popular introduction of Soup's character. (1974)

Spirit of the Mountain

Shelley Davidow 5–8

Set in South Africa and written partly as a diary, this book lets readers get a look into a young girl's struggle with anorexia and the help she finds from a local healer and from powers she doesn't understand. Alternately funny and scary, this book takes you on a realistic journey by a prize-winning author. (2009)

Story of the Treasure Seekers

Edith Nesbit 4, 5, 6

The subtitle is: *Being the Adventures of the Bastable Children in Search of a Fortune.* In an effort to save their inventor father from financial ruin, the six children find inventive ways to make a shilling or two in turn-of-the-century England. They dig for treasure, kidnap a neighbor, write and sell poetry, and more. (1899)

Strawberry Girl

Lois Lenski, *illustrated by author* 5

Set in rural Florida's strawberry growing region, this story of Birdie Boyer and small farm family life captures a time in a region of the United States that has passed into history. (1945)

★ Newbery Medal

Sun So Hot I Froze to Death

Arthur M. Pittis; *illustrated by Ausa M. Peacock* 4

This final volume in the "Waldorf Reader Series" focuses on American regional tales and is in four sections: Fabulous Tales, Hero Tales, Tall Tales, and A Scary Story. Within each section, a series of chapter stories focus on a different character. There are stories of Davy Crockett, Johnny Appleseed, Brer Rabbit, Pecos Bill, and others. There are also poems and lyrics to sing. Linguistically, these stories introduce the young reader to reading non-standard English, as well as geographical aspects of the Waldorf Grade Five social studies curriculum. (2005)

Sword in the Tree, The

Clyde Robert Bulla; *illustrated by Paul Galdone* 4, 5, 6

In the days of King Arthur, a boy who dreams of becoming a knight, must find his courage and protect his mother from an uncle who takes over the family castle. (1956)

Tale of Despereaux, The

Kate DiCamillo; *illustrated by Timothy Basil Ering*   4, 5, 6

Desperaux Tilling, a small mouse of unusual talents, the princess that he loves, a servant girl who longs to be a princess, and a devious rat determined to bring them all to ruin, make up the cast of this fairy tale. The subtitle is *Being the Story of a Mouse, a Princess, Some Soup, and a Spool of Thread.* (2003)

★ Newbery Medal

Teddy Bear Habit, The

James Lincoln Collier   5, 6

A twelve-year-old boy who thinks he's a loser and still takes his teddy bear with him wherever he goes, gets involved with a variety of characters and adventures in Greenwich Village, New York during the beatnik days. Full of intrigue, mystery, and lies that need to be untangled, this page-turner is credited with transforming many a lackluster reader into an enthusiastic one. (1967)

Thimble Summer

Elizabeth Enright   4, 5

Set in rural Wisconsin during the Depression and a drought, Garnet's family fortune turn around after she finds a silver thimble near their farm. Now feeling very lucky, Garnet, soon to be ten, spends the summer having adventures with her best friend Citronella, visiting town without adult accompaniment and preparing her pig for an appearance at the upcoming County Fair. (1938)

★ Newbery Medal

Three Candles of Little Veronica, The

Manfred Kyber; translated by Rosamond Reinhardt;
illustrated by Iris Guarducci   5, 6

Subtitled *The Story of a Child's Soul in this World and the Other,* Kyber interweaves the world of humans, animals, and angels, sensitively dealing with the subject of early death and the connections between the seen and unseen world. Beautifully illustrated, this story has touched many and become a cherished one. In 1972 it was translated from German. (1929)

Trumpet of the Swan, The

E. B. White   4, 5, 6

Knowing how to read and write is not enough for Louis, a voiceless Trumpeter Swan—his determination to learn to play a stolen trumpet takes him far from his wilderness home. This is the third of White's not-to-be-missed novels for children, the others being *Charlotte's Web* and *Stuart Little*. (1970)

Uncle Daney's Way

Jesse Haas   5, 6, 7

Cole's great-uncle moves in with them after a logging accident confines him to a wheelchair, but Cole's parents can't afford to keep his two-thousand-pound draft horse, Nip. Under his uncle's guidance, Cole learns to work the horse, and Pop finally has the help he needs to get a small logging business started. (1994)

View from Saturday, The

E. L. Konigsburg   5, 6

The author earned another Newbery with this story of four very individual students who develop a special bond and attract the attention of their teacher, a paraplegic, who chooses them to represent their sixth-grade class in an Academic Bowl competition. (1996)

★ Newbery Medal

Visit to William Blake's Inn, A:
Poems for Innocent and Experienced Travelers

Nancy Willard; *illustrated by Alice and Martin Provensen*   4, 5, 6+

This award-winning book offers children and adults a delightful collection of poems describing the curious menagerie of guests who arrive at an imaginary inn of poet William Blake. Blake's *Songs of Innocence and Songs of Experience* inspired the author. (1981)

★ Newbery Medal, Caldecott Honor

Voyages of Dr. Dolittle, The

Hugh Lofting 4, 5

The 1988 revised edition of the series has been updated to make the far-voyaging doctor who talked to animals more politically correct. There are, however, copies still available of the original editions, as well as a 1997 Newbery award-winning version redesigned for younger readers. (1922)

★ Newbery Medal

Westward Adventure: The True Stories of Six Pioneers

William O. Steele; *illustrated by Kathleen Voute* 4, 5

Written for young readers of history, this is a very accessible account of pioneer true-life adventures by a Newbery Honor author whose more than twenty juvenile novels vividly recapture America's pioneer past. (1962)

Wheel on the School, The

Meindert DeJong; *illustrated by Maurice Sendak* 5, 6

A young girl inspires her teacher, schoolmates, and small Dutch village to find a way to bring the storks back to their rooftops. It's full of life lessons about friendship, perseverance and community. (1954)

★ Newbery Medal

Whipping Boy, The

Sid Fleischman 4, 5, 6

Prince Horace is so naughty that everyone calls him Prince Brat. Because it is forbidden for him to be spanked, Jemmy, an orphan boy, is taken from the streets to be the prince's whipping boy. When the prince decides to run away, he takes Jemmy with him, and thereupon begins an adventure full of mischief and melodrama. (1986)

★ Newbery Medal

White Stallions of Lipizza

Marguerite Henry; *illustrated by Dennis Wesley* 5, 6

Hans, a Viennese baker's son, achieves his dream and is apprenticed to the Spanish Court Riding School where the amazing Lipizzan Stallions are trained. (1964)

Wild Animals I Have Known and 200 Drawings

Ernest Thompson Seton, *illustrated by author*   4

"Being the personal histories of Lobo, Silverspot, Raggylug, Bingo, the Springfield fox, the pacing mustang, Wully and Redruff" is how the author describes this illustrated collection of stories about real animals. (1898)

Wind in the Willows, The

Kenneth Grahame   4, 5+

The adventures of Mr. Toad, Rat, Badger, and Mole, the well-known, oh-so-human animal characters in this tale, have delighted adults and children for decades. However, the British men's club tone may not be for everyone. Best appreciated when read aloud by an adult, this novel of British manners and country living can be appropriate for even the very young listener. Selected episodes have been published as individual volumes to appeal to young independent readers. (1908)

Wind Song

Carl Sandburg; *illustrated by William A. Smith*   4+

From all of his poems, Sandburg selected these that particularly appeal to children. This is a collection to return to again and again for years to come. (1960)

Wish Giver, The: Three Tales of Coven Tree

Bill Brittain   4, 5, 6

When a strange little man comes to the Coven Tree Church Social promising he can give people exactly what they ask for, three young believers-in-magic each make a wish that comes true in the most unexpected way. (1983)

★ Newbery Honor

Witches, The

Roald Dahl   4, 5, 6

A young boy and his Norwegian grandmother, an expert on witches, together foil a witches' plot to destroy the world's children by turning them into mice. Dahl reads well aloud. Sometimes, younger listeners can savor the gruesome details more comfortably when in adult company. Mature independent readers may enjoy the thrills and chills alone. If Dahl is your cup of tea, there are others to sip such as *Fantastic Mr. Fox*, *James and the Giant Peach*, and, of course, *Charlie and the Chocolate Factory* and its sequel. (1983)

Wolves of Willoughby Chase, The

Joan Aiken   5, 6

Wicked wolves without and a grim, greedy governess within threaten two cous-ins. The girls have been left in the care of the cruel and calculating Miss Slighcarp, a distant relative who schemes to take their ancestral home, Willoughby Chase, away from the family. This first of a twelve-part series is set in Victorian England in the fictional reign of King James III. (1962)

Wonder Clock, The

Howard Pyle, *illustrated by author*   4, 5

These twenty-four fifteen-minute stories, one for each hour of the day, are full of medieval kings and princes, dragons, villains, ruffians, magical creatures, and their adventures and mishaps. Best read aloud, this collection of stories is more suitable to younger readers than most of Pyle's tales. The original illustrations by the famous artist are an important part of the magic of the book. (1887)

Wonderful Adventures of Nils, The

Selma Lagerlof; translated by Velma Swanston Howard;
illustrated by Hans Baumhauer   4, 5

Considered a masterpiece, this remarkably original work by the Nobel Prize-winning Swedish author records the adventures of a mischievous four-teen-year-old who is changed into a tiny being, transported across the Swedish countryside on the back of a goose, and learns about nature, geography, and folklore. (1907)

Zlateh the Goat and Other Stories

Isaac Bashevis Singer; translated by Elizabeth Shub;
illustrated by Maurice Sendak   4, 5, 6

Seven traditional folktales give the flavor of daily life in middle Europe in this much-honored children's collection from a Nobel laureate. Sendak, the illustra-tor, is one of the most honored American authors and illustrators of children's books. (1966)

★ Newbery Honor, School Library Journal Best of the Best Books

Grades Six
to Eight

AGES TWELVE TO FOURTEEN

Fiction and biographies that appeal to this age group often tell stories of trials that define character and test values. "Coming of age" to take one's place in society is signaled by the changes of puberty. Interest in what it means to be a man or a woman comes with those changes, and stories that address the question are most meaningful then. In the curriculum the questions of identity are addressed in a slightly different way in each grade. The life struggles of individuals who played a pivotal role in history are of natural interest to young people in the process of becoming who they are. History is taught through biography. Historical fiction is a rich genre for this age group once the historical context has been studied. Stories of interesting characters set in a well-characterized period of history in which there is a resonating interest make exciting reading.

Sixth Grade

Roman civilization and the the medieval life are usually studied in sixth grade. The rule of law made the *Pax Romana*. Sixth graders will spend more time discussing the rules of the game than they will actually playing, whether it is chess or volleyball. The accomplishments as well as the defeats of the Romans appeal to children who are eager to test themselves against standards. The stories of King Arthur's knights will do wonders to bring about a more chivalrous code of behavior on the playing field., as theThe ideals of sportsmanship are embodied in the tales.

Seventh Grade

Waldorf teacher Henry Barnes wrote,

> In the seventh grade the early struggles of puberty are beginning. Doubts arise in regard to authority, doubts in regard to many aspects of life. At this

time the children come to the study of the Renaissance when the unquestioned unity of the medieval world was shattered and men fought their way out from this harmony into a world of ideas and science…, the struggles in the age of the Reformation, the struggles in individual consciousness.

The Age of Exploration and the journeys that reshaped the map of the known world is also a history block well suited to the adventurous spirit of young adolescents. Works written for this age best address a widening interest in the real world, in history and science, in a context of the spirit of adventure and exploration. The Renaissance spirit is the spirit of junior high in which man is the measure of all things and all things remain possible.

Eighth Grade

In eighth grade the drama of modern world history engages and excites. The biographies of America's Founding Fathers and Mothers and the stories of other emerging democracies in the Age of Revolution make classroom or dinnertime debates worthy of Parliament or Congress.

The study of the world conflicts of the twentieth century prepares students for a high school experience in which independent historical judgment may grow. Biographies of presidents, civil rights leaders, scientists, artists, and inventors fuel personal dreams and ambitions and inspire individual interests and talents. Fiction that describes the discovery of one's own true character and the dilemmas of moral choice shines a light on the issues of our time as well as the challenges that students meet as they learn to stand up for their own values and beliefs.

Across Five Aprils

Irene Hunt   8+

The Newbery-winning author of *Up a Road Slowly* penned this coming-of-age novel, authentically reflecting the turbulence of the Civil War and the importance of family even when sons fight on opposite sides. Told from the viewpoint of the youngest son. (1964)

★ Newbery Honor

Adam of the Road

Elizabeth J. Gray   6, 7

In 1294, a minstrel and his son, Adam, adventure in the accurately depicted medieval England of the Magna Carta and the House of Commons. (1942)

★ Newbery Medal

Adventures of Huckleberry Finn, The

Mark Twain   8+

Twain's complex tale of a boy's moral journey, as he is forced to reevaluate what society has taught him about the institution of slavery in America, has been called the first and greatest American novel. It can inspire conversations about racism in America that ran as deep as the Mississippi on which Huck and the runaway slave, Jim, rafted. Simplified editions are available. (1884)

Adventures of Tom Sawyer, The

Mark Twain   8+

Tom's prankish boyhood is a fictional evocation of the author's youth in Missouri. Despite its popularity on juvenile reading lists, many find the southern dialects, which Twain introduced to American literature, challenging. Simplified and shortened versions are available. See Twain's *The Prince and the Pauper* for a book more suited to juvenile readers. (1876)

Amazing Maurice and his Educated Rodents, The

Terry Pratchett   7, 8

Maurice, a talking cat, recruits a group of intelligent rats and a boy with a penny whistle to run a scam based on the Pied Piper legend. The author won the British science fiction award for *Pyramids* in 1989. This award-winning novel, with its cheeky humor and outrageous plot, puts him on the list of top young adult authors in America as well. (2001)

✶ Carnegie Medal

America and Vietnam: The Elephant and the Tiger

Dr. Albert Marrin, photographed by author   8+

This is one of the only books for young people about the first war to be viewed on television. The author (whose other works for young adult readers are also recommended) offers concise information and answers questions while offering a picture of the times. Black and white photographs. (1992)

American Short Story

Edited by Thomas K. Parkes   8+

This is subtitled *A Collection of the Best Known and Most Memorable Short Stories by the Great American Authors.* With just over 1000 pages, this hearty collection features short stories from the past two hundred years, and includes the work of Washington Irving, Truman Capote, Nathaniel Hawthorne, Edgar Allan Poe, Mark Twain, Edith Wharton, William Faulkner, and many others. (1994)

And Now Miguel

Joseph Krumgold; *illustrated by Jean Charlot*   6, 7, 8

Miguel, the middle child of the Chavez family, lives near Taos, New Mexico, and longs to go with the men of his family to take their sheep to the summer pasture in the Sangre de Cristo Mountains, a rite of passage for boys in his community. Set in the 1950s, the story contrasts the old ways with modern change represented by the recently built Los Alamos atomic energy laboratory. (1953)

✶ Newbery Medal

Anne of Green Gables

L. M. Montgomery   6, 7

We first meet the series heroine, Anne Shirley, age eleven, adjusting to foster parents and a new home on Prince Edward Island, Canada. Subsequent titles follow her as she enters college, becomes a teacher, and marries: *Anne of Avonlea*, *Anne of the Island*, *Anne of Windy Poplars*, *Anne's House of Dreams*, *Anne of Ingleside*, *Rainbow Valley*, and *Rilla of Ingleside*. (1908)

Ark, The

Margot Benary-Isbert; translated by Richard and Clara Winston   7, 8

A farm becomes a growing concern and an old railroad car becomes an ark of life in this young adult novel about a family of East German refugees who start a new life in West Germany before the fall of the Berlin Wall. Translated from German. (1953)

Arm of the Starfish

Madeleine L'Engle   7, 8+

Adam, a brilliant student of marine biology working off the coast of Portugal, finds himself in the center of a power struggle between two groups of people— only one of which can be right. (1965)

Around the World in Eighty Days

Jules Verne   7, 8+

The story of inventor Phineas Fogg's race to circumvent the globe is a fast-paced adventure that has been a best seller for over a century. However, this journey is not science fiction, does not take place in a hot air balloon, and is Verne's portrait of the British Empire "on which the sun never set." Several translations from the French as well as many editions are available. (1873)

Banner in the Sky

James Ramsey Ullman   6, 7, 8

After his father dies on The Citadel, Switzerland's greatest mountain, Rudi, a nineteenth-century teen, realizes he must attempt the climb himself, even against his mother's wishes. Ullman writes this compelling story from experience. (1954)

★ Newbery Honor, ALA Notable Children's Book

Behind the Blue and Gray: The Soldier's Life in the Civil War

Delia Ray   8

The second volume of the author's photographically illustrated two-volume series traces the events of the Civil War from the first battle to the surrender, with emphasis on the experiences of the individual soldier. See also *A Nation Torn Apart.* (1991)

Best Short Stories of O. Henry, The

O. Henry (William Sidney Porter)   8+

These thirty-eight stories are selected from over six hundred that Porter wrote under the pen name O. Henry. Other collections are available, but look for inclusion of "The Gift of the Magi," which is perhaps his best known (a popular Christmas story) and "The Ransom of Red Chief." (1994)

Big Wave and Other Stories, The

Pearl S. Buck   8+

This collection includes the author's famous story of a Japanese boy who must face life after escaping the tidal-wave destruction of his family and village. Illustrated with eighteenth- and nineteenth-century Japanese prints. Readers who enjoy Buck's short stories may also wish to discover her novels set in Asia, such as *The Good Earth.* (1948)

Black Arrow: A Tale of the Two Roses

Robert Louis Stevenson   7, 8+

A tale of adventure is set in fifteenth-century England during the Wars of the Roses. The royal crown itself is the prize to the winner and young Richard Shelton is torn in his loyalties between the House of York and the House of Lancaster as he seeks to avenge the death of his father and becomes involved with the Band of the Black Arrow. (1888)

Black Pearl, The

Scott O'Dell   6, 7, 8

Diving off the Mexican coast of Baja, California, sixteen-year-old Ramon battles a monstrous devilfish to claim a rare black pearl. He does not foresee the trouble such a legendary gem can cause his family. (1967)

★ Newbery Honor

Book of Americans, A

Rosemary and Stephen Benét; *illustrated by Charles Child*   8

This witty collection of fifty-six poems is about famous Americans. Stephen Benét also wrote "The Devil and Daniel Webster," a very popular short story about another famous American. (1933)

Book of Pirates, The

Howard Pyle, *illustrated by author*   6, 7, 8

Now reprinted as *Howard Pyle's Book of Pirates*, this book was a hit before Disney's blockbuster. It is subtitled *Fiction, Fact and Fancy Concerning the Buccaneers and Marooners of the Spanish Main.* Copies of the original edition are now rare and valuable, but a recent reprint, with smaller black-and-white reproductions of the original art, makes this text available once again. (1921)

Born Free: A Lioness of Two Worlds

Joy Adamson   6, 7, 8

The author and her husband, a game warden in Kenya, rescue and raise a newborn cub they call Elsa. When the lioness is three, they must teach her to hunt so she can return to the wild world. Elsa's education is documented with excellent photos. (1960)

Borrowed House, The

Hilda Van Stockum   8+

During World War II, a young German girl, a member of Hitler's Youth, stays with her parents in occupied Amsterdam and comes to a realization about the war. (1975)

Boys' Sherlock Holmes, The

Sir Arthur Conan Doyle   8+

Ignore the gender designation on this selected collection: Holmes is a sleuth every reader should know. The complete collection awaits those who find this one whets an appetite for the urbane English detective and his loyal sidekick, Dr. Watson. (1892)

Bread Sister of Sinking Creek, The

Robin Moore   6, 7, 8

Stranded on the Pennsylvania frontier in 1776, independent fourteen-year-old Maggie discovers she has a gift for sourdough bread making, which will prove to be her survival. Recipes included. (1984)

Bridge to Terabithia

Katherine Paterson   7, 8+

A boy and girl form a deep friendship despite their different backgrounds and personalities and establish a secret meeting place they call Terabithia. The story deals with the death of one of them and the process of grieving for the survivor. It is the first of Paterson's two Newbery-winning novels for young adult readers. (1977)

★ Newbery Medal

Bronze Bow, The

Elizabeth George Speare   6

The author's second Newbery novel is set in the Middle East in the reign of Caesar Augustus as tensions between Romans, Jews, and the new Christian sect threaten to tear apart the shaky balance of power. Can the ideas of the controversial teacher, Jesus of Nazareth, offer an alternative to civil war and racial hatred? (1961)

★ Newbery Medal

Brother Dusty Feet

Rosemary Sutcliff   7, 8

In Elizabethan England, eleven-year-old Hugh Copplestone leaves home after too many beatings, taking his faithful dog, Argos, with him, and joins a band of traveling players for a life on the road. The text is more accessible to reluctant readers than many of this author's excellent historical fictions. (1952)

Bud, Not Buddy

Christopher Paul Curtis   6, 7, 8

A brave young orphan boy escapes his third foster home in search of a father he's never met. Set during the Depression, this is an inspiring, thought-provoking, and funny tale of overcoming circumstances that will touch your heart. (1999)

★ Newbery Medal, Coretta Scott King Award

Bull Run

Paul Fleischman   6, 7, 8

Northerners, Southerners, generals, couriers, dreaming boys, and worried sisters describe the glory, the horror, the thrill, and the disillusionment of the first battle of the Civil War in an easier-to-read, absorbing historical fiction. (1993)
★ Scott O'Dell Award for Historical Fiction

Burning Questions of Bingo Brown, The

Betsy Byars   6, 7

A sixth-grade boy is puzzled by the comic and confusing questions of youth and worried by disturbing insights into adult conflicts. Serious modern problems are lightened with humor and the hero is one of the author's most enjoyable characters. (1988)

By Secret Railway

Enid Meadowcroft   6, 7, 8

It's 1860 and twelve-year-old David is trying to help Jim escape to freedom on the Underground Railroad. (1948)

Calico Captive

Elizabeth George Speare   6, 7, 8

In 1754 an Indian raid on her small New Hampshire town leaves Miriam Willard a prisoner of the Indians, forced to take part in a harrowing march north. Knowing that all that awaits her at the end of the trail is an Indian gauntlet and a life of slavery, how can she go on? (1957)

Call It Courage

Armstrong Sperry   6, 7, 8

Alone in a sea-going canoe, the chief's son Mafatu must prove his courage and face his fear of the evil sea god who took his mother and nearly drowned him as an infant. (1940)
★ Newbery Medal

Captains Courageous

Rudyard Kipling   7, 8+

Set on the wild waters of the Grand Banks, this novel tells the story of a ship-wrecked millionaire's son who is rescued by the crew of a fishing schooner and taught a much-needed lesson about life at sea. (1897)

Carry On, Mr. Bowditch

Jean Lee Latham; *illustrated by John O'Hara Cosgrave*   7

This is a fictionalized biography of Nathaniel Bowditch, the mathematician and astronomer who realized his childhood desire to become a ship's captain and authored *The American Practical Navigator*. It is full of fascinating details about life at sea and navigation. Latham wrote many books about people who pioneered in science or technical fields. (1955)

★ Newbery Medal

Catherine, Called Birdy

Karen Cushman   6, 7, 8

The diary of fourteen-year-old Catherine recounts the many ways she escapes the suitors her father chooses as he attempts to arrange her marriage. Her attitude and the sense of humor are modern, but the story is set in medieval England in the year 1290. Some historical background on the position of women at that time would be helpful. (1994)

★ Newbery Honor, ALA 100 Best Young Adult Books of the 20th Century

Cay, The

Theodore Taylor   7, 8

When the freighter on which they are traveling is torpedoed by a German sub-marine during World War II, a twelve-year-old white boy, blinded by a blow on the head, and an old Negro are stranded on a Caribbean island where the boy acquires a new kind of vision, courage, and love from his old companion. *Timothy of the Cay* is the sequel. (1969)

★ Lewis Carroll Shelf Award

Changeover, The: A Supernatural Romance

Margaret Mahy   6, 7, 8

When her brother becomes fatally ill, his sister is the one who realizes he is under the influence of witchcraft. Mahy is a talented author from New Zealand. See *The Haunting*, which also won the Carnegie Medal. (1984)

★ Carnegie Medal

Chemical History of a Candle, The

Michael Faraday   ☀   7, 8

Faraday conducted a popular series of lecture demonstrations as a holiday entertainment for children. The six lectures and twenty-two demonstrations illustrate the basic phenomena of combustion and can be reproduced in a classroom or home laboratory with appropriate safety precautions. Some later editions included illustrations. (1861)

City: The Story of Roman Planning and Construction

David Macaulay, *illustrated by author*   ☀   6, 7

Macaulay, an award-winning children's author and illustrator, imagines a Roman city with buildings, roads, acqueduct, etc. and draws them with a draftsman's eye for detail, explaining the construction process in the text. The sense of being present in the place is very real in this book and in the others: *Cathedral: The Story of its Construction, Building the Book Cathedral* (about bookmaking, but also supplemental to *Cathedral*), *Castle, Mosque,* and *Unbuilding.* This series connects the subject of history with that of mechanics and exemplary geometrical drawing. (1974)

Crispin: The Cross of Lead

Avi (Edward Worthing Wortis)   6, 7, 8

Falsely accused of theft and murder, an orphaned peasant boy in fourteenth-century England during the reign of Edward III flees his village and meets a larger-than-life juggler who holds a dangerous secret. A sequel follows: *Crispin: At the Edge of the World.* (2002)

★ Newbery Medal

Dandelion Wine

Ray Bradbury   7, 8+

A twelve-year-old boy's magical summer in small town Illinois in 1928 has a bittersweet edge in Bradbury's semiautobiographical hit. In 2004, Bradbury received the National Medal of Arts, the highest award given to artists and art patrons by the U.S. government. (1957)

Danza!

Lynn Hall   6, 7

While in the United States with one of his grandfather's Paso Fino stallions, a Puerto Rican teenager discovers his true feelings about horses. The author has written many books about horses and dogs. (1981)

Dark Frigate, The

Charles Boardman Hawes   7, 8

When an orphaned seventeenth-century London boy goes to sea, he's forced to become a pirate and later a king's soldier. The exciting adventure concludes with a surprise ending. The language is a bit archaic, but the book becomes a page-turner once the pirates enter the scene. (1923)

★ Newbery Medal

Dark is Rising, The

Susan Cooper   6, 7, 8

Eleven-year-old Will Stanton and his siblings find themselves entering the world of magic as the legends of King Arthur come alive in this fantasy series. This is the second in a quintet that goes by this title. The others are *Over Sea, Under Stone*; *Greenwitch*; *The Grey King* (Newbery winner); and *Silver on the Tree*. (1973)

★ Newbery Honor, Boston Globe-Horn Book

Day No Pigs Would Die, A

Robert Newton Peck   6, 7, 8

When his pet pig reaches maturity, the reality of life on a Vermont pig farm tests the boy, Robert, who has been raised in the Shaker tradition. This novel is autobiographical. (1972)

Dobry

Monica Shannon 6, 7, 8

A Bulgarian peasant boy, Dobry, decides to leave the local village and land his family has farmed for generations in order to attend an art school in the far-away city of Sophia. The power of an idea to direct a life and the meaning of land to people who depend upon it are both conveyed in this story. (1934)

★ Newbery Medal

Dogsong

Gary Paulsen 6, 7, 8

Self-knowledge is the result of an Eskimo boy's decision to leave his modern village and make a demanding journey by dogsled. (1985)

★ Newbery Honor

Door in the Wall, The

Marguerite de Angeli, *illustrated by author* 6, 7, 8

While the plague and war with the Welsh rage through fourteenth-century London, ten-year-old Robin, son of a great lord, comes of age. Robin, who hopes to become a knight, finds he must make a great sacrifice to save a castle under siege. (1949)

★ Newbery Medal, Lewis Carroll Shelf Award

Double Life: Newly Discovered Thrillers of Louisa May Alcott

Louisa May Alcott; edited by Madeleine B. Stern, Joel Myerson and Daniel Shealy 8

Five melodramatic short stories, originally published for 1860s' newspaper readers in serial form, feature popular Victorian headline topics: doomed love, Mesmerism, and Indian cults. They were first published anonymously, and perhaps Miss Alcott would have wished they remained so, but the topics have become fashionable again. (1988)

Downright Dencey

Caroline Dale Snedeker　　　　　　　　　　　7, 8

In a Quaker community on the island of Nantucket just before the War of 1812, Dencey is a mystery to her mother whose stern exterior hides a heart that breaks every time her husband, captain of a whaling ship, goes to sea. The spirited little girl, who in an unQuakerly fit of temper throws a rock that wounds the town outcast, matures into a young woman of grace and courage. (1927)

★ Newbery Honor

Downriver

Will Hobbs　　　　　　　　　　　　　7, 8

Fifteen-year-old Jessie and other rebellious teenagers on a wilderness survival school team abandon their adult leader, hijack his boats, and try to run the dangerous white water at the bottom of the Grand. (1991)

★ ALA 100 Best Young Adult Books of the 20th Century

Dragonwings

Lawrence Yep　　　　　　　　　　　6, 7, 8

Moon Shadow leaves China to join his father, a famous kite-maker who dreams of building an airplane. Together they experience the 1906 San Francisco earthquake. (1975)

★ Newbery Honor, Lewis Carroll Shelf Award

Drums

James Boyd　　　　　　　　　　　　　8

Boyd's classic historical fiction about the American Revolution in the Southern colonies is paired with N. C. Wyeth's illustrative genius, making the 1995 Athenaeum Books for Young Readers edition the one to look for. (1925)

Drums Along the Mohawk

Walter D. Edmonds　　　　　　　　　　　8+

The author is remembered for a Newbery-winning children's book, *The Matchlock Gun*, and for this adult novel about pioneers in the Mohawk Valley during the Revolutionary War. In 1776, Gilbert and Lana Martin struggle to survive and sow the seeds of the future as the thunder of battle rumbles into their remote valley. (1936)

Early Thunder

Jean Fritz; *illustrated by Lynd Ward*   8

In 1775, as tensions grow between the British and the colonists, fourteen-year-old Daniel West faces a year of decisions in Salem, Massachusetts. Historian Henry Steele Commager recommended this novel as one that faithfully mirrors the life of Revolutionary Salem. Fritz is the author of an extensive series of biographies of the Founding Fathers. (1967)

Ender's Game

Orson Scott Card   6, 7, 8

Boy genius Ender Wiggin is sent deep into space to study military tactics on computer game models in order to save the world from aliens. Complex character development and moral issues make this better than it sounds, or so thought ALA's Young Adult Services and others who awarded it top honors. (1985)
　★ Hugo Award, ALA 100 Best Young Adult Books of the 20th Century

Escape from Slavery: Five Journeys to Freedom

Doreen Rappaport; *illustrated by Charles Lilly*   8

Five narrative accounts of slaves who managed journeys to freedom on the underground railroad give immediacy to the experience. (1991)

Fal: The Dragon Harper

Peter Patterson; *illustrated by Terry Thomas*   6, 7

This is an imaginatively told coming-of-age quest full of magic and dragons, challenges and triumph that will take the reader on a suspenseful and humorous journey. It includes music notation for the songs. (1992)

Famous Experiments You Can Do

Robert Gardner   6, 7, 8

The reader can replicate experiments in chemistry and physics, originally developed by scientists such as Archimedes, Galileo, Lavoisier, and Newton, by following the directions in this book. Adult supervision advised. (1990)

Grades 6 to 8

Far North

Will Hobbs 6, 7, 8

Gabe, his boarding school roommate, and a Dih-nay Tribe elder are stranded in the backwoods of the Northwest Territories as winter approaches. The old man's knowledge helps the boys build shelter and hunt for food, but survival ultimately requires persistence, cooperation, and courage. Young adult readers who enjoy this wilderness adventure will find more like it by Hobbs. See *Downriver* also. (1996)

★ ALA 100 Best Young Adult Books of the 20th Century

Fighting Ground, The

Avi (Edward Irving Wortis) 8

Thirteen-year-old Jonathan steals his father's gun and runs away to fight in the Revolutionary War. Within twenty-four hours of enduring suspense, excitement, and moral dilemmas, he discovers the real war is being fought within himself. (1984)

★ Scott O'Dell Award for Historical Fiction, ALA Best Books for Young Adults

Flour Babies

Anne Fine 7, 8

This is a humorous approach to the serious topic of teenage parents. Fourteen-year-old boys are given a school project to help them understand the burdens of parenthood. They must take care of a sack of flour as if it were an infant and keep a diary of their experience for three weeks. This is Fine's second Carnegie Medal. (1994)

★ Carnegie Medal, Boston Globe-Horn Book

Forever Free

Dorothy Sterling; *illustrated by Ernest Crichlow* 8

The events leading up to the signing of the Emancipation Proclamation, which freed over four million slaves, are described. (1963)

Frankenstein

Mary Shelley   8+

The most famous monster horror story is actually a romantic novel by a young woman who was only eighteen when she wrote it. Viking's 1998 edition includes artwork from the period and annotations that add to its interest for students reading it as an example of the Romantic period in literature. (1818)

Freedom Beyond the Sea

Waldtraut Lewin   7, 8

To escape the horrors of the Inquisition, which she witnesses, the sixteen-year-old daughter of a murdered Jewish rabbi disguises herself as a boy and joins the crew of Columbus's *Santa Maria*. This novel, originally published in German, is full of detailed historical information despite the somewhat romanticized plot. (2001)

Gathering of Days, A: A New England Girl's Journal 1830–32

Joan W. Blos   6, 7, 8

This novel is in the form of the journal of a fourteen-year-old girl. Kept the last year she lived on a farm in New Hampshire, it records daily events in the small town, her father's remarriage, and the death of her best friend. (1979)
★ Newbery Medal

Geron and Virtus: A Fateful Encounter of Two Youths:
A German and a Roman

Jakob Streit; translated by Nina Kuettel; *illustrated by Adam Agee*   6, 7, 8

Streit tells the story of two boys during the Roman campaign to conquer the Germanic tribes. This Roman/German encounter in history brought forth the birth of a new Europe and the transition to a new time. The story is about friendship, slavery, honor, and adventure. Enhanced by vivid illustrations. (2007)

Gettysburg Address, The

Abraham Lincoln   8

Dramatic black-and-white woodcuts of battlefield and wartime scenes by Michael McCurdy make a fitting setting for perhaps the most famous speech in American history and certainly a masterpiece of terse prose that deserves to be read aloud. Many other text versions are available, but this 1995 edition is one to admire. (1863)

Ghost Belonged to Me, The (Quartet)

Richard Peck   7, 8

The *Blossom Culp* series tells the story of a family in 1913 living in a small town in the midwest. Peck weaves the supernatural with comical situations. When thirteen-year-old Alexander finds a ghost haunting his barn, he turns to his remarkable neighbor, Blossom Culp, who has experience with these things. Her character reappears in *The Dreadful Future of Blossom Culp, Blossom Culp and the Sleep of Death*, and *Ghosts I Have Been*, which was honored by the *New York Times* and the ALA. (1975)

★ ALA Best of the Best Books

Giver, The

Lois Lowry   8+

Twelve-year-old Jonas is given the appointment to his life's work in the cult community in which he has been raised. His position causes him to question the cost of living in a society in which choice and controversy have been eliminated, and then to flee for his own survival. This riveting story stays with the reader for the issues it raises and gave Lowry her second Newbery prize. There is much to discuss here whether at home or in a classroom. (1993)

★ Newbery Medal, ALA Best Book for Young Adults

Glimpses of Louisa: A Centennial Sampling of the Best Short Stories of Louisa May Alcott

Louisa May Alcott; edited by Cornelia Meigs   8+

Alcott's biographer and noted authority on children's literature selected, edited, and introduced this Centennial collection. Out of hundreds of stories she selected these: "Onawandah," "An Ivy Spray and Ladies' Slippers," "My Red Cap," "Poppies And Wheat," "Kate's Choice," "Tessa's Surprises," "Mountain Laurel and Maidenhair," "Corny's Catamount," "Water Lilies" and "Laurie." (1968)

Golden Horseshoe, The

Elizabeth Coatsworth; *illustrated by Robert Lawson*   6, 7, 8

A story of coming-of-age and high adventure is set in colonial Virginia where Native American and Quaker cultures meet. Coatsworth's books may be somewhat difficult to find. (1935)

Good-bye, Mr. Chips

James Hilton   8+

A shy scholar takes a post as Classics Master at a small boarding school in the English countryside and remains there for the rest of his life. A consummate bachelor, he is cantankerous, fussy, eccentric, and greatly loved by the generations of boys who pass through his classes. (1934)

Great American Short Stories

Edited by Wallace and Mary Stegner   8+

Two editions exist of this popular collection of twenty-six stories by America's best writers, including Washington Irving, Nathaniel Hawthorne, Edgar Allan Poe, Mark Twain, Edith Wharton, James Thurber, William Faulkner, Henry James, John Steinbeck, Eudora Welty, and others. (1957)

Great Constitution, The:
A Book for Young Americans

Henry Steele Commager   8

Historian Commager's concise little volume manages to tell a great story—the dramatic but laborious process by which the delegates to the Constitutional Convention arrived at our nation's constitution—without getting lost in the details. It has been used in classrooms all over the country. A companion volume, *The Great Proclamation*, tells the story of the Emancipation Proclamation which Abraham Lincoln signed into effect. (1961)

Hand in Hand: An American History Through Poetry

Lee Bennett Hopkins; *illustrated by Peter M. Firore*   6, 7, 8

This is a poetical history as well as a topical anthology arranged chronologically by subject. Over seventy-five selections reflect the diversity of the peoples that came to North America and shaped the nation. Patriotic songs, speeches, and individual anthems by American poets, such as Whitman, Sandburg, Frost, and Langston Hughes, well-known contemporary poets, and a few new voices are represented. (1994)

Hang For Treason

Robert Newton Peck   8

A Vermont youth becomes involved with Ethan Allen and the Green Mountain Boys, despite his father's Tory leanings, in the early days of the Revolutionary War. Peck has quite a following as author of the popular *Soup* series. (1976)

Hang Tough, Paul Mather

Alfred Slote   6, 7, 8

A young baseball pitcher with an incurable blood disease (juvenile leukemia) is determined to get in as much time on the mound as possible. (1973)

Harry Potter and the Philosopher's Stone
(Sorcerer's Stone, American edition)

J. K. Rowling; illustrated by Mary GrandPré   6, 7, 8

An orphan becomes a student of sorcery at a special boarding school with other unusual children. This smashing British series grows increasingly scary and complex as Harry grows older. Redirection might be indicated for younger readers who latch onto the first one but cannot grow up as fast as the fictional protagonist in the sequels: *The Chamber of Secrets*, *The Prisoner of Azkaban*, and others. (1997)

★ ALA 100 Best Young Adult Books of the 20th Century

Hatchet

Gary Paulsen   7, 8

Thirteen-year-old Brian survives a plane crash in the Canadian wilderness where he is stranded for over fifty days. This is an exciting survival story with sequels: *The River*, *Brian's Winter*, *Brian's Hunt*, and *Brian's Return*. (1987)

★ Newbery Honor

Haunting, The

Margaret Mahy   7, 8

Barney is afraid to tell anyone about the messages he receives from relatives who have died. This novel is set in mid-twentieth century and filled with magic, mystery, fantasy, and the supernatural. See Mahy's other title, *The Changeover*. (1982)

★ Carnegie Medal

Hawk That Dared Not Hunt By Day, The

Scott O'Dell 7, 8

In the early sixteenth century, amid political turmoil and threats of plague, young Tom Barton accepts the risks of helping William Tyndale publish and smuggle into England the Bible he has translated into English. (1975)

Help Wanted: Short Stories About Young People Working

Edited by Anita Silvey 8+

A young person's first job is a special experience. The twelve stories collected here anecdote the changes the protagonists go through as a result of the kind of work they chose and take the reader into the journey with them. Authors include Gary Soto, Norma Fox Mazer, and Ray Bradbury. *(1997)*

Hero Ain't Nothin' But a Sandwich, A

Alice Childress 8

The life of a thirteen-year-old Harlem black youth on his way to becoming a heroin addict is seen from several points of view including his own. (1973)

★ ALA Notable Children's Book

Hero and the Crown, The

Robin McKinley 6, 7, 8

McKinley creates a fantasy adventure series that explores the struggle of good and evil through the perspective of strong female characters. This prequel to *The Blue Sword*, a Newbery Honor Book, follows the adventures of the Damarian king's daughter, Aerin, as she fights for the crown and love. (1984)

★ Newbery Medal, ALA Best Books for Young Adults

High Deeds of Finn Mac Cool, The

Rosemary Sutcliff 6, 7, 8

The stories of Finn and the grey dog and others of the brotherhood of the Fianna are based on the heroic stories of Fionn mac Cumhaill and the Fenian Cycle of Irish folktales. Sutcliff has earned a large following writing novels of historical fiction based on ancient tales. (1967)

His Dark Materials (Trilogy)

Philip Pullman   7, 8+

The Golden Compass is Book One in a British trilogy set in London about an alternate earth where magic is an ordinary fact of life. Lyra and her daemon familiar (an animal spirit that accompanies her through life) set out to solve a mystery involving the kidnapping of children for use in gruesome experiments. The ending is not entirely resolved and serves as a lead into the next two volumes, *The Subtle Knife* and *The Amber Spyglass*. The much-honored trio is popular with adults as well as mature young adult readers. (1996)

★ Carnegie Medal, ALA Notable Children's Book

Hobbit or There and Back Again, The

J. R. R. Tolkien   6, 7, 8

The adventures of the well-to-do hobbit, Bilbo Baggins, who lived happily in his comfortable home until a wandering wizard granted his wish. See also *The Lord of the Rings* trilogy for which this is a prequel. (1937)

Holes

Louis Sachar   7, 8

Due to a curse on his family, Stanley Yelnats is sent to a hellish juvenile correctional camp in the Texas desert where he is forced to dig for a treasure and finds his first real friend and a new sense of self. A rare winner of three major awards, *Holes* established its author as one of the most important voices in children's literature. (1998)

★ Newbery Medal, National Book Award

Homecoming

Cynthia Voight   7, 8

The first novel in this young adult series is about an abandoned family of four children ages six to thirteen. Led by the determined Dicey Tillerman, the four make their way from Rhode Island to Connecticut with courage, resourcefulness, and the sheer will to find a home together. Additional volumes in the Tillerman series are *Dicey's Song* (Newbery winner), *A Solitary Blue*, *The Runner*, *Come a Stranger*, *Sons from Afar*, and *Seventeen Against the Dealer*. (1982)

Hoofprint on the Wind

Ann Nolan Clark; illustrated by Robert Andrew Parker   6, 7

A boy is sure he saw a horse among the cliffs of an island off the coast of Western Ireland, but fellow islanders think he imagined it. (The region is called Connemara after Ireland's only indigenous breed, a hardy pony said to have pulled the Celts' war wagons.) (1972)

Hospital Sketches

Louisa May Alcott   8

Before Alcott created *Little Women*, she wrote a fictionalized account of her experiences as a volunteer Civil War nurse, "Nurse Tribulation Periwinkle," in a Washington, D.C. hospital. Based on her letters home, it is a glimpse into the attitudes and shocking realities of medical care during this time. Various reprints available. It is not suitable for young children. (1863)

House of Dies Drear, The

Virginia Hamilton   8

Mysterious sounds and events, in a house that was once part of the Underground Railroad in the days of slavery, convince the new occupants, an African-American family, that they are in grave danger. This mystery novel was so successful there is also a sequel: *The Mystery of Drear House: The Conclusion of the Dies Drear Chronicle* (1987). (1968)

How the Weather Works

Michael Allaby   6, 7, 8

This colorful introduction to how the weather works features entertaining and educational experiments and activities for the whole family, with complete directions for setting up a weather station in your home, helpful advice on how to keep accurate records, and forecasting techniques. Includes over one thousand color photos and illustrations, published by *Reader's Digest*. (1999)

I, Juan de Pareja

Elizabeth Borton de Treviño   7

Written in the manner of an autobiography, this novel is based on the true story of the slave who was willed to the great seventeenth-century Spanish painter, Velasquez. Although forbidden by law to practice any arts, Juan discovers his own artistic talents. The relationship of master and slave evolves into one of friendship and equality. (1965)

★ Newbery Medal

I'll Pass for Your Comrade: Women Soldiers in the Civil War

Anita Silvey   8

During the Civil War many women joined on both sides, not just to nurse and spy, but to fight alongside their men. This well-researched book includes period photographs, documents and resources for further exploration. (2008)

In Face of Danger

Mara Kay   8

While residing with a German family, English-born Ann Lindsay discovers that Frau Meixner, whose son is a member of the Hitler Youth, is hiding two Jewish girls in the attic. (1976)

Indian Captive: The Story of Mary Jemison

Lois Lenski, illustrated by author   6, 7, 8

This easy-to-read historical fiction is based on the true experiences of twelve-year-old Mary Jemison, who, after being captured by a Shawnee war party during the French and Indian War, is rescued and subsequently adopted by two Seneca sisters. In 1832 James Seaver interviewed Mary and edited her account for publication. Upon this record, the Newbery-winning author and illustrator based her version. (1941)

★ Newbery Honor

It's Like This, Cat

Emily Cheney Neville   6, 7, 8

This coming-of-age novel set in New York City tells of fourteen-year-old Dave, his family's problems and urban adventures as he takes outings into the neighborhood with the stray cat he has found. (1963)

★ Newbery Medal

Ivanhoe

Sir Walter Scott 6, 7, 8+

Set in the time of King Richard the Lion Heart, Scott's exciting novel is as good a tale of knights and ladies as any, but it takes a confident reader to manage the nineteenth-century British prose. An acquired taste, but addictive. (1819)

Jacob Have I Loved

Katherine Paterson 7, 8

An adolescent girl lives with her twin sister in the Chesapeake Bay area. This thought-provoking story is about sibling rivalry and jealousy in the 1940s. In 2006, the author received the Astrid Lindgren Memorial Award for the body of her work. (1980)
★ ALA 100 Best Young Adult Books of the 20th Century

Jip: His Story

Katherine Paterson 8

Jip is an orphan who lives on a farm in Vermont in 1855. As she does in *Lyddie*, the author manages to deal with real issues of the historical period in the context of a completely absorbing novel. (1996)
★ Scott O'Dell Award for Historical Fiction

Johnny Tremain

Esther Forbes 6, 7, 8

This historical fiction tells the story of the Revolutionary War, from the Tea Party through the Battle of Lexington, as seen through the eyes of a young Boston apprentice turned dispatch rider for the Committee of Public Safety. (1943)
★ Newbery Medal

Journey to the Center of the Earth

Jules Verne 6, 7, 8

Verne is considered the father of science fiction, but what keeps his books moving off library shelves is his ability to tell an exciting tale while making plausible guesses about unknown frontiers waiting for human exploration. Students of geology will enjoy comparing Verne's "science" to more recent discoveries. (1864)

Grades 6 to 8

Julie of the Wolves

Jean Craighead George; *illustrated by John Schoenherr*   ☀ 6, 7, 8

Wolves protect a thirteen-year-old Eskimo girl after she becomes lost. Her coming-of-age adventures and involvement with the wolves continue in two more volumes. The fourth volume is about the Inuit people but not Julie herself: *Julie, Julie's Wolf Pack*, and *Water Sky*. (1972)

★ Newbery Medal

Keeping Days, The

Norma Johnston   8

A coming-of-age tale in the genre of *Little Women* and *Little House* books, this one takes place in Yonkers, NY. An amazing girl tells of her life and family during a seven-month period in 1900. This is the first in a seven book series, followed by *Glory in the Flower*. The rest of the series may be out of print and hard to find but worth looking for. (1973)

Kidnapped

Robert Louis Stevenson   7, 8

David Balfour's uncle has him kidnapped to block the sixteen-year-old's inheritance. Life grows even more dangerous when David witnesses a murder and becomes involved in the struggle of the Scottish Highlanders against English rule. This, and three other popular Stevenson adventures, *Treasure Island, The Strange Case of Dr. Jekyll and Mr. Hyde*, and *The Black Arrow*, can be found collected in one Barnes and Noble volume. (1886)

Kim

Rudyard Kipling   7, 8

Orphaned Kim O'Hara travels through India and the Himalayas with an old llama from Tibet in this exciting story, which some consider Kipling's masterpiece. (1901)

King of Shadows

Susan Cooper; *illustrated by John Clapp*   ☀ 6, 7, 8

Nat Field, eleven-year-old orphan and Shakespearean actor in the London of 1999, wakes to find he has changed places with a Nat Field who lives and works in the London of 1599, at the original Globe Theater with Shakespeare himself. (1999)

King Solomon's Mines

H. Rider Haggard 7, 8

Adventurer Allan Quatermain discovers an ancient map that leads to a lost African tribe in a hidden country and the secret of Solomon's mines. (1886)

King's Fifth, The

Scott O'Dell 7, 8

In the early sixteenth century, seven people travel across the American Southwest in search of the legendary golden cities of Cibola. Captain Mendoza and his soldiers seek treasure; Father Francisco dreams of saving souls; Estaban maps the land for his Spanish king; and Zia, an Indian girl, accompanies the men as their guide. (1966)

✴ Newbery Honor

King's Iron, The

Robert Newton Peck 8

The author creates a memorable trio in the characters of a high-born Virginian, a crusty old woodsman and trapper, Durable Hatch, and Durable's Huron protégé, Blue Goose. Around them he weaves a historical fiction of the march to seize the cannons at Fort Ticonderoga during the American Revolutionary War. (1977)

Landing of the Pilgrims

James H. Daugherty, *illustrated by author* 8

A Newbery-winning author draws on the Pilgrims' own journals to give a moving account of their life and traditions, their quest for religious freedom, and the founding of America's Thanksgiving holiday. (1950)

Last Unicorn, The

Peter S. Beagle 7, 8

Ranked by some as a fantasy classic, this is an imaginative tale of a unicorn's quest for her lost fellows, assisted by a less than brilliant magician and a gullible scullery maid. (1968)

Legend of Sleepy Hollow, The

Washington Irving   8+

In the Hudson Valley of the eighteenth century, a superstitious schoolmaster, in love with a wealthy farmer's daughter, has a terrifying encounter with a headless horseman. Neither this nor another famous tale by this eminent American author, Rip Van Winkle, was intended for children, although many restyled juvenile versions are available. In the original version, as a ghost story, enjoy it read aloud. (1820)

Little Prince, The

Antoine de Saint- Exupéry, *illustrated by author*   6, 7, 8+

A pilot lands in the Sahara and meets a tiny prince from another planet who shares stories about the meaning of life and the beauty of nature in this allegorical tale that has been an adult cult classic. A recent translation from the French original is by Richard Howard. (1944)

Little Shepherd of Kingdom Come

John Fox   8

Continuously popular since it was first published only thirty-five years after the end of the Civil War, this novel is a moving story about a Kentucky mountain boy who chooses to fight for the Union as the boy and the nation undergo a trial of the spirit. Noted artist N. C. Wyeth illustrated some later editions. (1903)

Little White Horse, The

Elizabeth Goudge   6, 7, 8

In 1842 the valley of Moonacre is shadowed by the memory of the Moon Princess and the mysterious little white horse. Thirteen-year-old Maria, as tiny as she is determined, finds herself involved in the valley's history and resolves to restore it to peace and happiness. (1946)

★ Carnegie Medal

Little Women

Louisa May Alcott   6, 7, 8

The four very individual March family girls help their mother face the emotional and economic hardships of life in New England while their father is away fighting in the American Civil War. The popular saga continues in *Jo's Boys*, *Little Men*, and *Rose in Bloom*. (1868)

Long Way from Chicago, A

Richard Peck   7, 8

Joey and his sister spend a summer vacation during the Depression in a small town in Illinois where peculiar events occur. Peck's combination of humor and the supernatural earned him top honors. *A Year Down Yonder* is the sequel. (1998)

★ Newbery Honor

Lord of the Rings, The (Trilogy)

J. R. R. Tolkien   6, 7, 8+

A brilliant and complex trilogy plus a prequel tells of a heroic quest on the battlefield of Middle-earth with a cast of characters from Hobbits to Ents who will live in literary immortality. *The Fellowship of the Ring* is followed by *The Two Towers* and *The Return of the King*. The prequel, *The Hobbit*, is less dark and may be enjoyed as a separate story. (1954)

Lost Colony of Roanoke, The

Jean Fritz; *illustrated by Hudson Talbott*   8

For more than 400 years, people have speculated about the English colony of Roanoke (in present-day North Carolina), founded in 1585, but which mysteriously disappeared. Thoroughly researched, Fritz discusses the English exploration, the settlement itself, and current theories about the colony's outcome. (2004)

Lost World, The

Sir Arthur Conan Doyle   6, 7, 8

The creator of Sherlock Holmes also wrote the original "dinosaurs discovered still living in a hidden jungle" tale. This timeless adventure has inspired everything from *King Kong* to *Jurassic Park* and, from a reader's point of view, may still be the best of the lot. (1912)

Grades 6 to 8

Lyddie

Katherine Paterson 8

This novel by a prolific Newbery author takes place during the Industrial Revolution in New England. When Lyddie's family loses their farm, she is put to work. The formidable challenges the staunchly brave thirteen-year-old meets give an accurate picture of the mills, boarding houses, and industrial towns of the period, and the problems of child labor. See also *Jip: His Story*. (1991)

★ ALA 100 Best Young Adult Books of the 20th Century

M. C. Higgins, the Great

Virginia Hamilton 7, 8

As the slag heap from strip mining creeps closer and closer to his beloved home in the Ohio hills, fifteen-year-old "M. C." is torn between trying to get his African-American family away and fighting for their home. (1974)

★ Newbery Medal, Boston Globe-Horn Book

Man Without a Country, The

Edward Everett Hale 8

Written by a relative of patriot Nathan Hale, this famous story was created "for the single purpose of teaching young Americans what it is to have a country, and what duty they owe to that country" and is still able to spark a lively discussion. It tells the story of a traitor, U.S. Army Lt. Philip Nolan, who says in court that he wishes never to hear of the United States again. Accordingly, he is banished to sea and forced to live aboard boats for more than fifty-six years. (1863)

Martian Chronicles, The

Ray Bradbury 8+

The brown-skinned, yellow-eyed people of Mars live a beautiful, peaceful life rich with art, music, and philosophy until the humans from Earth land on their planet and attempt to colonize it in this classic collection of linked short stories. (1950)

Matilda Bone

Karen Cushman 6, 7, 8

Apprenticed to a medieval bonesetter, Matilda struggles to reconcile her privileged, pious upbringing with the coarser ways of common folk. This young adult coming-of-age novel has fascinating accounts of early medicine, a touch of romance, and humor. (2000)

★ School Library Journal Best Books of the Year

Meet the Austins

Madeleine L'Engle 6, 7, 8

The Austins, raised as loving Christians, are challenged by the arrival of a self-centered orphan, Maggy Hamilton. Twelve-year-old Vicky Austin knows she should sympathize with the troubled new member of the family, but Maggy makes it hard. Read more about the Austin family in *The Moon by Night, The Young Unicorns, A Ring of Endless Light,* and *Troubling a Star.* (1960)

★ Newbery Honor

Megan's Island

Willo Davis Roberts 6, 7, 8

Bewildered by her mother's frequent moves from place to place, the discovery of a strange birth certificate, and the presence of mysterious strangers, Megan searches for the secret of her past and her own identity. The author is a three-time-winner of the Edgar Allen Poy Award ("The Edgar") and has written many mysteries including *The Absolutely True Story: How I Visited Yellowstone Park with the Terrible Rupes.* (1988)

★ Edgar Allen Poe Award

Merchant's Mark, The

Cynthia Harnett 6, 7

In England in 1493, Nicholas, the son of a wealthy wool merchant, manages to unmask a plot designed to ruin his father's business. (1953)

Grades 6 to 8

Midwife's Apprentice, The

Karen Cushman   6+

A nameless, homeless girl is taken in by a sharp-tempered midwife and over-comes obstacles and hardships to make a place for herself in the world of medieval England. See also *Catherine, Called Birdy.* (1995)

★ Newbery Medal, ALA 100 Best Young Adult Books of the 20th Century

Missing May

Cynthia Rylant   6, 7, 8

After the death of the beloved aunt who raised her, twelve-year-old Summer and her Uncle Ob leave their West Virginia trailer in search of the strength to go on living. (1992)

★ Newbery Medal

Mistress Masham's Repose

T. H. White   6, 7, 8

Ten-year-old Maria, an orphaned heiress mistreated by evil guardians, discovers the descendants of the Lilliputians living on the grounds of her English man-sion. The author is better known for his works on the Arthurian legend, but this wonderful fantasy was a Book-of-the-Month Club selection when it was published. (1946)

Momo

Michael Ende; translated by Francis Lobb   6, 7, 8

Part fairy tale, part satire of our consumer society, this is the story of the orphan Momo and her quest to discover how time was stolen and where it was hidden. Translated from German. (1973)

Morning Star

H. Rider Haggard   7, 8+

The classic Egyptian novel is filled with magic, wandering Kas (or spirit-dou-bles), old gods, romance, and adventure. "One of the best recreations of ancient Egypt ever written," says author Roger L. Green. More adventure novels await and there is a Haggard Society website. (1912)

My Brother Sam is Dead

James Lincoln Collier and Christopher Collier   8+

Recounts the tragedy that strikes the Meeker family during the Revolution when one son joins the rebel forces while the rest of the family tries to stay neutral in a Tory town. Study guides are available for this popular young adult historical fiction. (1974)

★ ALA Notable Children's Book

My Side of the Mountain

Jean Craighead George   8+

Sam lives in a tree house he built in the Catskills, lives off the land, and raises a peregrine falcon in this illustrated novel. The second book, *On the Far Side of the Mountain*, is about his sister's mountain adventure. *Frightful's Mountain* is told from the falcon's point of view. For mature readers, but if this series appeals, look for other titles by this masterful nature writer who also writes for younger readers. (1959)

★ Newbery Honor

My War with Goggle-Eyes

Anne Fine   6, 7, 8

A mother's dull but dependable boyfriend, Gerald, tries to win Kitty's favor with reluctant participation in a nuclear protest demonstration that turns into a comedy of errors. The two-time Carnegie Medal-winning British author's antinuclear subplot never overshadows the main theme of acceptance and tolerance in relationships. (1989)

★ Carnegie Medal

Mysterious Island

Jules Verne; translated by W. H. G. Kingston and Agnes Kinloch Kingston   8+

Five prisoners of the Civil War escape in a balloon from Richmond, Virginia, and land on an uninhabited island, where they begin to reconstruct society, as they knew it. Sidney Kravitz revised the original translation from the French by Kingston in 2000. Simplified, less-detailed young adult or new reader editions exist as well, as they do for many of Verne's science fiction classics. This is a sequel to *Twenty Thousand Leagues Under the Sea*. (1875)

Mystery of the Periodic Table, The

Benjamin D. Wiker; *illustrated by Jeanne Bendick*   ☀   7, 8

The author leads us on an absorbing journey through the ages, on the trail of the elements of the Periodic Table as we know them today. He introduces scientists like Von Helmont, Boyle, Stahl, Priestly, Cavendish, Lavoisier, all incredibly diverse in personality and approach, which laid the groundwork for a search that is still unfolding. (2003)

Nation Torn, A: The Story of How the Civil War Began

Delia Ray   ☀   8

This introduction to the events that led up to America's Civil War has a balanced perspective and is an excellent resource. See also the sequel, *Behind the Blue and Gray.* Illustrated with photographs. (1990)

Never Cry Wolf

Farley Mowat   6, 7, 8

The Canadian North is the natural setting of this very funny, poignant, and true chronicle of a biologist sent to observe wolves in their native habitat. Mowat's book is credited with changing the public's view of the wolves. (1963)

Nightjohn

Gary Paulsen   8

The twelve-year-old slave, Sarny, knows the punishment for learning to read and write is bloody, but when the new slave, Nightjohn, offers to teach her, she readily agrees. This is a graphic and brutal depiction of slavery and one of Paulsen's most powerful novels for young adults. (1993)

North by Night: A Story of the Underground Railroad

Katherine Ayres   8

An immediate, first-person narrative brings the Underground Railroad to life through the eyes of a spirited sixteen-year-old girl whose family home is used to usher slaves to freedom. The preface gives the historic background and explains the author's research. Routes are shown on a map of Ohio's Underground Railroad. (1998)

North to Freedom

Anne Holm   6, 7, 8

After escaping from an Eastern European concentration camp where he has spent most of his life, twelve-year-old David struggles in the strange outside world to flee north to freedom in Denmark. It won the award for best children's book in Scandinavia under the title *David* or *I Am David*. (1963)

★ ALA Notable Children's Book, Lewis Carroll Shelf Award

Number the Stars

Lois Lowry   6, 7, 8

In Nazi-occupied Denmark, a ten-year-old girl's bravery is tested as she joins in a dangerous effort to help her Jewish best friend's family escape to Sweden. This easier-to-read historical novel is as important a story of the Danish resistance during WW II as it is about friendship. (1989)

★ Newbery Medal

Of Courage Undaunted: Across the Continent with Lewis and Clark

James H. Daugherty, *illustrated by author*   8

Lewis and Clark showed resourcefulness and courage on their journey through the wilderness from St. Louis to the Pacific. Written from original records and diaries of the expedition by a Newbery-winning author. (1951)

Old Yeller

Fred Gipson; *illustrated by Carl Burger*   6, 7, 8

The moving (tearful) story of a fourteen-year-old boy and his dog is set in the Texas hill country of the 1860s. Like *The Yearling*, this story pulls at the heart and captures the growing awareness of adolescence in any time or place. There is a simplified text version from Mallard Press, 1990, part of the Disney American Classics Series. (1956)

★ Newbury Honor

Grades 6 to 8

Other Side of Truth, The

Beverly Nardoo   7, 8

Two refugee Nigerian children are caught in the civil strife of the 1990s. Eighth-grader Sade and her fifth-grade brother, Femi, become immigrants in London after their mother is killed by assassins' bullets. They overcome the challenges of public school, foster homes, western bureaucracy, and fear of discovery as they try to find their outspoken journalist father. (2000)

★ Carnegie Medal

Otto of the Silver Hand

Howard Pyle, *illustrated by author*   6

One of our most gifted storytellers was also an artist and the art teacher of pupils Maxfield Parrish and N. C. Wyeth. Just the illustrations, twenty-five full page plus headpiece and tailpiece drawings for each of the fourteen chapters, are worth the search for one of several reprinted editions. The exciting story is of Otto, a poor boy living in medieval Germany, whose severed hand is replaced by a silver one and who survives to become a valued advisor to a king under the motto, "Better a silver hand than an iron hand." (1888)

Out of the Dust

Karen Hesse   8

In a series of poems, fifteen-year-old Billie Jo relates the hardships of living on her family's wheat farm in Oklahoma during the dust bowl years of the Depression. (1997)

★ Newbery Medal, Scott O'Dell Award for Historical Fiction

Outsiders, The

S. E. Hinton   7, 8

Hinton's first novel was published when she was just seventeen and brought a different reality to literature about the teen years. Her novel about clashes between two high school groups, the affluent insiders and the "greasers" has wide appeal and led to changes in literature for young adults. (1967)

Owl Service, The

Alan Garner   7, 8

During a summer vacation in a secluded valley in Wales, three young people find themselves driven by mythical characters to reenact an ancient tragic Welsh legend. Garner weaves a spellbinding fantasy. (1981)

★ Carnegie Medal

Perilous Road, The

William O. Steele   8

Fourteen-year-old Chris bitterly hates Yankee soldiers. He learns a difficult lesson about tolerance when he discovers his brother may be part of a Yankee supply troop near his Tennessee mountain home. Steele, who wrote exciting historical fiction for young people, vividly portrays early America in *The Lone Hunt, The Far Frontier, The Buffalo Knife, Flaming Arrows, We Were There With the Pony Express*, and others. (1958)

★ Newbery Honor

Pink and Say

Patricia Polacco, *illustrated by author*   8

This moving story of interracial friendship during the Civil War is based on a story passed down in the author's family. Sheldon "Say" Curtis, age fifteen, has never seen a black person up close until Pinkus "Pink" Aylee, also a young Union soldier, saves his life. During his brief stay in Pink's home, the wounded boy comes to understand his friend's unconquerable vision of freedom. When the boys return to their units, they are captured and taken to Andersonville, a dreadful prison. This easier-to-read story is richly illustrated with evocative paintings. (1994)

Postcards from No Man's Land

Aidan Chambers   8

The winner of the 2003 Michael Printz Award and the Carnegie Medal alternates between two stories: seventeen-year-old Jacob visits a daunting modern Amsterdam at the request of his English grandmother and a nineteen-year-old girl relates her experience observing British soldiers attempting to liberate Holland from German occupation. (1999)

★ Carnegie Medal, Michael Printz

Grades 6 to 8

Prince and the Pauper, The

Mark Twain   7, 8+

Twain did not write for children usually, even if his best-known works are about them. This tale of two children, an urchin and the crown prince, who exchange places in sixteenth-century London, was written about, as well as for, young people. (1881)

Proud Taste for Scarlet and Miniver, A

E. L. Konigsburg, *illustrated by author*   6, 7, 8

An award-winning author and illustrator of children's books and young adult fiction wrote this entertaining fictionalized biography of Eleanor of Aquitaine. While waiting for her husband, King Henry II, to join her in heaven, Eleanor and three persons who knew her, recount her dramatic life in twelfth-century France and England. (1973)

Queen's Own Fool: A Novel of Mary, Queen of Scots (Quartet)

Jane Yole and Robert J. Harris   7

When twelve-year-old orphan Nicola leaves Troupe Brufort and serves as the court fool for Mary, Queen of Scots, she experiences the political and religious upheavals in both France and Scotland. Nicola is based on Mary's historical jester, known as "La Jardiniere." This is the first of four historical novels set in Scotland. (2000)

Redwall

Brian Jacques   6+

It appears to be just another medieval fantasy peopled with anthropomor-phic animal characters enacting the mortal combat between the heroes and the antagonists, but fans argue it is actually a thought-provoking novel on the nature of good and evil. Violent, and at times downright gruesome, the rich cast of characters and the detailed accounts of medieval warfare have built an international following for the twenty-plus volumes of the series. And boys like it. (1987)

Rifles for Watie

Harold Keith   8

The sweeping panorama of historical fiction is rich and vivid in detail, with dozens of fully realized characters despite the easy-to-read text. The reader never doubts the reality of this story of a lesser-known part of the Civil War, the Western campaign. (1957)

★ Newbery Medal, Lewis Carroll Shelf Award

Rime of the Ancient Mariner, The

Samuel Taylor Coleridge   7, 8+

The 1970 Dover edition of Coleridge's spellbinding story poem about a seaman who kills a friendly albatross for sport and then is haunted by spirits has reproductions of the dramatic black-and-white engravings Gustave Doré created to illustrate the tale. (1798)

Rip Van Winkle

Washington Irving   6, 7, 8

An American classic, a story in the Gothic tradition, set in the days before and after the American Revolution, is about a man who falls asleep for one hundred years and awakes unaware that the Revolution has taken place. Versions rewritten in simpler language exist for younger listeners or readers. (1819)

River Between Us, A

Richard Peck

During the early days of the Civil War, the Pruitt family takes in two mysterious young ladies who have fled New Orleans to come north to Illinois. Interesting and well written, this book begins as a retelling of family history and ends full of surprises. (2003)

★ Scott O'Dell Award for Historical Fiction

Roll of Thunder, Hear My Cry

Mildred D. Taylor   6, 7, 8

Cassie Logan's story is based on the author's childhood in a poor southern black family during the Depression. The sequels take her to high school and the start of World War II in *Let the Circle Be Unbroken* and *The Road to Memphis*. (1976)

★ Newbery Medal, Coretta Scott King Award

Rosie the Riveter:
Women Working on the Home Front in World War II

Penny Colman   8

This book chronicles the federal government's successful publicity drive which gave 18 million women the incentive to enter the workforce and that led the way to reforms for women and minorities. It includes sixty archival black-and-white photographs. (1995)

★ ALA Notable Children's Book

Ruby in the Smoke

Philip Pullman   7, 8

In 1872, in the atmospheric underside of mid-Victorian London, down the dangerous fog-bound streets, a young woman, Sally Lockhart, tries to solve the mystery of her father's death. More of the story is told in *Shadow in the North* and *Tiger in the Well.* (1985)

★ ALA 100 Best Young Adult Books of the 20th Century

Science Experiments You Can Eat

Vicki Cobb   7, 8

In thirty-nine demonstrations performed with food stuffs and kitchen equipment, this fun but first-rate introduction to chemistry and physics investigates the characteristics of fats, carbohydrates, and proteins and the nature of acids and bases, solutions, suspensions, colloids, emulsions, and more while answering such questions as "why does bread rise?" and "what makes jelly gel?" Similar titles exist for younger readers; this one is good for upper grades. (1972)

Second Mrs. Giaconda, The

E. L. Konigsburg   7

Why did Leonardo da Vinci devote three years to a painting of the second wife of an important merchant when all of the nobles of Europe were begging for a portrait from the greatest artist of the Italian Renaissance? This two-time Newbery-winning author has created an intriguing answer to the puzzle behind the most famous painting of all time, "The Mona Lisa." (1975)

Shabanu

Suzanne Fisher Staples 7, 8

In modern Pakistan's remote desert, the courageous twelve-year-old daughter of a camel driver must deal with plans for her arranged marriage to a hateful landowner. *Haveli* is the sequel. (1989)

★ Newbery Honor, ALA 100 Best Young Adult Books of the 20th Century

Shark Beneath the Reef

Jean Craighead George 7, 8

On the island of Coronado, as a young Mexican fisherman comes of age, he faces an underwater challenge of a great white shark and, on land, becomes aware of the human conflicts around him. (1989)

Sherwood Ring, The

Elizabeth Marie Pope 6, 7, 8

As Peggy Grahame, sent to live with her Uncle Enos at her family's ancestral estate, adjusts to a lonely life, she discovers she is not quite as alone as she originally thought she was—ghosts who seem very interested in getting to know Peggy haunt the estate. (1958)

Shipwreck at the Bottom of the World:
The Extraordinary True Story of Shakleton and the Endurance

Jennifer Armstrong 6, 7, 8

A dozen versions of the story of Ernest Shackleton and the ship *Endurance* are available. This one not only tells a compelling story well, but also presents the geographical, meteorological, nautical, and scientific details of the Antarctic adventure that make palpable to young readers the jaw-dropping feat of bringing everyone safely home. Illustrated with forty photos from the expedition archives. (1998)

★ Boston Globe-Horn Book Honor

Sign of the Beaver, The

Elizabeth George Speare   6, 7, 8

In late eighteenth-century Maine, Matthew, age twelve and separated from his family by a series of mishaps, is rescued by a chief of the Beaver tribe. Over a period of months, Matthew teaches an Indian boy English and learns a great deal about hunting. When the tribe plans to travel, Matthew must make the most challenging decision of his life: to join them or remain behind waiting for the return of his family. (1984)

★ Newbery Honor, Scott O'Dell Award for Historical Fiction

Silent to the Bone

E. L. Konigsburg   7, 8

When a thirteen-year-old is struck dumb after his infant half-sister falls into a coma and their au pair blames him, Bran's best friend pieces together the truth and helps him recover his voice. (2000)

★ School Library Journal Best Books of the Year

Silver Sword, The

Ian Serraillier   8

When the Germans invade their home in Poland, the members of the Balicki family are torn apart, but they succeed in reuniting themselves in Switzerland at the end of World War II. (1956)

Single Shard, A

Linda Sue Park   6, 7, 8

The author, the daughter of Korean immigrants, takes us to twelfth century Korea for this story of a homeless orphan who lives under a bridge with a disabled man who raises him. With a life full of challenges and dreams, and faced with ethical dilemmas, he finds his passion and talent and makes a life for himself. (2001)

★ Newbery Medal

Skellig

David Almond 6, 7, 8

Unhappy about his baby sister's illness and the chaos of moving into a dilap-idated old house, Michael retreats to the garage and, among the debris and spider webs, finds a mysterious stranger who is something like a bird and some-thing like an angel. This British novelist's debut into young adult literature was selected in 2007 by judges of the Carnegie Medal as one of the ten most impor-tant children's novels of the past seventy years. (1999)

★ Carnegie Medal, Printz Honor

Slake's Limbo

Felice Holman 7, 8

Thirteen-year-old runaway Artemis Slake is not the only homeless person try-ing to survive in the sometimes-dangerous New York City subway system. This is an inspirational young adult novel. (1974)

★ Lewis Carroll Shelf Award, ALA Notable Children's Book

Slave Dancer, The

Paula Fox 8

A young boy, Jessie Bollier, recalls the summer of 1840 when he was kidnapped and forced to serve upon a slave ship and play his flute while the slaves were exercised. (1973)

★ Newbery Medal

Smoky the Cowhorse

Williames James, *illustrated by author* 6, 7, 8

A cowboy, who turned to writing only after a life in the saddle was over, has written a tribute to the American cow horse. As a horse story, it is as good as they come. As an authentic piece of the life of the American cowboy and his horse, it is priceless. (1926)

★ Newbery Medal

Snow Goose, The: A Story of Dunkirk

Paul Gallico, *illustrated by author*   8

A World War II story of an unlikely friendship between a reclusive hunchback painter, a shy young girl, and a wounded snow goose culminates in an act of heroism during the Battle of Dunkirk on the coast of southern England. (1941)

★ O. Henry Award

Soldier's Heart: A Novel of the Civil War

Gary Paulsen   8

Eager to enlist, fifteen-year-old Charley has a change of heart after experiencing both the physical horrors and mental anguish of Civil War combat. (1998)

Sound of Chariots, A

Mollie Hunter   8

A young girl growing up in Scotland after World War I tries to come to terms with her grief over her father's death and her increasing sense of the passage of time. (1976)

Sounder

William H. Armstrong   6, 7, 8

Moving story of the struggles of a poor black sharecropper family, their coon dog, Sounder, and a boy trying to reach manhood in the rural south of the late nineteenth century. *Sour Land* continues the story of the boy who survives to old age. (1969)

★ Newbery Medal, New York Times Outstanding Book of the Year

Stowaway

Karen Hesse; *illustrated by Robert A. Parker*   7

A boy bribes his way onboard the *Endeavour* with Captain James Cook and learns that adventure can be deadly serious business. Nicholas records his impressions, insights, and internal dialogues in this detailed diary. (2000)

★ School Library Journal Best Books of the Year

Summer of the Swans

Betsy Byars   7, 8

A fourteen-year-old girl is experiencing mixed emotions about herself and her younger brother who is a special needs child. When he becomes lost, the attentions of a boy who offers to help add another complication to a summer day already fraught with powerful feelings. (1970)

★ Newbery Medal

Swiss Family Robinson, The

Johann Wyss   6, 7, 8

A venerable ancestor to all survivor tales, this one relates the fortunes of a shipwrecked family as they adapt to life on an island with abundant animal and plant life. It has been reissued many times including abbreviated and simplified editions. (1812)

Tale of Two Cities, A

Charles Dickens   8+

This story of the French Revolution, set in London and Paris, is an excellent historical fiction as well as a terrific tale with a romantic hero, a beautiful heroine, and unforgettable villainy, as well as inspiring self-sacrifice. Dickens is at the top of his form. Once the taste is acquired, many more novels await the happy reader. (1859)

Tales from Shakespeare

Retold by Roger L. Green; *illustrated by Richard Beer*   7

With a foreword by Christopher Fry, these retellings of Shakespeare's stories differ from the classic version by Charles and Mary Lamb in modernity of style and in the emphasis upon telling the whole story as nearly as possible and introducing the majority of characters. Volume I, the comedies; Volume II, the tragedies and romances. (1964)

Tales from Shakespeare

Charles and Mary Lamb   7

The authors used Shakespeare's words as much as possible to retell twenty plays—six tragedies including *Pericles*, *Hamlet*, *Romeo and Juliet*, and *Othello*, and fourteen comedies—conveying all the Bard's wit, wisdom, and humanity. Alone, the tales are outstanding young adult literature in their own right, and they make an excellent introduction to the originals or preparation for a dramatic production. (1807)

This Dear-Bought Land

Jean Lee Latham; *illustrated by Jacob Landau*   8

In 1607 a fifteen-year-old boy joins the expeditionary force that hopes to establish a permanent colony in Virginia. This historical novel is by a Newbery-winning author. (1957)

Three Musketeers, The

Alexandre Dumas   7+

D'Artagnon joins the king's musketeers to serve the young Louis XIII in seventeenth century France in the first of three novels that make up the *d'Artagnan Romances*. Other volumes describe the next twenty years. (1844)

Tisha: The Story of a Young Teacher in the Alaska Wilderness

Robert Specht   7, 8

Boldness is the real-life virtue of a young woman, Ann Hobbs, who, in the 1920s, chose to teach in the coldest reaches of the North American continent. Here the weather itself is a danger, as well as isolation and tensions with the local inhabitants. The author reports her experience as a "told to" story. (1976)

Tituba of Salem Village

Ann Petry   8

The horror and hysteria surrounding the Salem witch trials is brought to life in this novel of Tituba, a native of Barbados. Sold as a slave to the Puritan Reverend Parris and accused of witchcraft, Tituba becomes one of the main figures in the Salem witch trials. (1964)

Treasure Island

Robert Louis Stevenson   6, 7, 8+

Set in the 1740s, this is a swashbuckling adventure of treasure seekers on a pirate ship captained by Long John Silver, as seen through the eyes of cabin boy Jim Hawkins. See also *Kidnapped.* (1883)

Tripods Trilogy, The

John Christopher   8+

In this story, alien creatures control humans over age fourteen by skull implants. Three thirteen-year-old boys strike for an outpost of freedom of uncapped people in *The White Mountains.* More white-knuckle science fiction suspense about the fight against the robotic Tripods is dished up in *The City of Gold and Lead* and *The Pool of Fire.* The trilogy expanded years later with a prequal *When the Tripods Came.* (1966)

Trumpeter of Krakow, The

Eric Philbrook Kelly   7

Poland of the Renaissance is the unusual setting for this tale written in part to present and preserve Poland's unique history and culture. After Hitler's invasion, the book earned a unique place in young adult literature. (1928)
★ Newbery Medal

Tuck Everlasting

Natalie Babbitt   6, 7, 8

Ten-year-old Winnie runs away from home and discovers the Tuck family and their secret—a spring that gives eternal life. Powerful issues of life and death, love and loyalty are gently confronted in this enjoyable fantasy. (1975)
★ Lewis Carroll Shelf Award, ALA Notable Children's Book

Twenty Thousand Leagues Under the Sea

Jules Verne   6, 7, 8

The mysterious Captain Nemo's submarine, the *Nautilus,* and the capability of sustaining life entirely off the bounty of the seas hardly seems like science fiction anymore, but it is still a good adventure story by a writer credited as the father of the genre. New complete translations from the French for purists, as well as simplified versions for younger readers or new readers, are available. (1869)

Twenty-One Balloons, The

William Pene Du Bois, *illustrated by author*   6, 7, 8

An old, bored mathematician has an adventure when he takes a trip across the Pacific Ocean by balloon and crash-lands on the island of Krakatoa. Adventures abound before the island's volcano explodes. A mixture of fun, fantasy, invention, and science, this book will delight young and old. (1947)

★ Newbery Medal

Two Little Confederates

Thomas Nelson Page   8

The first of these two stories published in *St. Nicholas* magazine in 1888 presents a boy's-eye view of the Civil War from the southern side. In the second, a spunky little southern girl reunites a fragmented family after the Civil War. The original black-and-white illustrations are reproduced in the facsimile edition. Page was a Virginia plantation owner, lawyer, and, finally, U.S. ambassador to Italy. (1888)

Uncle Tom's Cabin

Harriet Beecher Stowe   8+

Curiosity about a book that became a cultural icon and gave rise to a racial epithet may inspire some to read this novel that was more influential for its ability to raise abolitionist support than for any literary virtue. It is the story of "Uncle" Tom, a noble slave whose fortunes vary as his masters change. (1852)

Up a Road Slowly

Irene Hunt   7, 8

Set in the 1930s, this is the story of a young girl who, after the death of her mother, is sent to live with her strict but loving Aunt Cordelia (an elementary school teacher) and her ne'er-do-well uncle. At first, Julie has a hard time fitting in with the precisely ordered world of her aunt, but as she grows into adulthood, Julie begins to understand this self-possessed woman. (1966)

★ Newbery Medal

Walk Two Moons

Sharon Creech   7, 8

The struggle of thirteen-year-old Salamanca Tree Hiddle to understand and deal with her mother's disappearance unfolds while on a cross-country trip with her eccentric grandparents. The novel is complex with many subplots, and the language is lyrical. (1994)

★ Newbery Medal

Water Sky

Jean Craighead George   6, 7, 8

Lincoln goes to Barrow, Alaska, to live with friends of his father for a while and learns the importance of whaling to the Eskimo culture. He finds he must choose between his Eskimo ancestry and his belief in saving the whale from extinction in the Newbery Medalist's powerfully written novel. (1987)

Weirdstone of Brisingamen, The: A Tale of Alderley

Alan Garner   6, 7, 8

A young girl and her brother are catapulted into a battle between good and evil for possession of a magical stone of great power that is contained in her bracelet. The award-winning British author's knowledge of folklore, geographical region, and fine prose style imbues his story with thoughtful depth. *The Moon of Gomrath* is the sequel. (1960)

Westing Game, The

Ellen Raskin   6, 7, 8

This mystery involves sixteen remarkable characters invited to the reading of Samuel W. Westing's will. They could become millionaires—it all depends on how they play the tricky and dangerous Westing Game in a puzzle-knotted, word-twisting plot filled with humor and suspense. (1978)

★ Newbery Medal, Boston Globe-Horn Book

When the Rattlesnake Sounds: A Play

Alice Childress; *illustrated by Charles Lilly*   8

Underground Railroad heroine Harriet Tubman discusses freedom and slavery with her two coworkers in this play by the author of the much-honored book, *A Hero Ain't Nothin' But a Sandwich.* (1975)

Grades 6 to 8

Where the Red Fern Grows

Wilson Rawls 6, 7, 8+

A poor ten-year-old boy in the Ozarks works for two years to earn enough to buy two coon dogs. He and the dogs are inseparable as he teaches them to tree raccoons, enter competitions, and face a mountain lion. Boys like it, and grown men cry reading this one. (1961)

White Company, The/Sir Nigel

Sir Arthur Conan Doyle 6, 7, 8

In medieval England, a young squire serves Sir Nigel and travels with him to France to join the White Company, a daring band of archers. This 1988 edition, with an introduction, puts the two novels together as a set, but they can be found separately. The author, creator of Sherlock Holmes, regarded these two works as "the most complete, satisfying and ambitious thing that I have ever done." (1891)

White Stag, The

Kate Seredy 6

A retelling of the Hungarian national epic recasts Attila the Hun as the father of the Hungarian nation and describes the legendary migration from Asia to Europe of Attila and the Huns and Magyars. Also worth looking for are Seredy's *The Singing Tree* and *The Good Master* set in modern Hungary. (1937)
★ Newbery Medal

Wilderness Tattoo, The: A Narrative of Juan Ortiz

William O. Steele 7

Juan was a young guide to Spanish explorers, but was captured by the indigenous people and later rescued by Hernando de Soto. He became a guide to de Soto's troops in their fruitless search for gold. (1962)

Winged Watchman, The

Hilda Van Stockum 6, 7, 8

Suspenseful story of occupied Holland during World War II tells about the Verhagen family, a memorable set of individuals whose lives powerfully demonstrate the resilience of those who suffer but do not lose faith. Bethlehem Books reprints this author's books. (1962)

Witch of Blackbird Pond, The

Elizabeth George Speare   7, 8

Young Kit Tyler comes from Barbados to colonial Connecticut. When she befriends a widow thought to be a witch, townspeople begin to suspect her as well. (1958)

★ Newbery Medal

With Pipe, Paddle and Song:
A Story of the French-Canadian Voyageurs

Elizabeth Yates; *illustrated by Nora S. Unwin*   7, 8

Sixteen-year-old Guilluame has spent half of his life in his French father's Montreal chateau and half in his mother's Chippewa village. He signs up with a crew of voyageurs to journey into the wilds of Canada, trapping the furs that have made the New France of the 1750s prosperous. Newbery Award-winner Yates skillfully weaves history and the theme of coming to grips with the conflicting demands of two cultures. (1968)

Wizard of Earthsea, A (Trilogy)

Ursula K. Le Guin   7, 8

Sometimes called science fiction and sometimes fantasy, this trilogy is dark and complex enough to be popular with adults as well as teens. The protagonist Ged is tested in the uses and abuses of power in the context of dragons, wizards, and magic. The other titles are *The Tombs of Atuan* and *The Farthest Shoe*. This masterful storyteller won a literary award for each of these titles. (1968)

★ Boston Globe-Horn Book, Lewis Carroll Shelf Award

Wolf

Gillian Cross   7, 8

In this honored British import, Cassy, age thirteen, is forced to stay with her mother in a squatter's settlement of artists, where she joins the group in producing an educational program about wolves and inadvertently learns that her missing father is a notorious terrorist. (1986)

★ Carnegie Medal

Wolf by the Ears

Ann Rinaldi 8

An acclaimed historical fiction author tells the intense, provocative story of a slave, Harriet Hemings, who some believe was the daughter of Thomas Jefferson. (1991)

★ ALA Best Books for Young Adults

World's Desire, The

H. Rider Haggard and Andrew Lang 8+

A great storyteller and a brilliant classical scholar combine forces to write a sequel to the world's greatest epic poem, in which Odysseus seeks out Helen of Troy in Egypt. Lang was known for his translations of *The Odyssey* and *The Illiad*. (1890)

Wrinkle in Time, A (Quartet)

Madeleine L'Engle 7, 8+

In the first book, a brother and sister experience altered time and space as they search for their father, a missing scientist. This extremely popular science fiction adventure continues in *A Wind in the Door*, *A Swiftly Tilting Planet*, and *Many Waters*. The series is sometimes called a quintet with the addition of *In Acceptable Time*. (1962)

★ Newbery Medal

Yanks Are Coming, The: The United States in the First World War

Dr. Albert Marrin 8

Marrin writes a comprehensive but exciting history of America's role in World War I for young adult readers. He describes how American military forces helped the Allies turn the tide of World War I and how the United States mobilized industry, trained soldiers, and promoted the war to the people at home. (1986)

Yearling, The

Marjorie Kinnan Rawlings 7, 8

In the Florida backwoods, a young boy struggles to save a fawn he has raised. Numerous editions testify to the timeless appeal of this story. (1938)

★ Pulitzer Prize

Biographies

Biographies are the approach to history in the Waldorf curriculum. All history is taught by the telling of stories of the lives of individuals who helped give shape to the human drama we tell of ourselves. The selection of which biographies or autobiographies to share is left to the discretion of the teacher, but there is a general consensus that, for example, the Founding Fathers of the United States will be included in eighth-grade history. One teacher may choose to emphasize the life of George Washington, while another may select Benjamin Franklin as a focus for the study of the American Revolution and the role of the others will be woven into that framework.

Students may be asked to prepare a report to share with the class on one of the explorers of the Age of Exploration, or the class in second grade may use as a reader a version of the life of Saint Francis of Assisi. The life of the Buddha leads into the study of the culture of ancient India in fifth grade or the biography of Caesar Augustus becomes the pathway into the broader picture of the Roman Empire in sixth grade.

There are so many important individual stories that only a few may find their way into any particular teaching block, but the study of history as the story of individuals leads children into the genre of biography as a source of a lifetime of reading pleasure and, at least in Waldorf schools, to a love of the study of history and human civilizations. It is also the case that the challenges or achievements of real people such as Franklin Roosevelt or Churchill may provide inspiration to a life of public service or for perseverance in overcoming an obstacle. Such inspiration, drawn from the life of another, is often the reason adults give for reading biographies. Young people looking for role models after which to fashion their own identities are well served by biographies. Following the annotated list are additional recommended titles of famous individuals.

Biography

Abe Lincoln Grows Up

Carl Sandburg; *illustrated by James Daugherty*   6, 7, 8

This version adapted for young readers, is an alternative to the longer original that earned Sandburg his reputation as an authority on Lincoln. (1928)

Abraham Lincoln

Ingri and Edgar Parin d'Aulaire, *illustrated by authors*   6, 7, 8

An award-winning picture book biography, this is one in a series by the well-known writer/illustrator team featuring extraordinary lithographs and lively text. Others in the series: *Benjamin Franklin, Columbus, George Washington,* and *Pocahontas.* (1940)

★ Caldecott Medal

Always Inventing: A Photobiography of Alexander Graham Bell

Tom L. Matthews   7, 8

Matthews offers more about Bell's interests and inventions than just the telephone. Informative engravings, journal sketches, and family photographs illustrate this handsomely designed book. Includes resources for research. (1999)

★ School Library Journal Best Books of the Year

America's Paul Revere

Esther Forbes; *illustrated by Lynd Ward*   6, 7, 8

The inspiration for this young adult biography is Forbes's Pulitzer prize-winning full-length biography of one of America's early patriots. (1946)

Amos Fortune, Free Man

Elizabeth Yates; *illustrated by Nora Unwin*   8+

This is the inspiring biography of an eighteenth-century African prince who at age fifteen was captured, brought to America, and sold at auction. At age sixty, he bought his freedom. (1951)

★ Newbery Medal

Biography

And Long Remember: Some Great Americans Who Have Helped Me

Dorothy Canfield Fisher; *illustrated by Ezra Jack Keats*   ☀️   4, 5, 6

Here is a first introduction to biographies of great Americans: George Washington, Thomas Jefferson, John Paul Jones, Patrick Henry, Nathan Hale, Robert E. Lee, Ulysses S. Grant, George Washington Carver and others written by a well-respected children's author. (1959)

And Then What Happened, Paul Revere?

Jean Fritz   ☀️   4, 5, 6+

Light-hearted but accurate history, this title is just one in a series of biography-based American histories by this prize-winning author. With color illustrations by various artists, this is a good introduction to American history for young readers or older reluctant readers. Look for *Bully for You, Teddy Roosevelt*; *Just a Few Words, Mr. Lincoln*; *Why Not, Lafayette? Will You Sign Here, John Hancock? You Want Women to Vote, Lizzie Stanton? Shh! We're Writing the Constitution*; *George Washington's Breakfast*, and others. (1973)

★ Boston Globe-Horn Book Honor

Andrew Carnegie

Clara Ingram Judson   ☀️   6, 7, 8

Carnegie was a pivotal leader in business and philanthropy in the late nineteenth and early twentieth-century. Judson's successful series of biographies may still be found in libraries and book outlets. Look for: *Mr. Justice Holmes* (Newbery Honor); *Benjamin Franklin*; *City Neighbor: The Story of Jane Addams*; *George Washington: Leader of the People*, and others. (1961)

★ Newbery Honor

Anne Frank: The Diary of a Young Girl

Anne Frank; translated by B. M. Booyaart   8+

The diary of a young Jewish girl's coming-of-age during World War II describes her life in hiding from the Nazis. It is perhaps the most widely-read and effective reminder of the Holocaust. One edition offers a foreword by Eleanor Roosevelt. A later "definitive" edition restored passages omitted in the original. (1952)

Antoine Lavoisier: Founder of Modern Chemistry

Lisa Yount　　　　　　　　　　　　　　　　　　　7, 8+

In addition to the life story of the eighteenth-century "father of chemistry," hands-on activities are included that demonstrate the importance of his work. Black-and-white illustrations. (1997)

Archimedes and the Door of Science

Jeanne Bendick, *illustrated by author*　　　　　　5, 6, 7

Against the backdrop of Archimedes' life and culture in Greece of the second century B.C., the author discusses the man's work and his discoveries and later influence in mathematics, physics, and astronomy. Simple, often humorous, line illustrations and diagrams enhance the text. (1962)

Augustus Caesar's World: 44 B.C. to 14 A.D.

Genevieve Foster, *illustrated by author*　　　　　　6

This is an excellent introduction to the subject of Roman history for young readers. Important deeds of individuals are paralleled with other world personalities and events in an easy-to-read text enhanced with simple line illustrations. Foster traces the major civilizations of Rome, Greece, Israel, Egypt, China, India, and Persia from 4500 B.C. to the period of 44 B.C. and 14 A.D. (1947)

Balboa, Finder of the Pacific

Ronald Syme　　　　　　　　　　　　　　　　　　4–7

For true-adventure lovers, the daring early explorers of the globe are introduced in this author's extensive easy-to-read series that includes Balboa, as well as Alexander Mackenzie, Amerigo Vespucci, Captain Cook, Cartier, Champlain, Francis Drake, Henry Hudson, Hernando de Soto, John Cabot, John Charles Fremont, La Salle, Magellan, Walter Raleigh, and Verrazano. (1956)

Behind the Mask: The Life of Queen Elizabeth I

Jane Resh Thomas　　　　　　　　　　　　　　　7

Illustrated with well-known portraits, supplemented with a cast of characters, chronology, and a bibliography, this biography includes the myths, as well as the social and political realities, which shaped the age and the character of one of the most fascinating individuals in world history. (1998)

Biography

Beyond the Myth: The Story of Joan of Arc

Polly Schoyer Brooks   ☀ 6, 7, 8+

Young Joan of Arc accomplished what some call a miracle in rallying her French countrymen to defeat the English at Orleans in 1429. A challenging read, but full of detail about the "Maid of Orleans" and the time in which she lived. (1990)

★ ALA Best Books for Young Adults

Biographies for 8th Grade History:
Twenty Remarkable Men and Women

Susan Cook; *illustrated by author's students*   ☀ 8

A class teacher assembled stories of remarkable men and women from around the world including John Harrison, Eli Whitney, Sequoyah, Simon Bolivar, Benito Juarez, Frederick Douglass, Harriet Tubman, Elizabeth Cady Stanton, Clara Barton, Marie Curie, Janusz Korczak, Helen Keller, Mao Zedong, Jomo Kenyatta, Nelson Mandela, Martin Luther King Jr., Cesar Chavez, and Wangari Maathai. (2009)

Botticelli: A Biography

Elizabeth Ripley   ☀ 7

Ripley created a series of short biographies of Renaissance artists for young adult readers. Each one is illustrated with black-and-white reproductions of some of the most famous works. They may be found in libraries and used book outlets: *Michelangelo, Rembrandt, Durer, Raphael,* and *Titian.*(1960)

Captain Cook Explores the South Seas

Armstrong Sperry   ☀ 7

James Cook, born in 1728, went from shipyard apprentice to master navigator, mapmaker, and leader of British expeditions. This is a breathtaking account of some of those explorations. Newbery-winner Sperry grew up in Connecticut, near the sea, with a fascination for ships and sailing. See *Call It Courage* and *John Paul Jones: Fighting Sailor.* (1955)

Charles Lindbergh

Blythe Randolph
8

The fascinating highlights of the life of the American author-inventor-activist-aviator are presented in short chapters with black and white photos. Lindbergh's autobiography is also available for those who want a longer, more detailed account of the 1927 historic non-stop flight from New York to Paris, in the single-seat, single-engine monoplane *Spirit of St. Louis.* (1990)

Chaucer and His World

Ian Serraillier
6+

The author describes details of medieval life which are reflected in the work of the greatest poet of that period, considered the father of English literature. These include home and church, education, agriculture, medicine, trade and industry, and art and architecture. (1968)

Child of the Silent Night: The Story of Laura Dewey Bridgman

Edith Hunter; *illustrated by Bea Holmes*
4, 5, 6

Laura Dewey Bridgman, who lived from 1829 to 1889, was the first deaf and blind person to learn a language. Her courageous journey preceded that of Helen Keller by fifty years. (1963)

Childhood of Famous Americans (Series)

Published by Aladdin Books
4, 5, 6

This popular paperback series of over forty titles presents the middle elementary student an easy-to-read biography that engages interest by emphasizing the important events of childhood that shaped the destinies of famous Americans, Presidents and First Ladies as well as scientists, inventors, artists, sports figures, and heroes and heroines of American history are included. Older reluctant readers may also enjoy these volumes. (1983)

Clara Barton: Civil War Nurse

Nancy Whitelaw
8

This biography of the founder of the American Red Cross, illustrated with black-and-white photographs, is brief but accurately drawn from Barton's own diaries and published writings. It is written and designed to appeal to reluctant readers. Includes a glossary, index, footnotes and a suggested reading list. (1997)

Claudette Colvin: Twice Toward Justice

Phillip Hoose   8+

Nine months before Rosa Parks' history-making protest on a city bus, fifteen-year-old Claudette Colvin from Montgomery, Alabama was arrested and jailed for refusing to give up her seat to a white passenger. Colvin's story provides important historical context to the civil rights movement. (2009)

★ Newbury Honor Book

Columban

Jakob Streit; translated by Nina Kuettel;
illustrated by Christiane Lesch   ⚜   7

This powerful story tells of the life of St. Columban (540-614 A.D.) his travels from Ireland and his adventures and life in the Inner Hebrides. He is largely credited with the development of monastic life and Celtic Christianity. This title fits well into the transition between Roman and Medieval history, the period of European history sometimes unfairly called the Dark Ages, usually taught in the seventh grade in the Waldorf curriculum. (2010)

Commodore Perry in the Land of the Shogun

Rhoda Blumberg   ⚜   7

Commodore Perry's expedition to open Japan to American commerce in 1853 gave the West a first look at the isolated feudal society that existed there at the time. This much-honored book highlights the cultural interchange that altered both nations. (1985)

★ Newbery Honor, ALA Notable Children's Book

Copernicus: Struggle and Victory

Heinz Sponsel; translated by Monica Gold;
illustrated by Wilhelm Pretorius   ⚜   6, 7, 8

Originally published in 1949, this lively book is an established treasure in Germany. It depicts the life struggles and striving of the Polish astronomer, Nikolaus Copernicus and can enrich both science and history units. (2004)

Crossing, The:
How George Washington Saved The American Revolution

Jim Murphy   8

The author, who tells this exciting story of General Washington's leadership of the Revolutionary Army, has been a winner of Newbery Honors, three Orbis Pictus Awards, and the Margaret A. Edwards Lifetime Achievement Award. Illustrations include reproductions of portraits and several battlefield maps. Look for other works including *The Real Benedict Arnold*. (2010)

Daniel Boone

James H. Daugherty, *illustrated by author*   8

Daugherty served as illustrator for Stewart White's 1922 biography of Boone, *Daniel Boone: Wilderness Scout*, but this shorter volume, which he also authored, earned him a place on the Newbery shelf. It is unfortunately dated by the insensitive view of Native Americans, which may mar it beyond redemption for some. (1939)

★ Newbery Medal

Double Life of Pocahontas, The

Jean Fritz   8

This award-winning biography removes the romantic varnish from the legend of the sixteenth-century Native American who befriended the Jamestown colonists. It is an engrossing history of a woman who was exploited by both cultures in which she lived. (1983)

★ ALA Notable Children's Book, Boston Globe-Horn Book

Elizabeth Tudor: Sovereign Lady

Marguerite Vance   7

Known to history as Elizabeth I, this is the story of the queen who ruled during the golden age of the English Renaissance. Vance's biographies of women can be found in libraries and used book outlets. Look for *Scotland's Queen: The Story of Mary Stuart*; *Six Queens: The Wives of Henry VIII*; *Dark Eminence: Catherine de Medici and her Children*; *Marie Antoinette: Daughter of an Empress*, and others. (1954)

Biography

Emma's Poem: The Voice of the Statue of Liberty

Linda Glaser; *illustrated by Claire A. Nivola*   2, 3, 4

In 1880s New York, Emma Lazarus, a Jewish immigrant from Eastern Europe, helped more recent immigrants learn English and find jobs. Readers learn how the lines "Give me your tired, your poor, your huddled masses yearning to breathe free..." from Emma's sonnet were selected to be inscribed at the base of the Statue of Liberty. Bright paintings of watercolors and gouache enhance this true story. (2010)

English Governess and the Siamese Court, The

Anna Leonowens   8+

The autobiography behind the film drama and Broadway musical *The King and I* describes the experience of a courageous English widow who traveled with her young son to Siam (Thailand) to tutor a young prince. She found herself in conflict with the king, whose views on human rights and women's liberation were Eastern and Medieval as opposed to Western and Victorian. (1870)

Escape from Slavery:
The Boyhood of Frederick Douglass in His Own Words

Frederick Douglass;
edited and illustrated by Michael McCurdy   8

McCurdy has edited and illustrated this version of Douglass's first autobiography about his childhood through his first months as a freeman in hopes of making it more accessible to school children. It includes a foreword by Coretta Scott King. Interested readers may wish to consider one of the three full-length autobiographies. (1994)

Falconer, The

Christopher Sblendorio; *illustrated by Amy Inglis*   6+

A class teacher has written the life story of the man who was to become the Holy Roman Emperor during the early thirteenth century. This thoroughly researched biography captures the essence of the life of Frederick II of Hohenstaufen and will interest older children and adults as well. (2010)

Famous Signers of the Declaration

Dorothy Horton McGee   8

McGee narrates the events and details of the famous document through the lives of the patriots who signed it "at risk of our lives." Franklin, Jefferson, John Adams, Sam Adams, Hancock, and others are portrayed in all their contrasting characters. (1955)

Florence Nightingale

Cecil Woodham-Smith   8+

Liberally quoting from Nightingale's correspondences, it tells the story of her role in reorganizing British army hospitals, improving sanitation in India, establishing a nursing school, and more. This biography is written for adults but mature readers can appreciate it. See *Heart and Soul: The Story of Florence Nightingale* for another version for young adults. (1951)

Franklin Delano Roosevelt

Russell Freedman   8

As with the Newbery-winning Lincoln photo biography, Freedman unites a highly readable text from firsthand observations of family, friends, and Roosevelt's own diary with black-and-white photographs. He offers an intriguing and inspiring portrait of the president who led America through the Depression and WW II. (1990)

Frederick Douglass

Frederick Douglass; edited by Henry Louis Gates   8+

Gates compiled into one volume all three autobiographies: *Narrative of the Life of Frederick Douglass: An American Slave*; *My Bondage and My Freedom*; and *Life and Times of Frederick Douglass*. The first, written only seven years after he escaped slavery is best known, but the later versions reveal his eloquence and the scope of his work. This adult-trade volume is for the mature interested reader. Numerous young adult biographies are also available. (1994)

Biography

Free Woman on God's Earth

Jana Laiz and Ann-Elizabeth Barnes; *illustrated by Jacqueline Rogers*   3, 4, 5

Subtitled *The True Story of Elizabeth "Mumbet" Freeman, The Slave Who Won Her Freedom*, the authors tell the little-known story of a courageous woman who was a slave in the north for more than thirty years. Resilient and persevering, Mumbet convinces a compassionate lawyer to sue for her freedom in a Massachusetts court, paving the road for the abolition of slavery in Massachusetts in 1783. Sensitive black and white illustrations complement the text. (2009)

Freedom Train: The Story of Harriet Tubman

Dorothy Sterling; *illustrated by Ernest Crichlow*   8

Look for this biography of one of the leaders of the Underground Railroad, as well as this author's other books about the early struggles of African Americans to achieve freedom and legal rights. See also *Lift Every Voice*. (1957)

Galileo Galilei: Inventor, Astronomer, and Rebel

Michael White   7

The story covers Galileo's life and accomplishments as well as his conviction for heresy in 1633 for his support of the Copernican view of the universe. Full of the drama of persecution, court trial, and house arrest, it explains the background of the conflict between the scientists of the time and the Catholic Church. Color and black-and-white photographs enhance almost every page. (1999)

George Washington's World

Genevieve Foster, *illustrated by author*   6+

Important deeds of the individual are paralleled with other world events and personalities in an easy-to-read text enhanced with simple line illustrations. Beautiful Feet Press has reprinted this volume as well as the similarly styled *The World of Captain John Smith*, *The World of Columbus and Sons*, and *Abraham Lincoln's World*, which were originally published in the 1940s. (1941)

★ Newbery Honor

Great Little Madison, The

Jean Fritz   4, 5, 6+

Honors were heaped on Fritz's vivid picture of the fourth American president and the problems he and the Founding Fathers faced. This sometimes-humorous biography includes detailed accounts of First Lady Dolly Madison and his close friendship with Thomas Jefferson. (1989)

★ Orbis Pictus Award, School Library Journal Best Books of the Year

Great Lives (Series)

Published by Charles Scribner/ Atheneum
Paul Quinn   6, 7, 8

Each illustrated volume in this series is a collection of twenty-five or more brief biographies of individuals who contributed significantly to a particular field of human endeavor, written by an authority in that field. Although out of print, the titles and authors to look for are: *The American Frontier* (Patricia Calvert), *American Government* (Doris and Harold Faber), *American Literature* (Harold Faber), *Exploration* (Milton Lomask), *Human Culture* (David Weitzman, featuring archeologists and anthropologists), *Invention and Technology* (Milton Lomask), *Medicine* (Robt. H. Curtis, M.D.), *Nature and the Environment* (Doris and Harold Faber), *Painting* (Shirley Glubok), *Sports* (George Sullivan), and *World Religions* (William J. Jacobs). (1988–1997)

He Went with Christopher Columbus

Louise Andrews Kent   7

Kent wrote six "He Went with…" biographies of explorers. The others are: *He Went with Sir Francis Drake, He Went with Marco Polo, He Went with Champlain, He Went with Magellan,* and *He Went with Vasco da Gama.* (1940)

Heart and Soul: The Story of Florence Nightingale

Gena K. Gorrell   8

The story of the pioneer who founded the first professional nursing school in 1860 is fleshed out from many sources: family letters, official correspondence, personal letters from Queen Victoria, and photographs, some of which are collected from Nightingale's family. (2000)

Hitler

Dr. Albert Marrin ☀ 8

Marrin exposes the beguiling nature of totalitarianism and the childhood sources of Hitler's fanaticism in this illustrated biography of the leader of Nazi Germany. See also *Stalin: Russia's Man of Steel, The Yanks are Coming: The United States in the First World War,* and others. (1987)

★ School Library Journal Best Books of the Year

Invincible Louisa: The Story of the Author of "Little Women"

Cornelia Meigs ☀ 8

Meigs's biography recounts the life of one of the most noted women writers of the nineteenth century and her family. Alcott was strong-willed, adventurous, and loved to write. Feeling responsibility for the economic welfare of her family, she used her writing to supplement her father's erratic support. Living in a time of great social and economic change in America, it is no surprise she has become a heroine to many. (1933)

★ Newbery Medal

Joan of Arc

Louis-Maurice Boutet de Monvel, *illustrated by author* ☀ 4, 5, 6+

A facsimile edition of this picture storybook, one of the earliest works written for children, has been reproduced with care with luminous illustrations from the original, which is in the Pierpont Morgan Library. The story, although written for children, is an accurate and inspiring version of the life of the martyred French patriot who inspired her countrymen to defeat the English in the fifteenth century and paved the way for the coronation of Charles VII. (1953)

Kids at Work: Lewis Hine and the Crusade Against Child Labor

Russell Freedman; *illustrated by Lewis Hine* ☀ 8

Often going undercover posing as an insurance salesman, Hines, a teacher, photographer and activist, traveled the United States documenting child labor in factories, mills, mines, and fields in the days before protective labor laws were in place. His photographs movingly show children what their peers were subjected to and the economics of the early twentieth century. (1994)

Kite That Won the Revolution, The

Isaac Asimov; *illustrated by Victor Mays*   8

Among Asimov's many recommended titles is this biography of Benjamin Franklin that considers him as a scientist interested in electricity, as well as one of the leaders of the American Revolution. (1963)

Lee of Virginia

Douglas S. Freeman   8

Freeman's four-volume biography of General Robert E. Lee, the great Confederate general of the American Civil War, won the Pulitzer Prize in 1935 and remains one of the most respected biographies ever written. This version for young adult readers is reduced to 236 pages. (1958)

Lees of Arlington, The: The Story of Mary and Robert E. Lee

Marguerite Vance; *illustrated by Nedda Walker*   8

We meet the Lees as children before they became "the first family" of the Confederate South, he the great general, and she the plantation mistress who taught her women slaves to read. As with the author's biographies of European women, Vance's biographies of Americans feature the role of the Founding Father's mothers and wives. Look for *Martha, Daughter of Virginia* and *Patsy Jefferson of Monticello.* (1949)

Leonardo da Vinci

Diane Stanley, *illustrated by author*   5, 6, 7

The talented author/artist earned many awards for her picture book biography of the Italian genius, often referred to as the "Renaissance man" as a result of his accomplishments in so many arenas. Full-page color illustrations face each page of a very accessible text. Stanley has also written biographies of Michelangelo, Joan of Arc, Shakespeare, Elizabeth I and others. (1996)

✳ Boston Globe-Horn Book Honor Book, Orbis Pictus Award

Leonardo da Vinci: First Impressions

Richard McLanathan ☀ 7

This is an engrossing, well-organized narrative, with quality reproductions. Sketches from journals and notebooks give a glimpse of the man at work. Photographs of various locales that the great Italian Renaissance artist, inventor and scientist visited add a sense of time and place. The author has written books about other artists including Michelangelo and Rubens. (1990)

Life and Death of Crazy Horse, The

Russell Freedman;
illustrated and photographed by Amos Bad Heart Bull ☀ 8

Freedman has written almost fifty books and is skilled in bringing history to life through engaging biographies. With extensive research, he presents a balanced biography of one of the greatest Native Americans who led his people with courage and integrity. Photographs of drawings by a Sioux artist and cousin of Crazy Horse add to the richness of this important story in American history. (1996)

Lift Every Voice

Dorothy Sterling; *illustrated by Ernest Crichlow* ☀ 8

Subtitled *The Lives of Booker T. Washington, W. E. B. DuBois, Mary Church Terrell, and James Weldon Johnson*, this collection of four biographies, about the early struggles of African Americans to achieve freedom and legal rights, may be found in libraries and used book outlets. (1965)

Lincoln: A Photobiography

Russell Freedman ☀ 8

A photographic record of the effect upon Lincoln's face of his years of public service makes a moving testimony to the compassion and caring nature of his soul and of the burden of leadership. The simple text provides a historical context for understanding the changes in the face of the first president to be frequently photographed and would be appropriate for middle-grade readers also. (1987)

★ Newbery Medal, Golden Kite Honor

Little Brother of the Wilderness: The Story of Johnny Appleseed

Meridel Le Sueur; *illustrated by Suzy Sansom* 3, 4, 5

This is an easier-to-read version of the life of John Chapman that Holy Cow Press has reissued. Apples, apple juice, and applesauce are so much a part of school children's lives that the story of the pioneer who planted apple trees across the American wilderness is one of natural interest. It can also be read aloud to younger students. (1947)

Lives of Famous Romans

Olivia E. Coolidge 6

This is an excellent collection of brief biographies of Cicero, Caesar, Augustus, Virgil, Horace, Nero, Seneca, Trajan, Hadrian, Marcus Aurelius, Diocletian, and Constantine. (1965)

Madame Curie

Eve Curie 7, 8+

The Curies were a family of scientists, but daughter Eve chose a career as a writer. She penned this biography of her brilliant mother who was twice awarded the Nobel Prize. (1938)

Many Thousands Gone: African Americans from Slavery to Freedom

Virginia Hamilton; *illustrated by Leo and Diane Dillon* 8

Carnegie Medal-winning illustrators and a Newbery-winning author teamed to produce this collection of succinct profiles with black-and-white portraits of individuals who fought and defeated the institution of slavery including Sojourner Truth, Harriet Tubman, Frederick Douglass, and others less celebrated. (1993)

Marco Polo and the Medieval Explorers

Rebecca Stefoff 6, 7

This is one of over twenty titles in the World Explorers series. They are by different authors, covering everything from the early Vikings, to the sixteenth and seventeenth centuries, to the Apollo spacecraft. The virtues of the individual volumes are those of the author. Some are well reviewed and others are not. Pick and choose. It's a place to start if an explorer is your topic. (1992)

Biography

Michelangelo

Diane Stanley, *illustrated by author* ☀ 7

An affectionate, anecdotal text and distinguished illustrations bring to life the great Florentine Renaissance artist and the turbulent time in which he lived. This easier-to-read book would be suitable for introducing art history. See also *Leonard da Vinci.* (2000)

★ School Library Journal Best Books of the Year

My Life with Martin Luther King, Jr.

Coretta Scott King ☀ 8+

With so many biographies of her husband on the market, Mrs. King's has a claim of first-hand knowledge that none of the others can make. (1969)

Paul Revere and the World He Lived In

Esther Forbes ☀ 8+

Forbes departs from the legend and gives an historical account of the patriot and silversmith's life and of Boston at the time of the American Revolution. This full-length biography won Forbes the Pulitzer Prize in history. She went on to write other books about this hero. See also *America's Paul Revere*, illustrated and suitable for grade four and up. (1942)

★ Pulitzer Prize

Profiles in Courage

John Fitzgerald Kennedy ☀ 8+

Kennedy's Pulitzer Prize-winning book tells the stories of eight courageous American Senators who crossed party lines or went against popular opinion to stand up for their beliefs. These include John Quincy Adams, Daniel Webster, and Sam Houston. (1956)

★ Pulitzer Prize

Queen Eleanor, Independent Spirit of the Medieval World: A Biography of Eleanor of Aquitaine

Polly Schoyer Brooks   6+

Eleanor of Aquitane was perhaps the most powerful and influential woman in twelfth-century Europe. Each chapter of Brooks's biography highlights a different time of her life, from her childhood in Aquitaine, to her marriages and roles as Queen of France and later of England, and finally as Queen Mother helping her sons rule as kings of England. (1983)

 ✳ ALA Notable Children's Book, School Library Journal
    Best Books of the Year

Rachel Carson: Who Loved the Sea

Jean Lee Latham; *illustrated by Victor Mays*   6, 7, 8

Carson is best remembered for her book, *Silent Spring*, which was among the first to expose the effects of pesticides on the environment. This story of her growing up, and the influences that made her the pioneering marine biologist, nature writer, and environmental leader she became, is written by a Newbery-winning author. (1973)

Remarkable Voyages of Captain Cook, The

Rhoda Blumberg   7

In addition to being a fascinating account of the eighteenth-century cartographer, navigator, and explorer, this book offers a valuable cross-cultural perspective on how the British and the Tahitians failed to recognize and accept each other's beliefs. (1991)

 ✳ ALA Notable Children's Book

Samuel F. B. Morse, Artist-Inventor

Jean Lee Latham   6, 7, 8

This was originally published under the title *Medals for Morse* by a Newbury-winning author who has written many biographies for young people. Born in 1791, Morse began his career as an artist, painting murals in Boston and New York. Having gone to Yale College and studied art in Europe, he had many interests and talents, including early photography and telegraphy. (1954)

Stalin: Russia's Man of Steel

Dr. Albert Marrin   8

Dr. Marrin has written a forceful account for young adult readers of Communist Russia's ruthless leader. Illustrated with photographs. (1988)

★ School Library Journal Best Books of the Year

Starry Messenger

Peter Sis, *illustrated by author*   7

The subtitle is *A Book Depicting the Life of a Famous Scientist, Mathematician, Astronomer, Philosopher, Physicist: Galileo Galilei.* Watercolor, pen, and rubber-stamp illustrations support the text, although much is missing in terms of a complete biography. Rather, the artist creates scenes that show how Galileo stood against the darker aspects of his time. Younger, as well as older, students can appreciate this book. (1996)

Story of My Life, The

Helen Keller   7, 8

Other autobiographical books by Ms. Keller include *The Journal of Helen Keller* and *The World I Live In.* Many simplified or shorter versions of her life story that recount her extraordinary accomplishments despite being deaf/blind from early childhood are also available. Two related books that portray the relationship with her teacher, Anne Sullivan, are *The Miracle Worker* by Gibson and *Teacher* by Davidson. (1903)

Traitor: The Case of Benedict Arnold

Jean Fritz   6, 7, 8

Fritz attempts to explain General Arnold's betrayal of the American Revolution in terms of his childhood and personality. "He wanted to be a hero," she states, and instead became traitor to a side he believed was doomed to failure. Illustrations from archives, maps, index, and source list are included. Making American history accessible for young readers has earned this author many awards. See also *And Then What Happened, Paul Revere?* and *The Great Little Madison.* (1981)

★ School Library Journal Best Books of Year, ALA Notable Children's Book

Travels of Marco Polo, The

Marco Polo; edited by Milton Rugoff   7+

There are quite a few books about Polo, many written for young adults, but Polo's own extraordinary travelogue should not be overlooked. Signet's paperback edition (1961), edited by Milton Rugoff, includes an extensive introduction with a map, a family tree for Genghis Khan, and a history of the manuscript (handwritten originals of which were being discovered as late as 1934). Challenging but fascinating reading for junior high. (1477)

Undaunted Courage: Meriwether Lewis, Thomas Jefferson, and the Opening of the American West

Stephen E. Ambrose   8+

Though principally a biography of Meriwether Lewis, this narrative also provides fascinating portraits of President Thomas Jefferson, William Clark, Sacagawea, and other members of the group of explorers who journeyed from the Ohio River to the Pacific Ocean in the years 1803–1806. Scholarly and well documented, this account is at the same time a great adventure story and generates a sense of excitement and anticipation that mirrors the feelings Lewis and Clark must have had. (1996)

When the World Was Rome: 753 B.C. to 476 A.D.

Polly Schoyer Brooks and Nancy Z. Walworth   6+

The authors tell the fascinating history of the Roman Empire, from its founding of the republic in 753 B.C. to its dissolution. She tells the story through the biographies of Romulus, the Etruscan kings, Camillus, the two Gracchus brothers, Julius Caesar, Augustus Caesar, the two Pliny's, Galen and the first Christian Emperor, Constantine, whose death signaled the beginning of the end. (1972)

World Awakes, The: The Renaissance in Western Europe

Polly Schoyer Brooks and Nancy Z. Walworth   7

The story of the Renaissance as it emerges in Italy, Spain, France, and England is told through the biographies of Lorenzo de Medici, Leonardo da Vinci, Ferdinand and Isabella of Spain, Columbus, Francis I, Francis Rabelais, Elizabeth I and Shakespeare. As with the other two highly recommended histories by these authors, black and white photographs of the art of the period enliven the text. (1962)

World I Live In, The

Helen Keller   7, 8+

Keller's *The Story of My Life* changed the world. But this sequel to her autobiography remains almost unknown. Responding to skeptics who doubted that a person who was blind, deaf, and mute almost from birth could find words to describe her experience, she presents a striking word-picture of her reality, a moving account of an extraordinary woman's keenest impressions. (1909)

World of Captain John Smith, The

Genevieve Foster, *illustrated by author*   ⁂   5–8

Combining her career as an artist with a desire for her children to have a better understanding of history, Foster wrote a series of books that placed American history in the context of world events. In this one that spans the years 1580 to 1631, she includes stories of Smith's contemporaries: Shakespeare, Rembrandt, Galileo, the Puritans, and others. See also *Abraham Lincoln's World, George Washington's World, Augustus Caesar's World,* and *The World of Columbus and Sons* by the same author. (1959)

World of Walls, The

Polly Schoyer Brooks   ⁂   6

Subtitled *The Middle Ages in Western Europe,* the author's short biographies provide a vivid picture of life during the barbarian invasions, feudalism, the Crusades, and the important events that shaped the age. The narrative interweaves the biographies of Gregory the Great, Charlemagne, William the Conqueror, Eleanor of Aquitaine, Richard the Lion Heart, Francis of Assisi, Simon de Montfort and Geoffrey Chaucer. (1966)

York's Adventures with Lewis and Clark

Rhoda Blumberg   ⁂   7, 8

Subtitled *An African-American's Part in the Great Expedition,* this book recognizes the contributions made by York, an African-American slave who took part in the Corps of Discovery's expedition across the newly acquired American Northwest Territory. (2004)

★ Orbis Pictus Award

Additional Recommended Titles
of Famous Individuals

Abigail Adams (1744-1818), American First Lady

Abigail Adams: Witness to a Revolution (1995)
Nancy S. Bober   8

Benedict Arnold (1741–1901), American Revolutionary General and British Loyalist

Benedict Arnold: Traitor of the Revolution (1970)
Ronald Syme   8

Louis Braille (1809–1852), Inventor of Alphabet Allowing the Blind to Read

Louis Braille: The Boy Who Invented Books for the Blind (1971)
Margaret Davidson   4, 5, 6

Louis Braille: Windows for the Blind (1951)
J. Alvin Kugelmass; *illustrated by Edgard Cirlin*   6, 7, 8

Out of Darkness: The Story of Louis Braille (1997)
Russell Freedman; illustrated by Kate Kiesler   5–8

John Brown (1800–1859), American Abolitionist

John Brown: A Cry for Freedom (1980)
Lorenz Graham   8

George Washington Carver (circa 1864–1943), African-American Scientist

George Washington Carver: The Man Who Overcame (1966)
Lawrence Elliott   8

Biography

Christopher Columbus, Fifteenth-Century Italian Explorer

Christopher Columbus on the Green Sea of Darkness (1988)
Gardner Soule ☀ 7

Where Do You Think You're Going, Christopher Columbus? (1980)
Jean Fritz; *illustrated by Margot Tomes* ☀ 5, 6, 7

World of Columbus and Sons, The (1965)
Genevieve Foster; *illustrated by author* ☀ 6, 7

James Cook, Eighteenth-Century British Explorer

Far Voyager: The Story of James Cook (1970)
Jean Lee Latham; maps by Karl W. Stuecklen ☀ 7

Copernicus, Sixteenth-Century Astronomer

Copernicus: Founder of Modern Astronomy (2002)
Catherine M. Andronik ☀ 7

Vasco da Gama, Fifteenth-Century Portuguese Explorer

Vasco da Gama and the Portuguese Explorers (1993)
Rebecca Stefoff ☀ 7

Thomas Edison (1847–1931), American Inventor

Thomas Edison (1989)
Vincent Buranelli ☀ 6, 7, 8

Young Thomas Edison (1958)
Sterling North ☀ 6, 7, 8

Joycelyn Elders, M.D. (1933–), First African-American Surgeon General of the U.S.

Joycelyn Elders, M.D.: From Sharecropper's Daughter to Surgeon General of the United States of America (1998)
Joycelyn Elders and David Chanoff ☀ 8

El Cid, Eleventh-Century Spanish Military Leader

El Cid (1993)
Philip Koslow ☀ 6

Ferdinand and Isabella, Fifteenth-Century Monarchs

Ferdinand and Isabella (1968)
Melveena McKendrick ☀ 7

Benjamin Franklin (1706–1790), American Statesman and Scientist

Benjamin Franklin (1950)
Ingri and Edgar Parin d'Aulaire, *illustrated by authors* ☀ 4, 5, 6

Benjamin Franklin: Young Printer (1941)
Augusta Stevenson ☀ 4, 5, 6

Poor Richard (1941)
James H. Daugherty ☀ 6, 7, 8

What's the Big Idea, Ben Franklin? (1976)
Jean Fritz; *illustrated by Margot Tomes* ☀ 6, 7, 8

Galileo Galileo, Seventeenth-Century Astronomer

Galileo for Kids: His Life and Ideas, 25 Activities (2005)
Richard Panchyk ☀ 7+

Mohandas K. Gandhi (1869–1948), Indian Statesman and Spiritual Leader

Gandhi: Great Soul (1997)
John B. Severance 8

Mohandas Gandhi: The Power of the Spirit (1994)
Victoria Sherrow 8

Martha Graham (1894–1991), Modern American Choreographer, Innovator

Martha Graham: A Dancer's Life (1998)
Russell Freedman 6, 7, 8

Johann Gutenberg (circa 1398–1468), German Printer and Inventor

Fine Print: A Story About Johann Gutenberg (1991)
Joann Johansen Burch ☀ 7

Langston Hughes (1902–1967), African-American Poet

Black Troubadour: Langston Hughes (1970)
Charlemae Rollins 7, 8

Biography

Thomas Jefferson (1743–1826), American President

Thomas Jefferson: Father of Democracy (1953)
Vincent Sheean; *illustrated by Warren Chappell*   8

John Paul Jones (1747–1792), Hero of the American Revolution

John Paul Jones: Fighting Sailor (1953)
Armstrong Sperry   8

John F. Kennedy (1917–1963), American President

John F. Kennedy: Young Man in the White House (1991)
I. E. Levine   8

Robert E. Lee (1807–1870), U. S. Civil War Confederate Leader

America's Robert E. Lee (1951)
Henry Steel Commager and Lynd Ward   6, 7, 8

Robert E. Lee and the Road of Honor (1955)
Hodding Carter; *illustrated by William M. Hutchinson*   6, 7, 8

Abraham Lincoln (1809–1865), American President

Abe Lincoln: Log Cabin to White House (1956)
Sterling North   6, 7, 8

Abraham Lincoln (1943)
James H. Daugherty, *illustrated by author*   4, 5, 6

Abraham Lincoln (1940)
Ingri and Edgar d'Aulaire   4, 5, 6+

America's Abraham Lincoln 1957)
May McNeer   6, 7, 8

Abraham Lincoln's World (1944)
Genevieve Foster   7

Martin Luther, Sixteenth-Century Protestant Reformer

Martin Luther (1956)
Harry Emerson Fosdick   7

Martin Luther (2004)
Martin E. Marty   7

James Madison (1751–1836), American President

James Madison (1997)
Mary Malone8

Ferdinand Magellan, Sixteenth-Century Portuguese Explorer

Ferdinand Magellan and the Discovery of the World Ocean (1990)
Rebecca Stefoff7

Ferdinand Magellan: Master Mariner (1957)
Seymour Gates Pond7

Jacques Marquette and Louis Joliet, Seventeeth-Century French Explorers

The Explorations of Pere Marquette (1951)
James Arthur Kjelgaard7

Juan Ponce de Leon, Sixteenth-Century Spanish Explorer

Juan Ponce de Leon (1995)
Sean J. Dolan7

Beatrix Potter (1866–1943), Children's Author and Illustrator

Nothing is Impossible: The Story of Beatrix Potter (1969)
Dorothy Aldis4, 5

Sir Walter Raleigh, Sixteenth-Century English Explorer

Sir Walter Raleigh and the Quest for El Dorado (2000)
Marc Aronson7

Eleanor Roosevelt (1884–1962), American First Lady

Eleanor Roosevelt: A Life of Discovery (1993)
Russell Freedman8

Theodore Roosevelt (1858–1919), American President

Theodore Roosevelt (1988)
Zachary Kent8

Junipero Serra, Eighteenth-Century Spanish Missionary Explorer

Junipero Serra (1991)
Sean Dolan4–7

Biography

Harriet Tubman (1822–1913), African-American Underground Railroad Leader

Harriet Tubman: Conductor on the Underground Railroad (1955)
Ann Lane Petry   8

George Washington, 1732–1799, American First President

George Washington (1943)
James Daugherty, *illustrated by author*   6, 7, 8

Eli Whitney (1765–1825), American Inventor

Eli Whitney: Great Inventor (1991)
Jean Lee Latham   8

Mythology, Legends and Folklore

The titles in this section make up the core of many Waldorf language arts and literature blocks as well as social studies units on ancient civilizations. For an indication of which myths are best suited to a particular age or grade level, please review the individual section introductions for a given age group and the index of Waldorf curriculum blocks.

The folklore of a particular people is a natural companion to the study of the geography in which the culture arose. So for example, American tall tales are fun to share along with the study of North American Geography. Familiar characters such as John Henry, Pecos Bill, and Paul Bunyun come to mind. There is room for myths and folklore from other parts of the world in every grade.

Myths, legends and folklore are the articulation of the archetypes from which contemporary culture continues to draw meaning. Many of the stories here first originated in a purely oral tradition, and now, as then, many versions exist including "updated" or modernized tellings. Examples of these include versions of the Trojan War, Anansi tales, "Uncle Remus" stories and others. Each storyteller re-crafts the images much as an illustrator does in drawing pictures. We look for versions that keep the essential story alive. Modern re-imaginings that expand, alter, or significantly deviate from the originals may have their own literary value and are included elsewhere.

These are the stories we tell and retell because they address our deepest questions about birth and death, good and evil, and the journey to find meaning in an individual life. They are reflections of how a culture gives shape and purpose to the collective life of the group in which an individual must find his or her place. As the Greeks explained it, history tells the facts; myths tell the truth of human experience.

Mythology

Adventures of Rama: The Story of the Great Hindu Epic Ramayana

Retold by Joseph Gaer   5

Many versions of the stories from the Ramayana have been told. Gaer, who studied and wrote about the major religions, their origins and beliefs, retells the exciting epic hero tale of India for children. (1954)

Adventures with the Giants

Catherine F. Sellew   4

Volume one of a two-volume collection of Norse myths that is still available in libraries and used book outlets. The second volume is *Adventures with the Heroes*. (1950)

Adventures with the Gods

Catherine F. Sellew   5

This is a collection of sixteen short abridged versions of well-known Greek and Roman myths. Though long out of print, it is still worth looking for. (1945)

American Tall Tales

Adrian Stoutenberg; *illustrated by Richard Powers*   4, 5, 6

Features eight American regional folk heroes, including Paul Bunyan, Pecos Bill, Stormalong, Mike Fink, Davy Crockett, Johnny Appleseed, John Henry, and steel maker Joe Magarac. (1966)

American Tall Tales

Mary Pope Osborne; *illustrated by Michael McCurdy*   4, 5

Davy Crockett, Paul Bunyan, Johnny Appleseed, Pecos Bill, John Henry, and Sally Ann Thunder Whirlwind are among the nine heroes and heroines featured in this collection of traditional American tall tales, illustrated with wood engravings in full color. Tall tales are often set in a particular region of the United States and can enrich geography studies together with explorer biographies. (1991)

Mythology

Arabian Nights Entertainments, The

Andrew Lang; *illustrated by H. J. Ford*   6, 7, 8

Dover reprinted folklorist Andrew Lang's edited selections from Richard F. Burton's adult classic, *1001 Arabian Nights*. Lang's version, published in 1898 with Ford's black-and-white illustrations, offers twenty-six of the tales that Scheherazade told to save her life. These will appeal to older children who love magic and fantasy. (1898)

Arthurian Saga, The (Quartet))

Mary Stewart   7, 8+

Merlyn is the narrator for this quartet, which tells the saga of King Arthur. It starts with Merlyn's boyhood in *The Crystal Cave*, continues with Arthur's childhood in *The Hollow Hills*, follows Arthur's reign in *The Last Enchantment*, and ends with Mordred's story and the death of Arthur in *The Wicked Day*. This is a treatment for mature young adult readers. (1970)

Black Ships Before Troy: The Story of the Iliad

Rosemary Sutcliff; *illustrated by Alan Lee*   6, 7, 8

Preserved in this renowned author's exciting and popular retelling of the epic are a good many of Homer's original images of battle scenes that maintain the saga's integrity and enhance its effect. Some of these, however, may disturb younger or particularly sensitive readers. (1993)

Children of Odin: The Book of Northern Myths

Padraic Colum   4

Award-winning folklorist, Colum offers a dramatic retelling of the Norse myths ordered in a sequence that provides a narrative thread. (1920)

Children's Homer, The

Padraic Colum; *illustrated by Willy Pogany*   5

This volume, subtitled *The Adventures of Odysseus and the Tale of Troy*, weaves together Homer's *Iliad* and *Odyssey* into one excellent story, a retelling that young readers will enjoy until they can appreciate the original. (1918)

Clashing Rocks: The Story of Jason

Ian Serraillier   5+

This is one volume in a series of five, retelling the pre-Homeric legends of Greek heroes. Perhaps out of print but still available in libraries and used book outlets: *A Fall from the Sky: The Story of Daedalus*; *The Gorgon's Head: The Story of Perseus*; *Heracles the Strong*; and *The Way of Danger: The Story of Theseus*, all originally published in the 1960s. Serraillier's other works are also recommended. (1963)

Cloud Tea Monkeys

Mal Peet and Elspeth Graham; *illustrated by Juan Wijngaard*   2, 3, 4

Tashi's mother picks tea leaves every day with the other women of the village at the foot of the Himalayas as her daughter plays with her monkey friends. When her mother becomes ill and their livelihood threatened, Tashi finds a way to support the family through the ingenuity and generosity of her monkey friends. Wijngaard's traditional illustrations are lavish and bring the story to life. (2010)

Cut From the Same Cloth: American Women of Myth, Legend and Tall Tale

Robert D. San Souci; *illustrated by Brian Pinkney*   4, 5

An award-winning author retells twenty stories about legendary North American women, from folktales, popular stories, and ballads for this collection. Organized by region, the women come from the Native American, African-American, Mexican-American, and Canadian traditions. These tales can enrich studies of geography or social studies and the author's retellings are well done, as usual. See also, *Larger than Life: The Adventures of American Legendary Heroes,* a prequel to this one, featuring tall tales about Paul Bunyan, Pecos Bill, John Henry, and the like. (1993)

D'Aulaires' Book of Greek Myths

Ingri and Edgar Parin d'Aulaire, *illustrated by authors*   5

The art and the text combine to make this a preferred collection of stories that are given a natural order and chronology to introduce the mythological pantheon of Greek History. Other books by these authors are also highly recommended. (1962)

Mythology

D'Aulaires' Norse Gods and Giants

Ingri and Edgar Parin d'Aulaire; *illustrated by authors*   ☀   4

Thor, Odin, and other Norse mythological characters come to life in this collection by the distinguished Carnegie Medal-winning team. The text is simple enough to serve as a reader for fourth grade. (1967)

Dragon Slayer: The Story of Beowulf

Rosemary Sutcliff   6, 7, 8

A retelling of the exciting early British tale of the hero Beowulf who goes to the aid of the Danes when he learns of the prowling monster Grendel who is filling their nights with horror. A new translation of the original is now on many high school reading lists. This is an excellent preparation for the more challenging verse version, which has also inspired a film version. (1961)

Frog Girl

Paul Owen Lewis, *illustrated by author*   2, 3

Lewis creates a tale based on Native American myth of the Pacific Northwest. A chief's young daughter has to rescue frogs stolen by two boys and return them to their family in the depths of the lake. Her care for the animals saves her village from the rumbling volcano. The author's vibrant illustrations are sensitive to the culture and add to the magic of the story. Look for the author's *Storm Boy.* (1998)

Gilgamesh: Man's First Story

Bernarda Bryson, *illustrated by author*   ☀   5

This is a brilliant retelling of the ancient Sumerian story. When his beloved friend, Enkidu, is killed, King Gilgamesh's grief sends him to the underworld to seek the solution to the mystery of death. This is the grandfather of all hero journey epics and the only version of it available for children. Movingly told with illustrations inspired by Sumerian art. (1966)

Gods, Men and Monsters from the Greek Myths

Michael Gibson; *illustrated by Giovanni Caselli*   7, 8

Dramatic color paintings and line drawings illustrate this collection of twenty-seven stories of Greek gods and heroes including those of Jason, Theseus, and the Trojan War. Originally published in 1977, this 1991 edition is written at a junior high level. See *D'Aulaires' Book of Greek Myths* for a version for younger, independent readers. (1977)

Golden Fleece, The: And the Heroes Who Lived Before Achilles

Padraic Colum; *illustrated by Willy Pogany*   5

A masterful weaving of the legend of Jason and his Argonauts with classic Greek myths, including Orpheus, Prometheus, and Zeus's war with the Titans, to create a continuous epic saga. (1921)

Gorgon's Head, The

Ian Serraillier; *illustrated by William Stobbs*   5

Bethlehem Books distributes many of Serraillier's excellent retellings of classic myths and legends that might be difficult to find. The subtitle of this myth is *The Story of Perseus.* (1961)

Greek Civilization

Charles Kovacs   5

An experienced Waldorf class teacher retells the deeds of mythic heroes Heracles, Theseus, and Odysseus, the history of the Golden Age of Athens, and the conquests of Alexander the Great. This is a new edition of the original title, *Greece: Mythology and History.* Another collection of stories of ancient civilizations that Kovacs wrote for the classroom is *Ancient Mythologies: India, Persia, Babylon, Egypt.* Both are available from Wynestones Press. (2004)

Heroes of Greece and Troy: Retold from the Ancient Authors

Roger L. Green   5, 6

The tales of Perseus, Hercules, Jason, and the Argonauts—nineteen tales in all—are vividly retold in this single connected narrative of the Heroic Age, from the coming of the Immortals to the Trojan War, followed by the events of the Trojan War and the wanderings of Odysseus. Green's retellings are among the most accessible for younger readers, while retaining the poetic quality of the ancient texts. (1960)

Mythology

Horse Hooves and Chicken Feet: Mexican Folktales

Edited by Neil Philip
3, 4, 5

Familiar themes take on the flavor of Mexico and the Southwest in these smooth retellings selected by an experienced anthologist. (2004)

★ ALA Notable Children's Book

John Henry, an American Legend

Ezra Jack Keats, *illustrated by author*
3, 4

The legendary life of folklore's African-American steel-driving man, who was born and who died with a hammer in his hand, is recreated in the Newbery-winning author's text and full-color collage art. All of this author's works are recommended. See *Keats's Neighborhood*. (1965)

King and the Green Angelica, The: Stories and Poems from Old Norse and Anglo-Saxon Times

Isabel Wyatt and Joan Rudel
4

This British publication is a collection of adaptations and translations of Anglo-Saxon and Norse charms, poems, and folktales. (1975)

King Arthur and his Knights of the Round Table: Newly Retold Out of the Old Romances

Roger L. Green; *illustrated by Aubrey Beardsley*
6

Green's retellings are among the most accessible, particularly for younger readers, while retaining the poetic quality of the ancient texts. (1953)

King of Ireland's Son, The

Padraic Colum
2, 3, 4

This is an excellent retelling of a Celtic folktale by one of the best-known poets of the Irish Literary Revival. It reads well aloud but can also be enjoyed by independent readers. (1916)

King of Men, The

Olivia E. Coolidge
6, 7, 8

The British author was known for her biographies and historical fiction written for young adult readers. This is a fresh retelling of the story of King Agamemnon from Greek mythology. (1966)

Lights Along the Path: Jewish Folklore Through the Grades

Rebecca Schacht; *illustrated by Jacqui Morgan*   K–6

This collection of thirty-eight stories retold for children ages four to twelve are selected from the standpoint of child development. The book is divided into three sections by age. Beautiful illustrations and a sidebar containing interesting historical and cultural details enhance each tale. (2003)

Nights with Uncle Remus

Joel Chandler Harris   4–8

Seventy-one of Harris's most popular stories are here, told through the voices of four "slave" storytellers, including Uncle Remus. As a white boy growing up in the South, Harris overheard stories told in the slave quarters, which he later wrote down. Many have been published separately as retold by others, and are thus three times removed from the original folktales. Harris's versions have a unique place in early American literature. *The Complete Tales of Uncle Remus*, collected by R. Chase and published in 1955 with art from the original edition, is still available. Use discretion in selecting stories to read to younger children. It's not all Br'er Rabbit, and none of it is Disney although it inspired a cartoon film. (1880)

Norwegian Folk Tales from the Collection of Peter Christen Asbjørnsen and Jørgen Moe

Peter Christen Asbjørnsen and Jørgen E. Moe;
translated by Carl Norman and Pat Shaw;
illustrated by Erik Werenskiold and Theodor Kittelsen   1, 2

These were collected by two Norwegian childhood friends in the 1830's after the country's separation from Denmark in the nineteenth century. Translated into English in 1870, they represent the old Norse folklore and include "East of the Sun, West of the Moon" and other favorites. (1845)

Old Peter's Russian Tales

Arthur Ransome   3, 4, 5

This collection of Russian folktales, retold by the English author of the popular *Swallows and Amazons* series, is set inside a story about an old uncle, Peter, who tells the stories to his nephews as they pass the long nights of the cold Russian winter. They were written after Ransome visited Russia in 1913. A reissue in 2006 makes this once-rare collection available again. (1913)

Mythology

Once and Future King, The

T. H. White 8+

This marvelous retelling of King Arthur's legend is really four novels published as one volume. The first, *The Sword in the Stone*, upon which a Disney adaptation was based, focuses on Arthur's boyhood and training with his magician mentor, Merlyn. Full of invention and quite different in mood from most contributions to the saga, it is still not written for children, nor are the next three that inspired the drama, Camelot. The final novel of the saga, published posthumously in 1977, is *The Book of Merlyn*. (1958)

Paul Bunyon Swings his Axe

Dell J. McCormick, *illustrated by author* 4, 5

Other versions exist but this one has lasted to present seventeen authentic American folktales of the giant logger's exploits in the North Woods. (1936)

People Could Fly: American Black Folktales

Virginia Hamilton; *illustrated by Leo and Diane Dillon* 4, 5, 6

An award-winning author of folktales, animal fables, fantasy, and the supernatural retells these stories in a unique collection. Born out of the desire for freedom and the experiences of slaves, the stories carry the combined cultural heritage of two continents. Caldecott-winning artists illustrate them. (1985)

★ Coretta Scott King Award, School Library Journal Best Books of the Year

Robin Hood

Paul Creswick; *illustrated by N. C. Wyeth* 6

Wyeth's illustrations tell stories. The artist makes richer this timeless version of the famous legend of the outlaw who gave to the poor what he stole from the medieval lords. (1917)

Saint George and the Dragon

Margaret Hodges; *illustrated by Trina Schart Hyman* 3, 4, 5

The segment from Spenser's "The Fairie Queene," which recounts the legend of St. George, the Red Cross Knight, and the dragon, is retold with vivid language and equally vivid illustrations. (1984)

★ Caldecott Medal

Seeing Stone, The

Kevin Crossley-Holland 6

In late twelfth-century England, a thirteen-year-old boy named Arthur recounts how Merlyn gives him a magical seeing stone that shows him images of the legendary King Arthur, the events of whose life seem to have many parallels to his own. This trilogy by a Carnegie Medal winner continues in *The Crossing Places* and *King of the Middle March*. (2000)

★ The Guardian's Children's Fiction Award

Star Rider and Anna McLoon, The

Jakob Streit; translated by Nina Kuettel; *illustrated by Andrez Dauchez* 6, 7, 8

The first story is a seventeenth-century Irish legend about a young man who comes to learn of a dreadful destiny said to be laid upon him by the position of the stars at the moment of his birth. The second tale, "Anna McLoon," tells the modern story of Ireland's last traveling storyteller and the tales she told. (2010)

Stone Soup: An Old Tale

Marcia Brown, *illustrated by author* 2, 3, 4

When three hungry soldiers come to a town where all of the food has been hidden, they set out to make soup of water and stones, and the whole town enjoys a feast. Many versions of this tale have been offered since Brown retold and illustrated it. They have not improved upon it, and in some cases, critics agree, have detracted from it. (1947)

Story of Jumping Mouse: A Native American Legend

John Steptoe, *illustrated by author* 4, 5

This original Native American animal fable, a teaching story for adults, is retold here in a form suitable for younger listeners. The original "Jumping Mouse" story is part of an adult novel, *Seven Arrows* by Hyemeyohsts Storm, which may interest mature young adult readers. (1985)

★ Caldecott Honor Book

Mythology

Story of King Arthur and his Knights, The

Howard Pyle, *illustrated by author*   ☀   6

Versions of the Arthurian legend abound but few surpass this illustrated retelling, which was reissued in 1969 as *The Book of King Arthur*. Pyle evokes the mood of the age of chivalry and the archaic language in Malory's original, but is still accessible to young readers. More Arthurian tales are retold in *The Story of Sir Lancelot and His Companions, The Story of the Champions of the Round Table*, and *The Story of the Grail and the Passing of Arthur*. (1903)

Sword and the Circle, The: King Arthur and the Knights of the Round Table (Trilogy)

Rosemary Sutcliff   6

This is the first installment in the author's Arthurian trilogy, followed by *The Light Beyond the Forest: The Quest for the Holy Grail*, which includes the adventures of Lancelot, Galahad, Bors, and Percival as they pursue the Grail. In *The Road to Camlann* Mordred rises up against his father, King Arthur. Sutcliff was a prolific writer of excellent historical fiction for young adults. (1981)

Sword in the Stone, The

T. H. White   8

This is the first book in White's tetralogy based on the life of King Arthur. He introduces young Arthur, commonly called Wart, and focuses on his education by the wise tutor, Merlyn. See *The Once and Future King*. (1937)

Tales of a Korean Grandmother

Frances Carpenter   K, 1, 2

Carpenter has framed her stories within a story, a collection of thirty-two Korean folk and fairy tales as retold by an old Korean grandmother to her two granddaughters. This collection has been reprinted many times, testifying to its lasting value. She also wrote *Tales of a Chinese Grandmother* and others. (1947)

Tales of Ancient Egypt

Roger L. Green   ☀   5

Retold with dignity and humor, these authentic tales are taken from the temples and tombs of ancient Egypt and include the creation stories, as well as the Egyptian Cinderella. (1967)

Tales of Uncle Remus, The

Retold by Julius Lester; *illustrated by Jerry Pinkney*   3, 4, 5

Julius Lester retells the famous African-American folktales collected from slaves on Harris's family's plantation and first published in 1880. In this edition, Lester's simpler text may be enjoyed read aloud or read alone. Older students may wish to sample the original literature as Harris wrote it. (1987)

★ ALA Coretta Scott King Honor, Boston Globe-Horn Book

Thorkill of Iceland: Viking Hero Tales

Isabel Wyatt   4

In this collection, the hero, Thorkill of Iceland, is sent by King Gorm of Denmark on a mission to the land of Giants, a journey from which his enemies plan he will never return. A writer of tales whose works are highly recommended dramatically retells these stories from the old sources. Floris Books has reissued this and others by Wyatt. (2001)

Thunder of the Gods

Dorothy Hosford; *illustrated by Claire and George Louden*   4

Look in libraries and used book outlets for this out-of-print retelling of the Norse myths. (1952)

Trojan War and the Adventures of Odysseus, The

Padraic Colum; *illustrated by Barry Moser*   5

This reduction of the *Iliad* and the *Odyssey* weaves the two tales into one seamless epic adventure by a modern harper of renown. Who better to introduce Homer to young people? (1997)

True and Untrue, and Other Norse Tales

Edited by Sigrid Undset; *illustrated by Frederick T. Chapman*   1–4

This collection is based on the original stories collected by Moe and Asbjørnsen, the Grimm brothers of Norwegian folktales. Copies of their original collection, *East of the Sun* and *West of the Moon*, are collector's items now. (1945)

Mythology

Unicorn with Silver Shoes, The

Ella Young; *illustrated by Robert Lawson*   4, 5

This collection of Celtic tales is one of three volumes of collections that Young retold. The other two are *Celtic Wonder Tales*, illustrated by Maud Gonne, and *The Tangle-Coated Horse and Other Tales*. They are unique as part of the Irish literary renaissance of the early twentieth century. In 1991 this was republished and can be found with an online search. (1932)

Way of Danger, The

Ian Serraillier; *illustrated by William Stobbs*   5

Subtitled *The Story of Theseus*, the author retells the myths of the hero who founded Athens and battled many foes. Serraillier's retellings of classic myths and legends may still be found in online bookstores and libraries. (1962)

Weaving of a Dream, The

Retold and illustrated by Marilee Heyer   2, 3

As a vehicle for her finely and richly detailed art, the author retells the Chinese folktale of the old woman who spends three years weaving a brocade of a longed-for palace. When the fabric is blown away, the woman's three sons set out to find it. Stunning illustrations make the story memorable. (1986)

West Indian Folk Tales

Philip Sherlock   2, 3, 4

This collection, part of the *Oxford Myths and Legends Series*, retells twenty-one folktales of the West Indies, several of which are about Anansi or Anancy, a spider in the role of a trickster. (1966)

World Mythology Series, The

Published by Schocken 4–8

This eleven-volume series of myths and legends of the world's cultures offers a large format with full color and black-and-white, ultrarealistic illustrations. Neither the art nor the retellings are preferred over other versions, but the breadth of the series is welcome and therefore included. *Gods and Pharaohs from Egyptian Mythology* (Geraldine Harris); *Heroes, Gods and Emperors from Roman Mythology* (Kerry Usher and John Sibbick); *Warriors, Gods and Spirits from Central and South American Mythology* (Douglas Gifford); *Demons, Gods and Holy Men from Indian Myths & Legends* (Shahrukh Husain); *Spirits, Heroes and Hunters from North American Indian Mythology* (Marion Wood); *Gods and Heroes from Viking Mythology* (Brian Branston); *Kings, Gods and Spirits from African Mythology* (Jan Knappert); *Dragons, Gods and Spirits from Chinese Mythology* (Tao Tao Liu Sanders); *Druids, Gods and Heroes from Celtic Mythology* (Anne Ross); and *Fabled Cities, Princes and Jinn from Arab Myths and Legends* (Khairat Al-Saleh). (1980's)

Mythology

Celebrations, Games, Music, Crafts and Other Activities

In addition to the academic core blocks, all students in Waldorf schools receive lessons in instrumental music and singing, handwork and crafts, gardening (even if in very limited spaces or containers), fitness games and sports, and in most schools, one or two foreign languages and eurythmy, a movement art. Life skills such as mending and sewing, cooking and food preservation, relating to nature and the cycles of the year, and celebrating that cycle in a cultural context are also part of the curriculum for all students. As a result, many families find enrichment of family life is a benefit of being part of a Waldorf community. Less TV watching, more handmade gifts, nature walks, and an appreciation of forgotten traditions of our past are family benefits that may not be mentioned in the school brochure.

The following section is primarily an adult resource. These books offer support for families striving to create a richer tradition of ritual and a connection to the great cycles of the sun and moon that once gave a pattern to cultural life. Readers will find here suggestions for at-home traditions to bring rhythm, rhyme, and reasons for seasonal celebrations and daily routines.

It includes books that may be used to enrich or create festivals, birthdays, anniversaries, holidays, and special occasions at home or school. Here are music, games, and songs to share; crafts, decorations, and gifts to make; gardening and carpentry projects; and explanations of common traditions to enliven family and community gatherings for every season of the year. Ideas for creating nature or seasonal tables for home or school such as those displayed in Waldorf classrooms can be found here, as can recipes and directions for seasonal treats and activities.

I would like to acknowledge and thank my co-editor, Pamela Fenner, for her significant contribution to this section of the book. She researched new titles, wrote annotations for them, and expanded the list to include many more books that will serve families.

African and Caribbean Celebrations

Gail Johnson; *illustrated by Caroline Glanville*   Family

Born in England, the daughter of an English mother and Jamaican father, Johnson has a unique interest in Caribbean celebrations and their roots in Africa. Here she blends sharing the history and traditions with songs, games, recipes, crafts, and activities in a beautifully illustrated book that takes us through the year. (2008)

All Night, All Day:
A Child's First Book of African-American Spirituals

Edited and illustrated by Ashley Bryan   3–8

Out of the many African-American spirituals, Bryan has chosen twenty, including both the best-known as well as less familiar ones for this songbook. These emotional and inspiring songs are just waiting to be sung. The collection includes piano and guitar accompaniments and the editor's watercolor illustrations. (1991)

★ Coretta Scott King Award

All Year Round

Ann Druitt, Christine Fynes-Clinton and Marije Rowling;
illustrated by Marije Rowling   Family

The yearly calendar is very important for bringing rhythm into family life, especially when it includes festivals to look forward to and prepare for. This is a rich resource in searching for ideas, stories, songs, activities, and recipes to make home and festival life memorable as well as to create one's own traditions. (1986)

American Boy's Handy Book, The: What to Do and How to Do It

Daniel Carter Beard; Foreword by Noel Perrin   4+

This ultimate do-it-yourself activity book is full of projects that can keep a boy (and girl) busy for a long time. As a turn-of-the-century classic, the historical element is also interesting. Some projects may be dated, but can inspire the imagination to improvise and look for substitutes. For safety, some projects do require adult supervision. Look for the 2010 Centennial Edition. Other titles are *The American Girl's Handy Book: Making the Most of Outdoor Fun* and *The Field and Forest Handy Book: New Ideas for Out of Doors.* (1890)

American Songbag, The

Carl Sandburg   Family

While traveling the country, Sandburg collected ballads, spirituals, and work songs from every region and cultural group to document the diversity of this great land. He selected 280 American folk songs in this compilation and included the music, lyrics, and background notes for each. (1970)

Art of Writing Songs for Children, The

Colin Price   7, 8+

This practical book, written by the composer of *Let's Sing and Celebrate!* is designed for those who would like to learn to write their own songs for children, yet who have no more than an elementary familiarity with music notation. This do-it-yourself workbook has fourteen lessons with corresponding worksheets. A special section is devoted to the use of the music notation software "Sibelius." (2006)

Autumn: Nature Activities for Children

Irmgard Kutsch and Brigitte Walden; translated by Ronald Koetzsch   Family

This is the first of a series of four seasonal nature activity books. It is full of indoor and outdoor activities, based on practical experience in a children's nature center in Germany. Other titles are *Winter*, *Spring*, and *Summer*. (2005)

Baking Bread with Children

Warren Lee Cohen; *illustrated by Marije Rowling*   Family

Baking bread with children of all ages can be a rewarding experience for all. Here are delicious recipes to make bread for a snack or meal. Multicultural stories, songs, and blessings enrich the culinary adventures. (2008)

Barefoot Book of Blessings, The

Sabrina Dearborn; *illustrated by Olwyn Whelan*   Family

For those who offer blessings, this 2007 revision of *A Child's Book of Blessings* offers examples from many cultures and traditions for all kinds of activities around the day and year. Colorful, sensitive illustrations frame each selection from a "Water Blessing" to a "Blessing for a Journey." (1999)

Big Summer Activity Book, The

Anne and Peter Thomas; translated by George Hall   Family

From simple games to inspiring projects, this excellent resource is full of ideas for wholesome indoor and outdoor fun to keep your children busy the whole summer long. Includes 500 color photos, illustrations and tips for car journeys, snacks, health, and safety. Look for *The Children's Party Book* by the same authors. (2006)

Birthday Book, The: Celebrations for Everyone

Ann Druitt, Christine Fynes-Clinton and Marije Rowling   Family

Birthdays are important emotional events for any age, but especially for children. This book was designed to help you bring meaning and beauty to your celebrations. Filled with recipes, stories, songs, games, and ideas for cards, decorations, and presents as well as historical anecdotes, it will become a family resource even for older teens and twenty-first-year parties as well as birthdays on rainy days or while on vacation. (2003)

Birthday Parties: Best Party Tips and Ideas

Vicki Lansky; *illustrated by Jack Lindstrom*   Family

Vicki Lansky has been writing newsletters, magazine columns and publishing parenting books since 1974. The beauty of this book is in the information about the age appropriateness of different party ideas such as games, prizes, and favors. Full of organizing tips, recipes, and more. The revised edition addresses special dietary needs. (1986)

Calf for Christmas, A

Astrid Lindgren; translated by Polly Lawson;
illustrated by Marit Törnqvist   K–3

Set in rural Sweden, this is a charming story of disaster averted with a Christmas miracle. It is beautifully illustrated in watercolors. Lindgren, author of the *Pippi Longstocking* series and *The Tomten* is one the world's most translated authors. (2010)

Celebrations

¡Cante, Cante, Elefante! Sing, Sing, Elephant!

Mary Thienes-Schunemann;
illustrated by Lura Schwartz-Smith   Family

Thienes-Schunemann, a talented singer, composer, and Waldorf teacher, helps bring Spanish into children's lives with a bilingual songbook filled with traditional songs, finger games, dances and rhymes from Spanish-speaking countries. Translated by Rebeca Itzcowich and Rosario Villasanu-Ruiz Sven Schunemann, the book includes an accompanying CD. (2005)

Carpentry for Children

Lester R. Walker   ☀ 3+

Introduce the world of hand tools, workbenches, and projects to children with a range of ages and skills. Both practical and inspirational, Walker offers guidance right from the start in building a workshop and its basic elements. Wood projects include a birdhouse, racing car, bath toy, raft, doll house, puppet theater, and more. This and Walker's *Housebuilding for Children* will inspire adults to guide children creating houses with discarded materials and with safety. (1985)

Celebrating Christmas Together: Nativity and Three Kings Plays with Stories and Songs

Estelle Bryer and Janni Nicol   Family

Families who want to find new ways of celebrating Christmas will be inspired with this resource. Begin with creating an Advent calendar and crib scene or plan a Nativity play. The play can be read or performed and the book has staging directions, instructions for simple costumes and props, songs and accompanying music. The companion is *Christmas Stories Together*, a treasure trove of thirty-six tales for children age three to nine. (2002)

Celebrations of Light: A Year of Holidays Around the World

Nancy Luenn; *illustrated by Mark Bender*   Family

The text and paintings highlight twelve festivals, showing the diverse ways in which people around the world use light as a major part of their celebrations. Bender's bright airbrush illustrations have a strong geometrical quality. (1998)

Child's Garden, A

Molly Dannenmaier   Family

Create outdoor enchanted mini-paradises for children to play and pretend in, from mazes and peepholes to vegetable patches, water gardens, natural sandboxes, climbing trees and more. Play with sand, earth, and water or discover plants in an "Alphabet Garden." Subtitled *60 Ideas to Make Any Garden Come Alive for Children* and now in soft cover, its stunning, full-page photographs add to the wonder. (1998)

Child's Play 1 and 2: Games for Life

Wil van Haren and Rudolf Kischnick   Family

These 172 games are appropriate for the developmental stages of younger children and are suitable for nursery, kindergarten and grammar schools along with camps and family occasions. Time-tested games follow in *Child's Play 3: Games for Life for Children and Teenagers.* (1996)

Children's Book of Kwanzaa, The

Dolores M. Johnson   Family

Each year on December 26, the African-American holiday of Kwanzaa begins. What is the purpose of Kwanzaa? How did it get its start? Dolores Johnson gives detailed descriptions of Kwanzaa's principles and symbols. Subtitled *A Guide to Celebrating the Holiday,* this comprehensive resource also includes recipes, craft and gift ideas, as well as suggestions to help young readers and their families create their own special Kwanzaa celebration. (1997)

Children's Party Book, The: For Birthdays and Other Occasions

Anne and Peter Thomas; *illustrated by Anjo Mutsaars*   K–7

This popular and invaluable guide contains more than 240 ideas for indoor and outdoor games, plus craft activities for children from age three to twelve. The 2008 revised edition is a soft cover. The activities are presented clearly with illustrations, diagrams, and step-by-step practical descriptions, all coded for age suitability. Special topics include: how to celebrate that special birthday; how to make and perform a simple theater for young children; how to organize parties with a seasonal theme; and how to make attractive decorations. (1998)

Celebrations

Christmas Carol, A

Charles Dickens   8+

No Christmas should pass without a reading of the tale of Victorian Ebenezer Scrooge who was visited by spirits of the past, the present, and the future and got over his "bah, humbug" attitude as a result. They keep making movies of it, but nothing can replace the special effects of the real thing. (1843)

Christmas in the Family

Isabel Marion, *illustrated by author*   Family

Isabel Marion, a mother of five, was born in Scotland and has been creating family festivals for many years. Here is her collection of activities, stories, music, and recipes to enrich a Christmas holiday. (2006)

Clump-a-Dump and Snickle-Snack

**Johanne Russ; translated by Lyn S. Willwerth;
*illustrated by Deborah Kaufmann***   K–4

Subtitled *Pentatonic Children's Songs,* this collection has forty-two songs for children age four and above. Gnomes, fairies, sylphs, sprites, and all the "people" in a child's world animate these delightful songs. (1966)

Come Follow Me! Volume 1

Lorraine Nelson Wolf   Family

Subtitled *A Collection of Folk Songs for Young Children* these soothing favorites range from reverent to wonder-filled to whimsical, many of which are oriented toward nature and the changing seasons. Simple and arranged with piano, accordion, harp, or guitar accompaniment, this audio CD includes a booklet with lyrics. Look for Volume 2. (2004)

Crafts Through the Year

Thomas and Petra Berger   Family

This completely revised compilation of the authors' very successful *Christmas Craft Book, Easter Craft Book, and Harvest Craft Book* offers 200 different seasonal and holiday crafts and decorations. Look for *The Gnome Craft Book* and *Feltcraft: Making Dolls, Gifts and Toys* by the same authors. (2000)

Creative Felt: Felting and Making Toys and Gifts

Angelika Wolk-Gerche; translated by Anna Cardwell   Family

People have been making felt for thousands of years. This book teaches how to make it in easy, step-by-step stages, with helpful photographs and diagrams. The second half is full of ideas for things to make with felt, ranging from toys and dolls to beautiful accessories and gifts. (2007)

De Colores and Other Latin-American Folk Songs for Children

Jose-Luis Orozco; *illustrated by Elisa Kleven*   Family

Bursting with color and spirit, this collection of Latin American songs is a tribute to Latino culture. From traditional tunes to rhymes and hand games, *De Colores* has easy-to learn songs for all occasions and moods. Includes simple musical arrangements with English and Spanish lyrics. Slightly abridged in 2006 from the original edition, this is ideal for classroom use, multicultural studies, or just plain fun. (1999)

Donkey's Dream, The

Barbara Helen Berger, *illustrated by author*   1, 2, 3

A little donkey tells about the dreams he experiences on a journey carrying Mary on the road to Bethlehem and which culminates in the birth of Jesus. Berger's beautifully illustrated retelling of the Nativity story can make this a beloved book to read and reread annually. (1985)

Earth, Water, Fire and Air: Playful Explorations in the Four Elements

Walter Kraul; translated by Donald MacLean   Family

This how-to book has simple to complex projects to experiment with earth, water, fire and air. Written more for parents and teachers, it includes instructions for simple toys and machines such as a waterwheel, propeller plane, simple pendulum clock, hot-air balloon, yo-yo and others. The 2010 revision has new photographs, diagrams and a few new activities. (1984)

Earthways: Simple Environmental Activities for Young Children

Carol Petrash; *illustrated by Donald Cook*   K+

Adults today wish to encourage young children's sense of natural wonder and to treat the earth not as a commodity to exploit and damage, but as a cherished gift to love, respect and protect. Activities in this resource are graded in difficulty so that children will learn how to have fun and play safely with earth, air, fire, and water. (1992)

Family Treasury of Jewish Holidays, The

Malker Drucker; *illustrated by Nancy Patz*   Family

Drucker explains the customs, symbols, and stories associated with the major traditional Jewish holidays and the two "new" holidays, Yom HaShoah and Yom Ha'atzmaut. Stories to read aloud by authors such as Barbara Cohen and Isaac Bashevis Singer are included along with crafts, songs, and recipes. Hebrew illuminated manuscript paintings are the source of inspiration for the illustrations and borders. (1994)

Felt Wee Folk: Enchanting Projects

Salley Mavor; *illustrated by author*   Family

This book is filled with gorgeous, detailed photographs and easy-to-follow instructions for making wee folk and fairies. These projects are portable, can be done in a short time of one to two hours, and will not intimidate the beginner or craft-averse. (2004)

Felting Needle: From Factory to Fantasy

Ayala Talpai; *photographed by Gini Graham*   Family

The felting needle has been adapted from industry for various hand-felting and doll-making procedures. This engaging book is written for a wide range of skills and ages. Topics covered are instructions for set-up, safety, for basic and advanced techniques. Four felting needles are included to help you begin. (2000)

Festival of Lights: The Story of Hanukkah

Maida Silverman; *illustrated by Carolyn S. Ewing*   K–3

Here is a graceful and moving retelling of the miracle of Hanukkah that includes instructions for the traditional candle-lighting ceremony and a holiday song and game. (1999)

Festival of Stones, The: Autumn and Winter Tales of Tiptoe Lightly

Reg Down   K–3

Readers follow Tiptoe and her friends as they adventure through the festivals of Michaelmas, Martinmas, Halloween, Advent, the Festivals of Stones/Plants/Animals/Light and Christmas, encountering the heart and soul of the festivals along the way. (2006)

Festivals Together: Guide to Multicultural Celebration

Sue Fitzjohn, Minda Weston and Judy Large   Family

This treasury helps teachers and families celebrate festivals from a variety of faiths and cultures from around the world: Buddhist, Christian, Hindu, Jewish, Muslim, and Sikh. The stories, items to make, recipes, songs, customs and activities offer a lively introduction to different ways of life. The "Celebrating Festivals and the Season" titles from Hawthorn Press also include: *All Year Round; Festivals, Family and Food; Celebrating Irish Festivals; The Children's Year; The Islamic Year, The Birthday Book* and more. (1993)

Finger Strings: A Book of Cat's Cradles and String Figures

Michael Taylor   K+

Most children are captivated with string games, but may never go beyond learning the basic cat's cradle. The author introduces other string games along with rhymes and stories. The volume comes with two colorful strings and diagrams with instructions for eighty easy-to-follow activities. (2008)

First Book of Knitting for Children, A

Bonnie Gosse and Jill Allerton;
photographed by David Gosse and Bryan Anderson   1+

Looking for a learn-to-knit book with the approach used in Waldorf schools? Photographs, rhymes, and clear instructions help the beginner learn to knit and purl. Includes simple patterns to make enticing animals for play. Look for *Knitting for Children: A Second Book* for more and varied patterns. (2004)

Floating Lanterns and Golden Shrines:
Celebrating Japanese Festivals

Rena Krasno; *illustrated by Toru Sugita*   Family

The stories in this book will delight children while teaching them about the customs of Japan. All the major Japanese festivals are described, interwoven with stories, recipes, activities, and history. From New Year's Day to Obon, cherry blossoms to snow sculptures, the entire year is described. (2000)

Foxfire Book of Appalachian Toys and Games, The

Linda Garland Page and Hilton Smith   Family

Tired of electronic games and toys? This collection will take the reader back to a childhood playing inside and outside games and making playthings. The editors provide instructions for the games as well as for constructing playhouses, noisemakers, and puzzles. Some projects need adult supervision. (1985)

From Sea to Shining Sea:
A Treasury of American Folklore and Folk Songs

Amy L. Cohn; *illustrated by Molly Bang*   Family

From the shores of the Atlantic Ocean to the waters of the Pacific, America overflows with a rich multicultural heritage. Cohn's lavish and engaging collection of Americana in song and story is organized into thematic historical sections, each illustrated by an American artist who has won a Caldecott Medal or Honor Award. (1993)

Games and Songs of American Children

William Wells Newell   4–8+

Newell researched American children's games throughout the eastern half of U.S. at the turn of the nineteenth century. Revised often since its first publication, Newell's book features 190 games and play situations, songs and melodies some of which compare with those from other cultures. Adults who have an historical interest will enjoy this entertaining, basic book. (1883)

Games Children Play: How Games and Sport Help Children Develop

Kim-John Payne; *illustrated by Marije Rowling*   Family

This book offers an accessible guide to movement games with children ages three and upwards. There are games for mixed ages, playground games, and water games to help with swimming. They are all tried and tested with children and are the basis for the author's extensive teacher training work. Includes chapters with games for different age groups that deal with child development questions. (1997)

Gardening with Young Children

Beatrys Lockie   Family

Lockie, born in Holland, was both teacher and avid gardener. Here she shares her wisdom for bringing love of the garden and responsibility to the earth to young children through activities, cooking, crafts, stories, poems, and songs. Great resource for parents and teachers. (2007)

Gesture Games for Spring and Summer, Autumn and Winter

Wilma Ellersiek; edited and translated by Lyn and Kundry Willwerth   K–2

This book and learning CD set features hand gesture games, songs, and movement games for children in kindergarten and the lower grades. Beautifully performed songs from *Gesture Games for Spring and Summer* and *Gesture Games for Autumn and Winter* for adults to learn to sing with the children in your care. Contains nineteen songs of Spring/Summer and eighteen Autumn/Winter songs. (2005)

Giving Love—Bringing Joy

Wilma Ellersiek; *illustrated by Friedericke Lögters*   Family

The subtitle is *Hand Gesture Games and Lullabies in the Mood of the Fifth for Children Between Birth and* Nine. Anyone working with young children may want to use this book to incorporate gestures, touch and movement with music. Translated from German and edited by Lyn and Kundry Willwerth, there is an audio CD available, performed by Connie Manson. (2003)

Halloween: An American Holiday, An American History

Lesley Pratt Bannatyne   Family

Bannatyne gives us an engaging look at the history of this holiday from its formation in the British Isles, to its evolution in America. Relevant poems, songs, crafts, and recipes supplement the rich history of this popular holiday. (1990)

Hopscotch Around the World

Mary D. Lankford; *illustrated by Karen Dugan*   2–7

Lankford presents nineteen versions of this classic game gathered from cultures around the world along with rules, interesting facts and a world map to identify each location. This is a marvelous resource for home or classroom. (1992)

I Had a Friend Named Peter:
Talking to Children About the Death of a Friend

Janice Cohn; *illustrated by Gail Owens*   K–4

Dr. Cohn, a psychotherapist who also holds a doctorate in clinical social work, has specialized in helping adults and children cope with grief, loss, and life transitions. This is a useful resource for parents who are looking for ways to talk to their children about the death of a playmate and the fears that arise from that situation. (1987)

I Saw Three Ships

Elizabeth Goudge; *illustrated by Margot Tomes*   Family

This award-winning English author wrote more than forty publications, many of them for children. Polly Flowerdew, an orphan, lives with aunts and is longing for a visit from the Wise Men at Christmas. When she looks out her window on Christmas morning, she sees three sailing ships: one with a red sail, another with brown, and one with a sail like the wing of a swan. Reprinted in 2008, it continues to be a beloved and magical Christmas story. (1969)

In the Beginning There was Joy:
A Celebration of Creation for Children of All Ages

Matthew Fox; *illustrated by Jane Tattersfield*   K–3

This biblical creation story is full of hope, wonder, and the joy inherent in any creative act. Fox celebrates creation as a gift and Tattersfield's superb, bright illustrations bring a special quality to each page. This book is worth trying to find online or in used bookstores. (1995)

Islamic Year, The: Surahs, Stories and Celebrations

Noorah Al-Gailani and Chris Smith; *illustrated by Helen Williams*   Family

Explore and celebrate Muslim festivals with this inspiring treasury of stories, surahs, songs, games, recipes, crafts, and art activities. A selection of folk tales illustrates the core values underlying Islamic culture with gentle humor and wisdom. Authors include variations in traditions in different countries, from Turkey and Uzbekistan to West Africa. This is a unique resource for educators and parents who want to share the spiritual wealth of Islam with children. (2002)

Jabulani! Ideas for Making Music

Carole Shephard and Bobbie Stormont; *illustrated by Kate Sheppard*   Family

If you'd like to create music or participate in musical and rhythmic activities, this book and CD may provide all the needed tools. It is packed with musical activities, games, and useful tips for using music with storytelling, drama, and even sports. Teachers, play workers, parents, and players of all ages will find a wealth of inspiration and practical information. (2005)

Jewish Holidays All Year Round: A Family Treasury

Ilene Cooper; *illustrated by Elivia Savadier*   Family

With an explanation of the Jewish calendar in the preface, each chapter explains the history and significance of a different holiday. Cooper includes activities, recipes, and illustrations representing various traditions. Color photographs are from the Jewish Museum in New York City. (2002)

Journey to Gameland: How to Make a Board Game from Your Favorite Children's Book

Ben Buchanan, Carol J. Adams and Susan Allison;
illustrated by Doug Buchanan   4–7

Learn step-by-step how to create obstacles and rewards to make a fun board game using the characters and plot of a favorite story as a jumping off point. Written by an eleven-year-old boy with the help of his family, this book can inspire your child and family to do likewise. (2001)

Celebrations

Keepers of the Animals:
Native American Stories and Wildlife Activities for Children

Michael J. Caduto and Joseph Bruchac   4, 5, 6

A resource for elementary school teaching, one can read or learn the stories, then tell them aloud. The traditional tales are followed by suggested related activities. There is a second volume: *Keepers of the Earth: Native American Stories and Environmental Activities for Children.* Both volumes have introductions by recognized Native American authors. (1988)

Kids Knitting: Projects for Kids of all Ages

Melanie Falick   Family

Beautiful photographs, illustrations and clear instructions make using this book an appealing way for beginners to learn to knit. From finger knitting to making your own needles, puppets and backpacks, these projects are enhanced by cultural information, washing and blocking tips and much more. (2003)

Kinder Dolls: A Waldorf Doll-Making Handbook

Maricristin Sealey   Family

Filled with diagrams, patterns, and illustrations, *Kinder Dolls* show that making dolls can be done easily and with great variety. This manual covers everything from safety to ethnic variations, and even includes tips on where to get the materials to make these beautiful, treasured dolls. Look for *Making Waldorf Dolls* by the same author. (2001)

Kneeling Carabao and Dancing Giants: Celebrating Filipino Festivals

Rena Krasno; *illustrated by Ileana Lee*   Family

Over thousands of years, people from many cultures around the world travelled and settled in the Philippines. Krasno introduces festivals, folktales, the history, geography, customs and how the modern Philippine nation developed. This collection also includes recipes, craft instructions, and games. The illustrations of Ileana Lee, a native Filipino, have a vibrant folk-art quality. (1997)

Let's Sing and Celebrate!
105 Original Songs for Seasons and Festivals: A Waldorf Songbook

Colin Price   Family

This book is the perfect resource for the time-challenged teacher, with songs grouped in easy to find categories, and an appendix packed with relevant information. In this songbook you will find the grade appropriateness of each song suggested. Only the melody is provided for the younger children, and a piano accompaniment is given for older children. (2003)

Lost Angel, The

Elizabeth Goudge   6+

Goudge's collection of short stories for the Christmas season are suitable for children twelve and older and adults. If out of print, look for it in the library, used and online bookstores. The prolific and beloved author won the Carnegie Medal for *The Little White Horse*. (1971)

Lullabies: An Illustrated Songbook

Illustrated by various artists; music arranged by Richard Kapp   Family

This is a beautiful pairing of art and music, with thirty-seven lullabies both traditional and from different cultures. The book contains lyrics and sheet music and will delight new parents as well as grandparents. An audio CD is sold separately as *Lullabies A Songbook Companion*. (1997)

Making Crafts from Your Kids' Art

Valerie Van Arsdale Schrader   Family

Ever wonder what to do with children's artwork besides hanging it on the refrigerator, storing it in drawers, or in boxes in the attic or basement? Whether you're a mother, grandmother, aunt or someone who loves kids, you can use the ideas in this book and your own creativity to transform their art into projects that celebrate their imagination and, at the same time, are functional and fun. (2003)

Making Dolls

Sunnhild Reinckens   Family

Three enchanting hand-made dolls grace the cover of this book and will inspire readers to try making one. The color photographs and simple diagrams show how to make seventeen kinds of dolls. Whether one is making a baby doll, a gnome or a doll for a doll's house, there are clear instructions for forming the head, the soft body and creating hairstyles and facial features. The author believes it is better to make a doll, however simple, than to purchase one in a store. (2003)

Making Fairy Tale Scenes

Sybille Adolphi; *illustrated by Uta Bottcher; photographed by Thomas Kink*   Family

Natural materials such as wool, felt, and cotton are easy to find and can be used to craft fairy tale scenes and familiar characters such as Cinderella, Tom Thumb, Snow White and others. Patterns, instructions, diagrams, and bright color photographs lead both children and adults through the creative process. Look for other delightful craft books by Floris Books. (2009)

Making Fairy-tale Wool Animals

Angelika Wolk-Gerche; translated by Deborah Brandow   Family

What could enhance one's storytelling more than by making little animals and figures for play using fairy-tale wool? This is a high quality carded unspun fiber, in natural colors or plant dyed and purchased as wool roving. The popularity of using this material has spread beyond Waldorf kindergartens. This book gives clear instructions for parents or teachers, advanced or beginner. Children can complete many projects. Bright color photographs will inspire readers' creativity. (2000)

Mary's Little Donkey and the Flight to Egypt

Gunhild Sehlin; translated by Donald MacLean and Hugh Latham; *illustrated by Jan Verheijen*   K–3

This tender story of the stubborn dirty little donkey that bears a pregnant mother to Bethlehem where her baby is born and then on to Egypt may become a favorite to read aloud or alone. The author was a teacher in Sweden and also worked with children in Jerusalem and Amman. (1987)

Miss Mary Mack and Other Children's Street Rhymes

Beverly Collins and Stephanie Colmenson; *illustrated by Alan Tiegreen*   K+

Here is a delightful collection of over 100 traditional rhymes for hand-clapping, ball bouncing and other street activities. "Miss Mary Mack" is itself one of the most recognizable rhymes. An index with first lines will help readers find their favorites. Also includes pen and ink illustrations and a bibliography of additional resources. (1990)

Moon Watchers: Shirin's Ramadan Miracle

Reza Jalali; *illustrated by Anne Sibley O'Brien*   2, 3, 4

The author, originally from Iran but a resident of Maine for more than twenty years, has written a quiet picture story of one Maine family's experience looking for the new moon to begin the celebration of Ramadan. It is a time when Muslims around the world pray, fast, and pay special attention to doing good deeds. Told through the eyes of nine-year-old Shirin, this Persian-American story is a resource for parents, librarians, and teachers. Watercolor illustrations. (2010)

Moonbeams, Dumplings and Dragon Boats

Nina Simonds, Leslie Swartz and the Children's Museum, Boston;
illustrated by Meilo So   Family

Subtitled *A Treasury of Chinese Holiday Tales, Activities and Recipes*, this collection will inspire families to explore the history and customs of five Chinese holidays. Each one includes tasty recipes, family activities, stories and directions for making crafts. (2002)

N. C. Wyeth's Pilgrims

Robert San Souci; *illustrated by N.C. Wyeth*   Family

N. C. Wyeth was one of America's most renowned twentieth-century artists. In 1940 he painted a fourteen-panel mural of the first Thanksgiving for the Metropolitan Life Insurance Company. Many of these murals illustrate San Souci's retelling of the stories of Myles Standish, Squanto, and the Pilgrims. Independent readers can take turns reading aloud while passing the book around so younger listeners can enjoy the gorgeous art. (1991)

Nature Connection, The: An Outdoor Workbook for Kids, Families, and Classrooms

Claire Walker Leslie, *illustrated by author*   3–8

Whether you live in the suburbs, country, or city, families will enjoy using this interactive workbook together. The author/illustrator is a naturalist and guides readers with fun, creative activities to observe, record, and draw what they see, hear, and touch in the outdoors. Rediscover the world outside all twelve months of the year. (2010)

Nature Corner

M. van Leeuwen and J. Moeskops   Family

Children may become more aware of the cycle of the year when they have a nature table at home or school. This book has instructions for making items that can be placed with objects found on nature walks to make a seasonal display. (2008)

Newbery Christmas, A

Selected by Martin H. Greenberg and Charles G. Waugh   4+

This special collection is subtitled *Fourteen Stories of Christmas by Newbery Award-Winning Authors.* These include authors such as Eleanor Estes, E. L. Konigsburg, Madeleine L'Engle, and Katherine Paterson. (1991)

Nicest Gift, The

Leo Politi   3, 4

Carlito lives in a Los Angeles barrio with his parents and his beloved dog, Blanco. The dog gets lost on a trip to the market and Carlito is desolate when Christmas Day arrives and his lost dog still hasn't been found. Leo Politi was a popular, award-winning author and illustrator and the first Californian artist to win a Caldecott Medal. (1973)

Night Before Christmas, The

Clement C. Moore   Family

This read-aloud poem appeals to all and Tasha Tudor's illustrations make her 1975 edition especially appealing for younger listeners. Also known as *A Visit from St. Nicholas,* many other versions exist and some with reproduced illustrations from other noted artists such as Thomas Nast and Jessie Wilcox Smith may be of historic interest for older readers. (1823)

Old Fashioned Thanksgiving, An

Louisa May Alcott   3–6

There are several illustrated adaptations of Alcott's richly detailed story in which seven children in nineteenth-century New England attempt to prepare for the holiday while mother is away caring for grandmother. It can appeal to a wide age group when read aloud. (1882)

Oxford Book of Carols

R. Vaughan Williams, Percy Dearmer and Martin Shaw   Family

This is the most famous and complete of all carol collections with 197 carols. Most are for the Christmas season, but some are for Passiontide, Easter, and other seasons of the year. This popular collection has been periodically revised. (1928)

Peter and Lotta Celebrate Christmas: A Story

Elsa Beskow, *illustrated by author*   1, 2

Peter and Lotta celebrate Christmas in Sweden with their aunts and uncle. They help them bake treats and decorate the house for the holiday, and learn the secret of where the presents come from. Beskow is the most popular children's author/illustrator in Sweden. Her books appeal to beginning readers and pre-readers. (2002)

Pinatas and Smiling Skeletons: Celebrating Mexican Festivals

Zoe Harris and Suzanne Williams; *illustrated by Yolanda G. Woo*   Family

Learn about Mexican traditions and festivals of la Natividad, Three Kings' Day, Carnaval, Corpus Christi, Independence Day, and the Day of the Dead. Bright folkloric illustrations capture the very essence of ancient hieroglyphs and modern retablos or small portraits of Catholic saints painted on wood or metal. Appropriate songs and recipes enhance each celebration. (1998)

Polar Express, The

Chris Van Allsburg, *illustrated by author*   K–6

A magical train arrives on Christmas Eve and takes a boy to the North Pole to receive a special gift from Santa Claus. As magical as the story are Van Allsburg's illustrations. This has become a treasured story for many adults and children. (1985)

★ Caldecott Medal

Celebrations

Pull the Other One! String Games and Stories, Book 1

Michael Taylor   1+

String games are played all over the world, and are often accompanied by songs and stories. This series of tales by a teacher affectionately called the "String Man" is accompanied by clear instructions and explanatory drawings with excellent activities for strengthening finger movement and facile thinking. A rainbow string is included. The author's Book 2 is *Now you See It* (2001)

Puppet Theatre

Maija Baric; *illustrated by Kristiina Louhi*   Family

Many children enjoy seeing or putting on puppet shows. Whether they are finger, hand or peek-a-boo puppets, they can be made from all sorts of materials at home or school. With instructions and illustrations, Baric shows how to transform wooden spoons, pieces of string, holey socks, outgrown clothes and other scrap materials into beautiful, durable and functional theatrical puppets. She also shows you how to create the staging and sound effects for performances. (2007)

Rise Up Singing: The Group Singing Songbook

Peter Blood and Annie Patterson; *illustrated by Kory Loy McWhirter*   Family

"Once upon a time, wasn't singing a part of everyday life?" asks Pete Seeger in the introduction. This comprehensive collection of songs may entice adults and children alike to join in singing. Nearly 1200 songs are from many categories: folk revival favorites; Broadway show tunes; hymns, spirituals, and gospel standards; songs about peace, freedom, labor, and the environment; and sea chanteys. The revised songbook is easier to read and use than ever before. (1988)

Rose Windows and How to Make Them

Helga Meyerbroker   Family

People gaze with wonder at the rose windows in medieval cathedrals and here is just the book to make similar transparencies from colored tissue paper to hang in a window for light to shine through. Using simple materials and following the step-by-step instructions, one can create simple or complex rosettes or scenes built up with layers of paper. These are fun projects for home or school. (1994)

Saint Nicholas

Jakob Streit   K–3

From Nicholas' childhood through his often adventurous adulthood and on into his sainthood, Streit weaves the history and legends of St. Nicholas. The Christmas season is filled with light and love and this story warms the heart and soul. (2003)

Second Waldorf Song Book

Brien Masters   Family

This second collection from Brien Masters emphasizes songs in two, three, and four parts, as well as rounds and canons. The pieces are arranged in groups according to the number and types of voices required. This volume is suitable for both classroom and choral use. (1993)

Sing a Song of Seasons

Mary Thienes-Schunemann; *illustrated by Lura Schwarz Smith*   Family

In this collection, subtitled *Songs from the Seasons of Nature to Sing with Young Children,* readers can learn the music to sing with children all through the year. Follow the simple melodies in the spiral-bound book or learn them using the CD. Soft pencil illustrations accompany the music. The series also includes: *This is the Way we Wash-a-Day, The Christmas Star, Sing a Song with Baby, Sing Through the Day* and ¡Cante, Cante, Elefante! Sing, Sing, Elephant! (1997)

Sing Through the Day: Eighty Songs for Children

Mary S. Swinger   Family

One could sing all day with children. Here are simple and easy songs for getting up, going to bed, playing, dancing, birthdays, holidays, animals, and even about the rain. A marvelous resource for teachers in day care and preschools, not just families. Includes a learning CD with children's voices. (1968)

Sing Through the Seasons: Ninety-Nine Songs for Children

Mary S. Swinger   Family

Even if adults aren't used to singing with children, this easy-to-follow songbook and CD can help one begin. International in scope, some songs are familiar and others are translated from other languages. (1970)

Singing Day, The: Songbook and CD for Singing with Young Children

Cindy Verney; *illustrated by Claude Munoz*   Family

Turn a child's daily routine into a musical journey with songs for getting dressed, going out, food and mealtimes, car journeys, bath time, lullabies, finger and toe games, birthdays, festivals and special occasions. The 2006 companion book is *The Singing Year.* (2003)

Singing Games for Families, Schools & Communities

Anna Rainville; *illustrated by Helen Caswell and Lee Ann Welch*   Family

Song, dance and play are woven together in this special collection. Readers may recognize forms, themes and melodies from many cultures. Use these for enlivening classrooms, backyards, living rooms, seasonal festivals, birthday parties, picnics, block parties, faculty meetings, teacher workshops, and conferences. Includes a CD. (2006)

Snowmen: Snow Creatures, Crafts, and Other Winter Projects

Leslie Jonath and Peter Cole; *photographed by Frankie Frankeny*   Family

No need to hide inside on a snowy day. Take this book outdoors and have fun. From the simple to the spectacular to the stupendously silly, *Snowmen* gives you thirty ideas for making snowmen, snow creatures, and a vast array of characters and objects. Or stay inside and do indoor snow-themed activities. The spectacular color photographs add excitement and inspire the imagination. (1999)

Sock Doll Workshop: 30 Delightful Dolls to Create and Cherish

Cindy Crandall-Frazier   Family

For anyone who makes all sorts of creatures using those single socks lost in the laundry will delight in this fun resource. Using simple tools and materials, readers will be inspired to create a special doll for someone to love. Crandall-Frazier, a homeschooling mother and Waldorf kindergarten teacher, is also the author of *Single Crochet for Beginners,* a perfect resource for the Waldorf third-grade handwork curriculum. (1995)

Songs for Earthlings: A Green Spirituality Songbook

Julie Forest Middleton   Family

This is a songbook of sacred multi-denominational songs, chants and rounds celebrating Earth and inhabitants. Includes songwriters from America and around the world and from many spiritual traditions with words and easy music. Many have guitar chords and arrangements. This collection is marvelous for community singing. (1998)

Sticks and Stones and Ice Cream Cones: The Craft Book for Children

Phyllis Fiarotta   Family

This title and its companion *Snips and Snails and Walnut Whales: Nature Crafts for Children* have been favorite books of teachers and parents for years. Recipes are easy to follow and there is a wide variety of craft projects with simple instructions. It may not be available as other titles, but may be found online. (1973)

Sunflower Houses

Sharon Lovejoy, *illustrated by author*   Family

With the subtitle, *Inspiration from the Garden – A Book for Children and Their Grown-Ups*, this will be a family treasure for activities in the garden as well as reading in the home. Interacting with nature is so important for children and this resource inspires as well as informs. See the author's other titles: *Roots, Shoots, Buckets & Boots* and *Toad Cottages and Shooting Stars* (2001)

Time to Keep, A

Tasha Tudor, *illustrated by author*   Family

Subtitled *The Tasha Tudor Book of Holidays*, Tudor draws on her childhood in New England for this charming picture book. Her year of holiday traditions and the special markings of the changing seasons will become a family treasure. (1977)

Toymaking with Children

Freya Jaffke   Family

This is an excellent handbook for parents of young children, with clear instructions for making a variety of wooden and soft toys. A revised and enlarged edition includes colored photographs and new sections: the meaning of play, how certain toys stimulate children, and how to select the appropriate toys for individual children. (1984)

Celebrations

Treasury of Children's Songs: Forty Favorites to Sing and Play

Dan Fox   Family

This popular songbook is an updated version of *Go In and Out the Window*, first published in 1987. Forty classic childhood songs are drawn from popular traditions around the world, many sung for generations. Illustrated with treasures from the Metropolitan Museum of Art and with commentary on the art and music, this collection also includes simple arrangements for accompaniment. (2003)

Under the Sky:
Playing, Working, and Enjoying Adventures in the Open Air

Sally Schweizer   Family

Whether a child lives in the city or country, the importance of playing outdoors cannot be overstated, especially in light of the rise of children's obesity. The author presents a world of possibilities for children in urban or rural areas. Subtitled *A Handbook for Parents, Carers, and Teachers*, this guide is for anyone wishing to cultivate children's play and activities for all seasons. (2009)

Waldorf Book of Breads, The

Collected by Marsha Post; *illustrated by Jo Valens*   Family

One of the many activities children like to do is help with cooking and especially making bread. Baking bread is a weekly activity in a Waldorf kindergarten. Not only is this activity a rich sensory experience, but children and adults get to taste the delicious and nutritious results of their efforts. Spiral binding makes this book easy to use. Look for others in the series, *The Waldorf Kindergarten Snack Book* and *The Waldorf School Book of Soups*. All have soft whimsical illustrations. (2009)

Waldorf Song Book, The

Brien Masters   2–5

This collection consists of over 100 songs arranged by age and time of year. Some rounds and multiple-part songs are familiar and others are less known and only to be discovered. Look for the author's *Second Waldorf Song Book*. (1988)

Whittle Your Ears: Poems, Songs, and Plays for Children

Barbara Dawson Betteridge   3–6

A supporter of Waldorf Education wrote this collection of poems, songs and plays over a period of fifty years. With a fresh approach to sound and language, Betteridge's book appeals to parents and their children along with teachers. (2007)

Winter Solstice, The

Ellen Jackson; *illustrated by Jan Davey Ellis*   3–4

In this picture book, learn about the scientific reason for the shortest day of the year as well as how people of many cultures throughout history have responded to the ever-growing darkness of winter. Companion volumes include *The Summer Solstice, The Autumn Equinox* and *The Spring Equinox*. (1994)

Winter Solstice, The: The Sacred Traditions of Christmas

John and Caitlin Matthews   Family

This family resource gives new meaning to the whole winter season, not just to Christmas. Folklore expert John Matthews traces the history behind many of the sacred traditions of the holiday season and provides refreshing and practical suggestions for celebrating the Winter Solstice as a joyous, life-affirming, spiritual festival. Includes illustrations and photographs. (1998)

Wonder of Lullabies, The: Singing with Children Series

Mary Thienes-Schunemann; *illustrated by Lura Schwartz-Smith*   Family

Here are fifteen beautiful and timeless lullabies from around the world, including: *All Night All Day, Hush Little Baby, Brahms' Lullaby, Golden Slumbers, and Bayushki Bayu.* These easy-to-learn songs are appropriate for all ages of children and adults. The book includes a CD. (2000)

Celebrations

Appendix

Acknowledgements

I would like to thank my teachers and mentors who made my career as a teacher possible. My insights into child development as well as my personal tastes and critical judgment which shape this book are profoundly influenced by my understanding of Rudolf Steiner's view of the developing human being which I first encountered in 1984 at the Waldorf School of the Peninsula in Los Alto, CA. It is of course only my own understanding for which no one but me can be responsible.

After I became a teacher, I was inspired to continue studying and teaching for twenty years by the example and contagious passion of individuals most of whom may not even be aware of the powerful influence they had. My life has been so enriched by my experiences as a teacher and student of Steiner's work that the debt of appreciation can only be acknowledged, never repaid.

A list of names to thank would be too long, but would include those who taught or lectured at Rudolf Steiner College, the Artemis School of Speech and Drama in East Grinstead, England, and my dear colleagues at Waldorf School of the Peninsula. The young student teachers that listened and learned with such enthusiasm re-inspired me.

I am especially indebted to the parents in my classes, study groups or workshops whose urgent questions and fresh perspectives reshaped my views and forced me to clarify them. And of course, my students—some of whom are mature adults with families—cannot possibly realize how much I owe them. It would be so satisfying to think that this book might find its way into their hands and help them as young parents to enrich their children's lives. I would sign each such book, "with all my love and gratitude, Mrs. Latimer."

I do want to acknowledge my debt to Karen Rivers whose role in the original edition was central. In addition, Pam Fenner and I are truly grateful to the teachers, librarians, school administrators, reading specialists, parents and even young students who sent in their suggestions and reading lists since the last revision. These were faithfully collected and delivered to me in a large box!

While we are responsible for the final selections, we are bound to acknowledge that this booklist is a reflection of the collective experience of many teachers, not just our own.

—K. L.

Appendix

A serendipitous encounter over lunch at a teachers' conference in California led to my meeting Karen Latimer. Within a short time I realized she was just the person to begin a complete revision of my lower school reading list. Karen was retiring from a career in elementary school teaching, loved children's literature and had experience in book publishing. It was a project she could manage in between temporary teaching assignments, consulting and tutoring. Some of the most valuable experience came through her literacy work for the Redwood City Public Library.

Though on opposite coastlines, we have benefitted enormously from the advances in technology for communication and particularly for research. Karen has been enthusiastic about the project and so patient even as the timeline stretched beyond our expected date of completion. I look forward to Karen's sharing her enthusiasm, knowledge of children's literature, and her favorite titles with others when the finished books arrive.

One of the most difficult tasks was reviewing the booklist in its various stages of selection and organization to make sure it met the needs of teachers, not just parents and librarians. We are grateful to the support of many professional colleagues and friends. Sabrina Babcock, Stephen Bloomquist, Meg Gorman, Arthur Pittis and Lyn Thurrell didn't hesitate when asked for commentary and suggestions. Each made time during their respective busy schedules teaching or during vacations, conferences and spare weekends. As deadlines neared, it was Meg who helped brainstorm and finally discern the title much as she did for our high school reading list. Bless you!

Christine Davidson, Christine Hunt and April Davis handled copyediting during different stages of development. Mary Echlin and Anne Riegel edited the early introductions with sensitivity and expertise. Colin Price kindly gave permission to use material from "Five Frequently Asked Questions" originally printed in *Renewal Magazine*, Spring/Summer, 2003. Patrice Maynard, former class teacher and presently Outreach Director for the Association of Waldorf Schools of North America (AWSNA) offered valuable suggestions and provided current information about Waldorf/Steiner Education. We are grateful to Zahava Fisch for her research skills and her commitment to this project.

With thanks to all involved in this book, we hope these selections will inspire others to discover and share a lifetime of reading with the next generation.

—P. J. F.

Waldorf/Steiner Education®

Our highest endeavor must be to develop free human beings, who are able of themselves to impart purpose and direction to their lives. The need for imagination, a sense of truth, and a feeling of responsibility—these three forces are the very nerve of education.

—Rudolf Steiner

The first Waldorf/Steiner school was founded in 1919 for the children of the employees of the Waldorf-Astoria cigarette factory in Stuttgart, Germany by Austrian philosopher and teacher, Rudolf Steiner. Other schools soon opened throughout Europe. In 1928 a group of Americans opened the first Waldorf/Steiner school in the United States in New York City,

Waldorf Education has grown from its humble beginnings in North America to include more than 160 independent schools across the continent, 250 early childhood centers, seventeen teacher training institutes, one school entirely adapted for children with special needs, one school adopted by Native Americans, and eight schools with educational programs designed in partnership with farms practicing organic or biodynamic agriculture. This independent school movement has grown to have a huge reach and influence across the continent and remains as exciting and challenging as the day it started.

Waldorf Education is based on a profound understanding of human development that addresses the needs of the growing child. Waldorf teachers strive to transform education into an art that educates the whole child—the heart and the hands, as well as the head.

Waldorf Education approaches all aspects of schooling in a unique and comprehensive way. The curriculum is designed to meet the various stages of child development. Waldorf teachers are dedicated to creating a genuine inner enthusiasm for learning that is essential for educational success.

Preschool and Kindergarten children learn primarily through imitation and imagination. The goal of the kindergarten is to develop a sense of wonder in the young child and reverence for all living things. This creates an eagerness for the academics that follow in the grades. Preschool and Kindergarten activities include:
• Storytelling, puppetry, creative play
• Singing, eurythmy (movement)
• Games and finger plays

Appendix

- Painting, drawing and beeswax modeling
- Baking and cooking, nature walks
- Foreign language and circle time for festival and seasonal celebrations

Elementary and middle-school children learn through the guidance of a class teacher who stays with the class ideally for eight years. The curriculum includes:

- English based on world literature, myths, and legends
- History that is chronological and inclusive of the world's great civilizations
- Science that surveys geography, astronomy, meteorology, physical and life sciences
- Mathematics that develops competence in arithmetic, algebra, and geometry
- Foreign languages; physical education; gardening
- Arts including music, painting, sculpture, drama, eurythmy, sketching
- Handwork such as knitting, weaving, and woodworking

The Waldorf high school is dedicated to helping students develop their full potential as scholars, artists, athletes, and community members. The course of study includes:

- A humanities curriculum that integrates history, literature, and knowledge of world cultures
- A science curriculum that includes physics, biology, chemistry, geology, and a four-year college preparatory mathematics program
- An arts and crafts program that includes calligraphy, drawing, painting, sculpture, pottery, weaving, block printing and bookbinding
- A performing arts program offering orchestra, choir, eurythmy and drama
- A foreign language program
- A physical education program

In recent years, there are also public schools, charter schools, and home-based schools using methods inspired by Waldorf Education.

While each Waldorf or Steiner school is autonomous, there are features in the curriculum that are common to most schools.

Main Lesson

History, language arts, science, and mathematics are taught in Main Lesson Blocks of three to four weeks during the daily morning main lesson hours. During this uninterrupted two-hour period, the class teacher, who ideally remains with the class from grade one through grade eight, presents one subject. A concentrated in-depth focus is developed using a wide variety of activities integrating art, music, movement, and storytelling into each curriculum subject.

The rest of the day is devoted to subjects that need constant practice and review, such as mathematics or reading, along with a rich array of disciplines including foreign languages, instrumental and choral music, handwork, woodworking, eurythmy, and physical education which are usually taught by teachers specializing in these areas.

Main Lesson Books

No textbooks are used. Out of the rich experience the teacher has offered, students create beautiful illustrated books detailing the concepts, summarizing the stories, and recording experiments from their main lesson blocks. At the end of the school year, every student has a unique and personal record of the year to take home.

GRADES 1–8

Primary Grades 1–3
Pictorial introduction to the alphabet
Writing, reading, spelling, poetry, and drama
Language arts taught through folk and fairytales, fables, legends,
   and Old Testament stories
Nature Stories, house building, and gardening
Numbers, Basic mathematical processes of addition, subtraction,
   multiplication, and division

Middle Grades 4–6
Norse mythology, history and stories of ancient civilizations
Local and world geography, animal kingdom, plant kingdom,
   and elementary physics
Writing, reading, spelling, grammar, poetry, and drama

Review of the four mathematical processes
Fractions, percentage, and geometry

Upper Grades 7–8
Medieval history, the Renaissance, world exploration, American history,
   and biography
Mathematics, geography, basic physics, chemistry, astronomy, and physiology
Creative writing, reading, spelling, grammar, poetry, and drama

Special subjects also taught are:
Handwork: knitting, crochet, sewing, cross-stitch, basic weaving,
   toy-making, and woodworking
Music: singing, pentatonic flute, recorder, string instruments, wind, brass,
   and percussion instruments
Foreign languages (varies by school): Spanish, French, Japanese, German
   or others
Art: watercolor painting, form drawing, beeswax and clay modeling,
   perspective drawing
Movement: eurythmy, gymnastics, group games

* Waldorf® is a registered mark of the Association of Waldorf Schools of North America.

Resources: Waldorf/Steiner Education

As of early 2012 there were more than 1000 independent Waldorf/Steiner schools, 2000 kindergartens and 629 institutions for special education located in sixty countries throughout the world. Waldorf Education is truly global—not only in its scope, but also in its approach. Wherever schools are found, the Waldorf curriculum cultivates within its students a deep appreciation for cultural traditions from around the world while all the while being deeply rooted in its local culture and context.

Participants in Waldorf Education® are proud of the influence they have had on many aspects of educational and parenting culture. There are many resources available on the internet for additional exploration.

North America
Association of Waldorf Schools of North America (AWSNA)
awsna@awsna.org
http://www.awsna.org/

Why Waldorf Works
http://www.whywaldorfworks.org/

Waldorf Education Frequently Asked Questions
http://www.whywaldorfworks.org/02_W_Education/faq_about.asp

Member School List
http://www.members.awsna.org/Public/SchoolListPage.aspx

United States Waldorf Teacher Training Links
http://www.whywaldorfworks.org/08_TeacherPrep/training_centers.asp

Online Waldorf Library (OWL)
http://www.waldorflibrary.org/

Canada Waldorf/Steiner Schools
The Waldorf School Association of Ontario (WSAO)
http://www.waldorf.ca/

Waldorf Early Childhood Association of North America (WECAN)
http://www.waldorfearlychildhood.org/

Other International Associations
Australia Waldorf/Steiner Schools
http://www.steiner-australia.org/

European Council of Steiner/Waldorf Education (ECSWE)
http://www.ecswe.org/

International Associations and Waldorf Schools by Country
http://www.waldorfschule.info/en/waldorfschule-bund/adresses/>international-associations-and-waldorf-schools/index.html

International Association of Steiner/Waldorf Early Childhood Education (IASWECE)
http://www.iaswece.org/index.aspx

UK Waldorf/Steiner Schools
Steiner Waldorf Schools Fellowship Ltd. (SWSF)
http://www.steinerwaldorf.org/index.html

Other Resources
Alliance for Childhood
http://www.allianceforchildhood.org/

Bob and Nancy's Site
http://www.bobnancy.com

Baldwin Project, The
http://www.mainlesson.com

Christopherus Homeschool Resources
christopherushomeschool.org

Friends of Waldorf Education
http://www.freunde-waldorf.de/en

Informed Family Life
http://informedfamiy life.org

Lifeways
http://www.lifewaysnorthamerica.org

Millennial Child
http://www.MillenialChild.com

Research Institute for Waldorf Education (RIWE)
http://www.waldorflibrary.org/ResearchBulletin.htm

RSF Social Finance
http://www.rsfsocialfinance.org

Studies on Waldorf Education
http://www.waldorfanswers.org/Studies.htm

The Waldorf Foundation
http://www.waldorfschule.info/en/waldorfschule-bund/waldorf-foundation/index.html

Waldorf Teachers Job Listing Site
http://www.waldorfteachers.com

Publishers

Adonis Press
http://www.adonicpress.org

AWSNA Publications/Books&More
http://www.awsna.org/catalog
publications@awsna.org

Floris Books
http://www.florisbooks.co.uk

Gilead Press
http://www.gileadpress.net

Hawthorn Press
http://www.hawthornpress.com

Immortal Books
http://www.immortalbooks.com.au

Lemontree Press
http://www.lmntreepress.com

Lightly Press
http://www.tiptoes-lightly.net

Living Arts Books
http://www.livingartsbooks.com

Mercury Press
http://www.mercurypress.org

Michaelmas Press
http://www.michaelmaspress.com

Rudolf Steiner College Press
http://www.steinercollege.edu/
RSC-press

Songbird Press
http://www.songbirdpress.biz

SteinerBooks
http://www.steinerbooks.com

SWSF Publications
http://www.steinerwaldorf.org/
livingeducation.html

WECAN Publications
http://www.waldorfearlychildhood.org

Whole Spirit Press
http://www.wholespiritpress.com

Wynestones Press
http://www.wynstonespress.com

There's More to Reading than Meets the Eye

By Barbara Sokolov

Everyone who comes in contact with Waldorf education is sure to notice how beautiful it is, from the enchanting natural toys and seasonal themes in the kindergarten rooms, to the incredible chalkboard drawings in each classroom. Visitors and prospective parents enjoy the amazing array of children's artistic creations -- the paintings and drawings, knitted dolls and animals, woven baskets, beeswax figures, and wood carvings, just to name a few. The music that the children play, their singing, and the wonderful plays each class performs are truly impressive. They admire the main lesson books written and illustrated by the students, books that artistically reflect the rich curriculum of a Waldorf school. And of course they can't help but notice the happy faces of the children.

But invariably the question arises of how and when children are taught to read in a Waldorf School. The growing anxiety in our society over declining reading skills is so pervasive that suddenly, all the wonders and beauty of a Waldorf education pale in the shadow of the reading issue. "But Waldorf schools take a laid back approach to reading," people say. "Waldorf students are not taught to read in first grade like public school students."

As a mother of four Waldorf students, I have often heard such remarks, and each time a cry of protest wells up inside of me. "Take a deeper look," I want to shout. There's more to reading than you may think at first glance.

People generally think of reading as the ability to recognize the configuration of letters on a page and to pronounce the words and sentences represented there. This is the mechanical outer activity of reading that is easy to recognize. So, when people talk about teaching children to read, they mean teaching them to decode the symbols that stand for sounds and words.

I have taught for a number of years in public and parochial schools that use this standard approach. In kindergarten, children as young as four years and eight months, are required to memorize the alphabet, a set of abstract symbols, and to learn the sounds that go with them. This process, called reading readiness, is dry and abstract, foreign to the very nature of small children.

In the primary grades, children continue to work on the outer mechanical aspect of reading. Students spend long periods of time reading simplistic texts that correspond to the level of their decoding abilities. Readers and textbooks contain stories and information written with restricted vocabularies and simple sentence structure. There is little to ignite young imaginations, toevoke wonder, or to stimulate appreciation for the beauty and complexity of language.

By the time such students reached my fifth and sixth grade classroom, they were all capable of decoding the words on a page, with varying degrees of fluidity. Some were good readers, but for many of my students, the words and sentences did not come together into a coherent whole. They had difficulty understanding or remembering what they read. On the surface, these children appeared to be reading, but with such limited comprehension, can it really be called reading?

Clearly, there is more to reading than meets the eye! Besides the superficial process of decoding words on a page, there is a corresponding inner activity that must be cultivated for true reading to occur. Waldorf teachers call it "living into the story." When a child is living into a story, she forms imaginative inner pictures in response to the words. Having the ability to form mental images, to understand, gives meaning to the process of reading. Without this ability, a child may well be able to decode the words on a page, but he will remain functionally illiterate.

Of course non-Waldorf teachers recognize the importance of the inner activity of reading too. They refer to it as reading comprehension skills. In the middle and upper grades of elementary school, tremendous effort is spent trying to expand students' vocabularies and to somehow work on comprehension. This is an arduous task, largely because reading is being taught in a way that is out of sync with children's natural capacities. The teacher in the upper grades must address reading comprehension problems and also deal with the tremendous antipathy children with difficulties feel towards reading.

It is very difficult to teach fifth or sixth graders, who have trouble with reading comprehension, how to create mental pictures. This inner capacity seems to have never properly developed in many. In contrast, kindergarten and primary grade children, left unhindered, are naturally busy creating imaginative inner pictures. They love listening to stories and actually live in the visual realm of imagination. How tragic that, in most schools, kindergarten and primary grade students are diverted from developing and strengthening this inner capacity so essential to true reading, in favor of learning dry abstract symbols and decoding skills.

The same thing can be said for vocabulary enrichment. Everyone knows how effortlessly young children develop a sense for language and how quickly and unconsciously their vocabularies grow. They hear new words in stories and conversations and somehow have a sense for their meaning. They may not be able give dictionary definitions, but somehow new words fit into the images that flow through a child's mind when she hears stories.

How unfortunate it is that in the early grades most children are not exposed to rich complex language, simply because such language would not be compatible with their limited decoding skills. Just at the time when their minds are most open to language acquisition they are working with artificially limited vocabularies in school! Of course, vocabulary building is an ongoing process throughout the school years and beyond. But it is much easier for older children to learn new vocabulary if they already have a well-developed sense of language, and a large pool of words and mental images to build upon.

It is apparent that the growing illiteracy problem in this country is not caused by the lack of technical decoding skills. For most of the children with reading deficiencies, it is a crisis in comprehension, a crisis largely brought about by the early introduction of abstract decoding skills and by ignoring the powerful tools of imagination and artistic activity that are the natural avenues of learning for young school children. Ironically, the only cure put forward by the educational establishment is to work harder and earlier on decoding skills, which only exasperates the problem further.

The conventional method of teaching reading must be turned inside out in order to take advantage of children's naturally developing capacities for learning. And this is precisely what happens in Waldorf Schools. On the very first day of kindergarten, children in a Waldorf school begin learning to read. True, it is not the technical, dry, outer aspect of reading that they are asked to work on. Instead they are engaged with the far more important inner aspect of reading.

Working with a real knowledge of the developing child, Waldorf teachers begin teaching reading by cultivating children's sense of language and their inner capacities to form mental images. Vivid verbal pictures and the use of rich language are constantly employed in the classroom. Difficult vocabulary and complex sentence structure are not held back in the telling of tales. Children sing and recite a vast treasury of songs and poems that many learn by heart. Children live into the world of imaginative inner pictures, totally unaware that they are developing the most important capacities needed for reading comprehension, for reading with understanding. They learn naturally and joyfully.

Imaginative stories, songs and poetry do not end in kindergarten. Rudolf Steiner points out that children between the age of about seven to fourteen have, above all, the gift of fantasy. So it only makes sense that children learn best if the curriculum is brought in such a way that it captivates their imaginations. In his book, Kingdom of Childhood, Steiner says, "We should avoid a direct approach to the conventional letters of the alphabet which are used in the writing and printing of civilized man. Rather should we lead the child in a vivid and imaginative way, through the various stages which man himself has passed through in the history of civilization."

My own children experienced the joy of learning the letters of the alphabet through imaginative stories and through the painting or drawing that accompanied each one. The letter "K", for instance, may be introduced by telling a fanciful story about a king. Then the teacher may draw a picture of the king standing in a pose that looks similar to the letter "K." This process hearkens back to the picture writing of early man, and gives our modern symbols real and living qualities to which children can relate. Although it took the entire year of first grade to present the alphabet in this way, my children were never bored. They were living into their fantasy, living with a wellspring of imaginative pictures. They were, in fact learning reading comprehension, long before they learned decoding. Amazingly, Waldorf children learn the hard part first without even knowing it! They live into the stories, they create inner pictures, and they understand the words. Then comes the easy part, learning to decode letters that are no longer so abstract and foreign, and to read the printed word

So, the first book that my daughter, Anna, read when she was "finally taught to read" was not a dull primer, but beautiful prose by E. B. White, *Charlotte's Web*. True, she learned to decode later than many of her public school counterparts, but she learned to read fluently, with understanding and enjoyment, much sooner than most. Take a look at the sophisticated novels and poetry that upper grade Waldorf students are reading. Take in an eighth grade production of Shakespeare, and you will see the wisdom of the Waldorf approach to reading

Working with a true knowledge of the human being, a true understanding of the stages of child development, the Waldorf teacher is able to educate children in ways that enable them to blossom forth with joy. As Rudolf Steiner says, "It is indeed so that a true knowledge of man loosens and releases the inner life of soul and brings a smile to the face.

Formerly a public and parochial school teacher, Sokolov was a class teacher at the San Francisco Waldorf School, San Francisco, CA http://www.sfwaldorf.org/

1. Rudolf Steiner, *The Kingdom of Childhood. Introductory Talks on Waldorf Education*
   Anthroposophic Press, 1995, p. 23
2 lbid, p. 22
From *Renewal: Spring Summer 2000*, Volume 9 Number 1

Fairy Tales and Stories
for Different Ages

By Joan Almon

When selecting fairy tales for young children, it is helpful to know which tales tend to be appropriate for different ages. These are to be taken as light indications, not hard and fast rules. Reading a few tales from each category gives a picture of the progression of difficulty of the tales. One can then choose according to the needs and maturity of the child(ren) involved. The source of an individual story may be indicated beside each name.

These are the very simplest tales and sequential tales, suitable for three and young four-year-olds:

Sweet Porridge *(Grimm #103)*
Silverhair (Goldilocks) and the Three Bears *(Spindrift)*
Little Louse and Little Flea *(Spindrift)*
The Giant Turnip *(Autumn Book)*
The Mitten
The Gingerbread Man
The Johnny Cake *(English Fairy Tales)*
The Hungry Cat *(A Lifetime of Joy)*
The Little House *(Spindrift)*
The Old Woman and Her Pig *(English Fairy Tales)*
The Cat and the Mouse *(English Fairy Tales)*
The Little Boy Who Wanted to be Carried Along *(A Lifetime of Joy)*
When the Root Children Wake Up
Little Red Hen
The City Mouse and the Country Mouse

These simple tales are slightly more complex than those listed above. The mood is usually cheerful and without too much sorrow and struggle. Quite good for four- and young five-year-olds:
The Three Billy Goats Gruff *(Spindrift)*
The Three Little Pigs
The Wolf and the Seven Little Kids *(Grimm #5)*

The Pancake Mill *(Let Us Form a Ring)*
Mashenka and the Bear *(Spindrift)*
The Elves *(Grimm #39)*
Star Money *(Grimm #153)*
Huggin and the Turnip *(The Seven Year Old Wonder Book)*

In the next category, many of the tales are associated with the term "fairy tale." There is more challenge and detail than in the above list, obstacles are encountered but they do not weigh too heavily on the soul of the child. These are good for five- and young six- year-olds:

The Frog Prince *(Grimm #1)*
Mother Holle *(Grimm #24)*
Little Red Cap *(Grimm #26)*
The Bremen Town Musicians *(Grimm #27)*
The Golden Goose *(Grimm #64)*
The Spindle, The Shuttle and the Needle *(Grimm #188)*
The Hut in the Forest *(Grimm #169)*
The Queen Bee *(Grimm #62)*
The Snow Maiden *(A Lifetime of Joy)*
The Seven Ravens *(Grimm #25)*
Snow White and Rose Red *(Grimm #161)*
Little Briar Rose *(Grimm #50)*
The Princess in the Flaming Castle *(Let Us Form a Ring)*
Twiggy *(Let Us Form a Ring)*
The Donkey *(Grimm #144)*
Lazy Jack *(English Fairy Tales)*
Tom-Tit-Tot *(English Fairy Tales)*
Rumpelstiltskin *(Grimm #55)*

The last category are those tales which are much loved by children but in most cases are better told in the first grade rather than in the kindergarten or early childhood classes. The challenges are more difficult in them and the force of evil more strongly described. Some kindergarten teachers may tell one or two of these tales at the end of the year if they have a number of children turning seven:

Little Snow White *(Grimm #53)*
Jorinda and Joringel *(Grimm #69)*
Hansel and Gretel *(Grimm #15)*

Cinderella *(Grimm #21)*
Rapunzel (Grimm #12)

Fairy Tale Resources

Complete Grimm's Fairy Tales, The
Hunt, Margaret and James Stern, editors, with introduction by Padraic Colum
and commentary by Joseph Campbell

English Fairy Tales
Joseph Jacobs, editor

Seven Year Old Wonder Book, The
Wyatt, Isabel

Spindrift and *Autumn* books
Available through Rudolf Steiner College Bookstore
http://www.steinercollege.edu/store/

The following are available through the store of the Waldorf Early Childhood
Education of North America: *http://store.waldorfearlychildhood.org/*

A Lifetime of Joy (formerly *Plays for Puppets*)
Zahlingen, Bronja

Let Us Form a Ring
Foster, Nancy

Interpretations of Fairy Tales

Once Upon a Fairy Tale
Glas, Norbert
Two volumes. Fascinating look at the "real meaning" of fairy tales.

The Wisdom of Fairy Tales
Meyer, Rudolf
The meaning of fairy tales and how they can have a positive influence on the
developing child.

Appendix

The Poetry and Meaning of Fairy Tales
Steiner, Rudolf
Contains two lectures given in 1908 and 1913 in Berlin

The Interpretations of Fairy Tales
Wilkinson, Roy
Summaries and commentaries of fairy tales and their effects on the healthy soul life.

Almon is the former Chair of the Waldorf Early Childhood Association and is the current Coordinator of the U. S. branch of Alliance for Childhood. http://www.allianceforchildhood.org/

Index of Titles

Roman type indicates books that have annotations or are listed.
Italic type indicates books that are referred to within annotations.

Appendix

B

Appendix

Appendix

M

Appendix

Index of Authors

Appendix

Appendix

Index of Illustrators

Appendix

Appendix

Index of Series/Sequels

U

V

W

Index of Anthologies/Collections

Appendix

Index of Waldorf Blocks

The following are titles suggested for common Waldorf Main Lesson Blocks. This is not a definitive list as each teacher chooses resources for his or her set of students. See Waldorf/Steiner Education for additional information.

United States History

Index of Subjects

This list of familiar and special subjects or topics may help the reader locate books of a particular interest. While it covers a wide range of categories, it is not meant to be a definitive list, only suggestions. Annotations for many of these books include additional titles that may apply to the same subject.

We have also included books whose setting may be in countries or cultures outside of the United States. They are listed by country as well as by continent. Likewise, we've included titles in four geographical regions within the United States.

Adventure

Across the Wide Dark Sea: The Mayflower Journey, 25
Adam of the Road, 95
Adventures of Rama: The Story of the Great Hindu Epic Ramayana, 179
Adventures of Tom Sawyer, The, 95
Adventures with the Giants, 179
Around the World in Eighty Days, 97
Banner in the Sky, 97
Bed-Knob and Broomstick, 55
Black Arrow: A Tale of the Two Roses, 98
Black Stallion, The, 57
Captain Cook Explores the South Seas, 152
Captains Courageous, 102
Charles Lindbergh, 153
Children's Homer, The, 180
Chitty Chitty Bang Bang: The Magical Car, 59
Of Courage Undaunted: Across the Continent with Lewis and Clark, 127
Dark Frigate, The, 104
Downriver, 106
Down the Mississippi, 61
Dragonsblood: An Environmental Fairy Tale, 62
Far North, 108

Geron and Virtus: A Fateful Encounter of Two Youths: A German and a Roman, 109
Golden Fleece, The: And the Heroes Who Lived Before Achilles, 183
Gone-away Lake, 66
Half Magic, 67
Hitty: Her First Hundred Years, 68
Hobbit or There and Back Again, The, 114
Holes, 114
Journey to the Center of the Earth, 117
Keep the Wagons Moving, 71
Kidnapped, 118, 139
Kim, 118
King Solomon's Mines, 119
Leonardo Da Vinci: First Impressions (McLanathan), 162
Lost World, The, 121
Magic Maize, 74
Moon in the Cloud, The (Trilogy), 76
Morning Star, 124
My Side of the Mountain, 125
Mysterious Island, 125
North to Freedom, 127
Phantom Tollbooth, The, 38
Pigeon Post, The, 39
Pippi Longstocking, 39

Africa/African Life and Culture

African-American Life and Culture
See United States: African-American
Life and Culture

Alphabet

Ancient Civilizations
See Egypt, Greece, India, Rome

Animals

Appendix

Appendix

Explorers/Exploration

Fables

Appendix

Festivals/Celebrations

France/French Life and Culture

Friendship

Games

Gardening

Appendix

Holidays
See also Festivals/Celebrations

Christmas

Appendix

Appendix

Mexico/Mexican Life and Culture

Music

Poland/Polish Life and Culture

Portugal/Portuguese Life and Culture

Appendix

Appendix

Appendix

About the Editors

Karen Latimer

Karen is a second generation Californian and received her B.A. in English from San Francisco State College, Waldorf Teacher Education from Rudolf Steiner College, and Child Development Education in California's Junior College System. Her first career out of college was in textbook publishing. She went to work for Harper & Row's Canfield Press Division in San Francisco, then moved to New York to work at Alfred A. Knopf followed by Harper's College Press.

Now married and with a young daughter, Karen moved back to California. Her family grew with the birth of a son and she enjoyed an active role in her children's parent cooperative nursery school. An interest in early childhood education developed through parenting classes through the school. Her children led her to Waldorf Education and a second career as a teacher. She helped found the Waldorf School of the Peninsula, now in Los Altos, CA and taught there from 1984 until 2003. Not long after her retirement, she began to substitute teach, mentor and consult in Waldorf Education. She taught evening classes at the Bay Area Waldorf Teacher Training Extension Programs in San Francisco and Los Altos. Between assignments, she began work on this book project.

A routine visit to the local library in 2004 led to a position as a literacy worker for Project READ, one of the most recognized literacy programs in the country. Project READ operates out of the Redwood City Public Library, which received the coveted "five star rating" of the new public library national rating system instituted by *School Library Journal*. She worked to introduce more children to the joys of literature and helped teach literacy skills to children and adolescents with arts, crafts, songs, and puppet shows.

Library budget cuts gave Karen an opportunity to retire in earnest, but remain a volunteer tutor. She developed new interests: gardening, travel, and choral singing and, to her abiding pleasure, reading everything from mysteries and historical fiction to the latest nonfiction. A new granddaughter arrived as this book went into production and Karen looks forward to introducing the next generation to the joy of *Make Way for Ducklings*.

Appendix

Pamela Johnson Fenner

Pam grew up in a large family in a small New England manufacturing town near the seacoast. The first book she learned "by heart" as a child was Robert McCloskey's *Make Way for Ducklings* and it continues to be one of her favorites. After receiving a B.S. in Biology from Chatham College, Pittsburgh, PA, she received a Master of Arts in Teaching Science (MAT) from Harvard University, Cambridge, MA. She taught high school biology in Brookline, MA and general science in a Lexington, MA middle school.

During twenty-one years in northern California, she and her husband were parents of three daughters. Pam worked as a childbirth educator, marketing assistant for an arts organization, administrative assistant in a software company, and a teaching assistant for her local public school district's Early Childhood Education (ECE) program. One of her most rewarding experiences was working with a reading specialist and leading small groups in remedial work. For three years she served as a member of the Curriculum Advisory Group for the Board of Trustees of the Dixie School District in Terra Linda, CA.

Pam graduated from the Holistic Childbirth Institute and later completed her Waldorf Teacher Education at Rudolf Steiner College. She launched her publishing company, Michaelmas Press and published *Waldorf Student Reading List* and the school's parent handbook, later to become *Waldorf Education: A Family Guide.* She worked for two Waldorf schools in community development and admissions.

Returning to her hometown in 1995, she published five titles including a high school reading list, *Books for the Journey*, and three years later helped found Tidewater School in Eliot, ME. She occasionally consults to schools and parent organizations. Pam has served as a member of the Board of Directors of several local historic and civic organizations as well as the Independent Publishers of New England (IPNE). She enjoys travel, gardening, choral singing, educational conferences—and especially exploring the shelves of a library or an independent bookstore.

OTHER PUBLICATIONS

Beyond the Rainbow Bridge: Nurturing Your Children From Birth to Seven

Barbara J. Patterson and Pamela Bradley

As comforting to the adults in our fast-paced world as a fairy tale is to a child. This award-winning book is based on a successful parenting class led by a seasoned early childhood teacher. Parents and teachers will learn healthy rhythms, creative discipline, birthday stories and doll-making. Includes Q and A with each chapter. Soft pencil illustrations and photographs. Adopted in parent-child classes nation-wide. Published in languages.

ISBN: 978-0-9647832-3-2 $17.95

Books for the Journey: A Guide to the World of Reading

Pamela J. Fenner, Anne Greer and John Wulsin, Jr.

"The only reading list you'll ever need,"
 says Billy Collins, former US Poet Laureate

This multi-disciplined resource for families, libraries and bookstores is a comprehensive 1500-title reference to search for the perfect book to stretch teens' reading choices, enhance curricula, motivate reluctant readers, and to indulge oneself. Each section has a "Reader's Roadmap." Indexed. Finalist: Foreword Magazine Book-of-the-Year Award, Education

ISBN: 978-0-9647832-4-9 $24. 95

Waldorf Education: A Family Guide

Pamela J. Fenner and Karen Rivers

Often called "Waldorf 101", this is the #1 introduction to Waldorf Education available. This comprehensive book is a collection of articles describing Waldorf Education—the curriculum, philosophy, history, celebrations, and traditions. Used is school communities world-wide.

ISBN: 978-0-9647832-1-8 $24. 95

Celebrating Whittier: New England's Quaker Poet and Abolitionist America's 1907 Centennial

Pamela J. Fenner

John Greenleaf Whittier, 1807–1892, was a significant part of our national history. Through rich illustrations from the 1907 Centennial documents from all across America, readers will discover why Whittier was revered for his struggle to free the slaves, honored for his character, and loved for his poetic rendering of the past.

Indexed. ISBN: 978-0-9647832-2-5 $19.95

John Greenleaf Whittier

John "Ben" Pickard Presentations/booklets by Whittier scholar
and great-grandnephew of the poet and abolitionist

Whittier and his Idiosyncratic Relatives: Fame and its Effects of Those Close By

Reading Whittier: A Discover of Forgotten Poetic Values

Whittier and his Elizabeths

Whittier as a Local Poet

A House Becomes a Home: The Women of the Amesbury Whittier House

Michaelmas Press
P. O. Box 702 • Amesbury, MA 01913-0016
www.michaelmaspress.com

VOLUME DISCOUNTS AVAILABLE